Hiking the Shining Rock & Middle Prong Wildernesses

Hiking the Shining Rock & Middle Prong Wildernesses

Tim Homan

PEACHTREE
ATLANTA

Published by
PEACHTREE PUBLISHERS
1700 Chattahoochee Avenue
Atlanta, Georgia 30318-2112
www.peachtree-online.com

Interior illustrations by Vicky Holifield
Book design and composition by Robin Sherman
Maps by Tim Homan; Loraine Joyner; XNR Productions, Middleton, WI

Printed in the United States of America in August 2012 by RR Donnelley & Sons,
Harrisonburg, VA
10 9 8 7 6 5 4 3 2 1
First Edition

Library of Congress Cataloging-in-Publication Data
        Homan, Tim.
          Hiking the Shining Rock & Middle Prong Wildernesses / written by Tim
        Homan ; illustrated by Vicky Holifield. -- 1st ed.
            p. cm.
          ISBN 978-1-56145-666-6 / 1-56145-666-7
          1. Hiking--North Carolina--Shining Rock Wilderness--Guidebooks. 2. Hiking--
        North Carolina--Middle Prong Wilderness--Guidebooks. 3. Shining Rock
        Wilderness (N.C.)--Guidebooks. 4. Middle Prong Wilderness (N.C.)--Guide-
        books. I. Holifield, Vicky. II. Title.
          GV199.42.N662H66 2012
          917.56--dc23
                                                            2012001620

This book is dedicated to Maggie Nettles,
longtime hiking buddy and friend.

Her mountain joy was always as radiant
as the sunsets we watched from the fire ring.

Camp Geezer will never be the same
without Maggie and her blue blanket.

Acknowledgments

I wish to extend special thanks to the following people for their help:

- David Brown, Steve Craven, Gary Crider, Bob Gadd, Elizabeth Little, Page Luttrell, Bill Martello and his wife Regina, Nelson Morgan, Carol Myers, Roger Nielsen, Chris and Jan Pitman, Charles Ratliff, Linda Russell, Brad Sanders, Diane Monaghan Sanders, and Brown Widener for hiking with me;
- Chris Kelly, Wildlife Biologist for the North Carolina Wildlife Resources Commission, for answering questions about peregrine falcon reintroduction;
- Kate Dixon, with Friends of the Mountains-to-Sea Trail, for answering my questions concerning the history of the MST;
- Ted Oprean, forester at the Pisgah Ranger Station, for helping me understand the convoluted history of the Shining Rock region's forests;
- Vicky Holifield for her editing, writing lessons, and botanical drawings;
- Gary Crider, Josh Leventhal, Page Luttrell, Maggie Nettles, and Roger Nielsen for their photographs;
- Loraine Joyner for her save on the maps;
- Page Luttrell, my wife, for her typing and ongoing computer lessons.

—*Tim Homan*

Contents

Abbreviations Used in This Guide

ALT—Art Loeb Trail
ALT-3—Section 3 of the Art Loeb Trail
AT—Appalachian Trail
BBD—Beech Bark Disease
BRP—Blue Ridge Parkway
CMC—Carolina Mountain Club
dbh—diameter at breast height
FS—Forest Service
GPS—Global Positioning System
GSMNP—Great Smoky Mountains National Park
HWA—Hemlock Woolly Adelgid
IGT—Ivestor Gap Trail
MST—Mountains to Sea Trail
NC—North Carolina
NF—National Forest
NPS—National Park Service
USFS—United States Forest Service
USGS—United States Geological Survey

The Scope of This Guide

The primary focus of this guide encompasses the high, mountainous terrain located within the Shining Rock Wilderness; the Middle Prong Wilderness; the Blue Ridge Parkway corridor north of the parkway (from Richland Balsam to the west almost to US 276 in the east); and the pocket of nonwilderness Forest Service property bordering the Shining Rock Wilderness to the north, NC 215 to the west, and the BRP corridor to the south. The largest of North Carolina's national forest wildernesses, Shining Rock preserves 18,483 acres, the Middle Prong, 7,460. Separated by a single highway, NC 215, the combined wildernesses currently total 25,943 acres (40.5 square miles). The pocket of FS land north of the parkway adds another 5,044 acres. All together, these three areas total 30,987 acres (48.4 square miles). The narrow part of the BRP corridor north of the parkway adds an unknown but relatively insignificant acreage to the total.

This guide details a network of thirty-four trails or trail sections plus one sidepath totaling 101.7 miles, all but 7.0 miles of which tread north of the parkway. This network connects three NC counties (Haywood, Transylvania, Jackson), two national forests (Nantahala and Pisgah), plus one national park (BRP). The Haywood-Transylvania boundary—Haywood to the north, Transylvania to the south—runs along the parkway corridor from US 276 to NC 215. Nearly all the FS holdings north of the parkway reside in Haywood County. From Mount Hardy Gap to Richland Balsam, the Haywood-Jackson line roughly parallels and crosses the parkway. Devils Courthouse, ALT-1, and segments of MST-5 travel through Transylvania County. Bearpen Gap Trail and the westernmost 2.2 miles of MST-1 range into Jackson County. Both wildernesses rise to over 6,000 feet in Haywood County.

The FS land south of the parkway and west of NC 215 to Richland Balsam shelters the easternmost large acreage of the Nantahala National Forest. Bearpen Gap Trail and the westernmost 2.2 miles of MST-1 thread through the BRP corridor and the Nantahala NF. All the other trail mileage detailed in this guide, north or south of the parkway, either roams through the BRP corridor or the Pisgah NF. Both wildernesses lie completely within the Pisgah NF.

On a larger physiographic scale, this region of repeated patterns—its humped ridges dipping between tall peaks, its steep slopes cradling deep coves—is part and parcel of the Great Balsam Mountains, the longest of the east-west cross ranges in the Southern Appalachians. The core area covered by this guide—north from the parkway through both wildernesses—features a high and rugged landscape. Here, nine different Great Balsam Mountain summits thrust 6,000 feet into the sky. Richland Balsam is the tallest of the nine at 6,410 feet.

The core area lies within a deep bowl rimmed by long and elevated ridges. The two most prominently labeled crests forming the inverted arch of the bowl are Pisgah and Lickstone. Pisgah Ridge, which walls in fully half of the curve, sweeps from the bottom of the bowl in the south all the way around its northeastern perimeter.

The grain of the mountain land inside the bowl ranks up with a strong north-south orientation. Fork Ridge, the main divide within the Middle Prong Wilderness, descends south to north. Shining Rock Ledge, the main divide splitting the eastern side of the core, rolls in a north-south direction. Stretching from the parkway corridor to the top of Cold Mountain, the ledge spans 7½ miles, measured as a raven flies right above the zigs and zags of its crest. The third prominent interior ridge,

Fork Mountain, descends to the northwest from Tennent to High Top before bending to the north immediately across the Shining Rock Wilderness boundary.

The half loop of ridges along the bowl's periphery and the lofty crests inside the basin physically force the plentiful Southern Appalachian rainwater toward two different directions, dividing drainages on a landscape scale like a sharply pitched roof. The steep terrain inside the bowl is a great, pouring fountain, one that gathers into streams rushing cold and clear, veining the high hollows and the bottom furrows of every cove. All of the fast-water branches, all of the trout-water creeks, prongs, and forks feed the upper Pigeon River watershed. And all of the smaller watercourses contribute to one of the four larger streams born in the bowl—Little East Fork Pigeon River, East Fork Pigeon River, Middle Prong, and West Fork Pigeon River. The bowl opens to the north; the grain of the land and elevation loss usher all water in that direction.

The dendritic drainage of the Pigeon River basin joins and journeys with our country's most extensive watershed. The east and west forks of the Pigeon combine their currents to become the Pigeon River, which delivers its mountain water generally north and northwest toward the French Broad. The Holston and French Broad Rivers unite just outside of Knoxville, where they lose their freight and names to the Tennessee. Conveyed in turn by the Ohio and Mississippi, the highland Dixie water rilling off Shining Rock Ledge—along with copious donations from Montana and Pennsylvania—finally flows into the Gulf of Mexico near New Orleans.

The Shining Rock Wilderness trail system—frequently connecting rivers and smaller streams to high ridges—interlaces eleven trails or trail sections totaling 40.0 miles. This mileage includes only those trails or portions of trails that are completely within the wilderness. The Art Loeb Trail (part of Section 3 and all of Section 4) winds through Shining Rock for 8.7 miles, the longest distance of any single treadway.

The Middle Prong Wilderness trail system encompasses five trails or trail sections (part of MST-1 and all of MST-2) and one sidepath up to Mount Hardy totaling 19.6 miles. This mileage includes all of the Green Mountain Trail, the northernmost nonwilderness mile of the Haywood Gap Trail, and the short trail segments within the de facto wilderness BRP corridor north of the parkway. The MST meanders along the high slopes of the southern portion of the Middle Prong for 6.4 miles, the longest length of tread within the network.

The web of trails penetrating the pocket of nonwilderness FS land between the Shining Rock Wilderness and the parkway (MST-5 dips south of the parkway for 0.5 mile) includes eighteen trails or trail sections totaling 35.6 miles. South of the parkway, two short trails plus ALT-1 and part of MST-1 add an additional 6.5 miles to the connected network of routes in this guide.

The arch and roll of Shining Rock Ledge raises the horizon to over 6,000 feet six times within the pocket of nonwilderness FS land and the Shining Rock Wilderness. From south to north, the ledge wedges highest into the sky at Black Balsam Knob (6,214 feet) before rising again to Tennent Mountain (6,070 feet). Once inside the wilderness, the ridge roller-coasters over Grassy Cove Top (6,055 feet), Grassy Cove Top's northern knob (approximately 6,015 feet), Shining Rock (approximately 6,010 feet), and finally famous Cold Mountain (6,030 feet). The FS land sandwiched between Shining Rock and the parkway boasts two more 6,000 footers: Sam Knob (6,060 feet) and Chestnut Bald (barely over 6,000 feet), its cap just over the line into the parkway corridor.

The Middle Prong Wilderness rears up into 6K highcountry in two places: the upper-north slope of Mount Hardy and the even loftier upper-east slope of Richland Balsam. The perimeter of the Middle Prong does not climb to nor legally claim the crowns of either of these peaks. The summits of both slant to their highpoints within the parkway corridor, wild land that butts up against the wilderness. The steeply pitched Middle Prong terrain rises to approximately 6,050 feet on Mount Hardy and approximately 6,320 feet on Richland Balsam.

Both wildernesses sweep downslope to their respective low points along the banks of the West Fork Pigeon River. Shining Rock's lowest point is approximately 3,050 feet, giving the wilderness a substantial 3,005-foot elevation differential between highest and lowest land. Middle Prong's low point is approximately 3,120 feet, giving it an even greater elevation differential, 3,200 feet. An elevation change of this magnitude—3,000 feet and more—guarantees a diverse forest in the Southern Appalachians.

The Shining Rock Region

The mountain kingdom of the Cherokee once held claim to today's Haywood County. Numerous Cherokee hunting and trading trails crisscrossed the county, and one of their small towns, known as Old Kanuga, was located near the banks of the Pigeon River, probably near present-day Canton. Old Kanuga was an isolated outlier town, by far the easternmost Cherokee settlement that far north in NC.

The smallpox epidemic of 1738–1739 killed nearly half the entire Cherokee Nation within a year. Another round of small-pox revisited its horrors upon the Cherokee twenty years later. In the summer of 1760, more than 1,600 men led by Colonel Montgomery waged war upon the Cherokee; the fighting for territory continued for decades without long letup. Smallpox, military defeat, and the steady encroachment of European set-tlers forced the Cherokee into a series of land-cession treaties. The remaining residents of Old Kanuga Town probably retreated into the mountains further west by 1770.

By the early 1780s, the incoming tide of European migration had forded the French Broad and was pressing upon the frontier of the Great Balsam Mountains. John Davidson and James Chambers—Revolutionary War veterans who received large land grants from the state of NC in lieu of cash—were the first recorded Europeans to build cabins along the Pigeon River near present-day Canton. Chambers was living upon his grant prior to 1790, the year he died. Increasing numbers of pioneers moved into the eastern part of the county (founded in 1808 and much larger then than now) in the early decades of the nineteenth century, clearing the larger, flatter floodplains and coves for farming homesteads. Self-reliant settlers established small communities up both the west and east forks of the Pigeon River prior to 1808. As long as fertile and flat land was still abundant, there was no need for early farmers to plant corn on the slanting slopes of the Shining Rock–Middle Prong area. They did, however, use the nearby highlands for hunting and as free range for hogs and cattle.

In the nineteenth century, commercial logging in western NC was restricted to high-value trees standing within reasonable skidding distance of streams large enough to float logs to a sawmill. During the late 1800s, nearly half of Haywood County was still covered in primary forest—northern and cove hardwoods plus hemlock on the lower elevations, spruce and fir at elevations above 4,200 to 4,400 feet. Nearly all of the high-elevation, southern section of the county—federal FS land today—remained in primary forest.

Large-scale industrial logging began on the southern side of Haywood County in 1906. In that year, Champion Fibre Company built a pulp mill and tannin extraction plant in Canton and began buying huge tracts of mountain land. From 1906 to 1909, Champion purchased much of the rugged country within today's wilderness and the future FS land south of the Shining Rock Wilderness and north of the BRP. The company also established a logging community named Sunburst in the floodplain flat beside the West Fork Pigeon River, the site of the contemporary Sunburst Campground.

The Champion Fibre Company conveyed its Haywood County holdings to the Champion Lumber Company in 1911 (no relationship between the two Champions). The new landlords cut mainly red spruce and Fraser fir that grew in large and nearly pure stands. Champion Lumber laid an extensive system of logging railways and moved Sunburst further down the West Fork to the present location of Lake Logan. Sunburst's large band sawmill processed timber for the construction market and government contracts, which included the military's robust demand for the light and strong spruce wood essential in airplane design back then.

Champion Lumber deeded its timberland, mill, and equipment to the Suncrest Lumber Company during bankruptcy proceedings in 1918. By 1923 Suncrest owned all of the land and timber within the original boundaries of the Shining Rock Wilderness. In the fall of drought-year 1925, a wildfire believed to have been sparked by a Suncrest locomotive burned 25,000 acres in southern Haywood County. The fire, which started in tinder-dry logging slash, burned incredibly hot and fast. This devastating conflagration burned so hot that it baked the humus down to shallow bedrock, scalding the ground below the shallow rootline of spruce and sterilizing the soil.

The southern boundary of the big fire ran along the present-day parkway from Richland Balsam in the west to Pigeon Gap in the east. The wildfire's perimeter extended northward well beyond both of today's wildernesses. Fortunately, the blaze spared moist coves and hollows such as those at the upper ends of Shining Creek and Greasy Cove Prong.

Suncrest logged the sharply folded landscape of the two wildernesses until 1926. From 1918 to 1926 the company cut 168,527,164 board feet of red spruce. In 1926 Suncrest Lumber went bankrupt and sold its Haywood County holdings to Sherwood Forests Inc. of Asheville, NC. Sherwood Forests bought the mountain land—much of it scarred land nobody wanted—as a speculative venture during the western NC land boom of the 1920s. In 1935, the federal government purchased Sherwood Forests' real estate, approximately 44,000 acres, for inclusion in the Pisgah Ranger District of the Pisgah NF.

Early on, FS management consisted of repairing the worst of the erosion and planting trees to begin the reforestation process. In 1938, the FS began large-scale plantings of red spruce within the area burned by the 1925 fire. Unfortunately, several large plantations of spruce saplings served as fuel for another drought-year fire in 1942, when several large fires broke out in Haywood and Transylvania Counties. These fires scorched over 13,000 acres within the Pisgah NF, 12,000 acres of that total within Haywood County north of the present-day parkway.

The 1942 fire burned roughly 5,000 acres within the boundaries of the '25 fire—all of that twice-blackened earth north of the parkway and east of NC 215, and most of it south of Shining Rock (the mountain). Flat Laurel Creek halted the fire between the two Sams—Sam Knob burned, Little Sam Knob's still-extant stand of planted red spruce did not.

The FS continued to set out spruce saplings through 1943, but their efforts produced mixed results. While a high percentage of the saplings survived, their growth rate was stunted due to the fire-depleted soil. World War II ended the extensive reforestation of red spruce.

Time passed. Vegetation began to heal the patient land. Resurgent forests began climbing the slopes toward treeless highcountry, planting the flags of their canopies on higher ground every year. Nearly four decades after the 1925 fire, the Wilderness Act of 1964 established the National Wilderness Preservation System. Originally encompassing 13,600 acres, Shining Rock became a charter member of that new system when President Johnson signed Public Law 88-577 on September 3 of that year. Shining Rock became one of only three small national forest wildernesses in the east to receive that designation in 1964. (The other two were Linville Gorge, also located in

North Carolina's Pisgah NF, and Great Gulf in New Hampshire.)

Beginning in the early 1970s, the FS conducted a series of prescribed burns in the pocket of nonwilderness Pisgah NF land south of the Shining Rock Wilderness and north of the parkway. The primary purpose of these small, controlled burns was to improve wildlife habitat in general, and, more specifically, to improve winter habitat for the eastern population of the golden eagle. The last in that series of prescribed burns occurred in the early 1990s.

Two decades after Shining Rock's first designation, the North Carolina Wilderness Act of 1984 (Public Law 98-324) created the 7,460-acre Middle Prong Wilderness and increased the size and legal resumé of the Shining Rock Wilderness.

Note: Much of the information in this brief history came from the thick loose-leaf binder I was allowed to sift through at the Pisgah Ranger Station and the equally thick book, *The Annals of Haywood County North Carolina* by W. C. Allen, first published in 1935.

The Blue Ridge Parkway

The vision that would become the Blue Ridge Parkway began in 1933 when President Franklin D. Roosevelt visited Shenandoah National Park. While the president inspected the ongoing construction of the Skyline Drive, Virginia Senator Harry F. Byrd recommended extending the roadway southwestward all the way to the Great Smoky Mountains National Park. Roosevelt promptly endorsed the proposal, and on November 24, 1933, Interior Secretary Harold Ickes approved the construction of the new "Park-to-Park Highway" as a public works project designed to help stimulate the Great Depression economy.

Ickes hired Stanley L. Abbott, a young landscape architect, to oversee planning for this ambitious undertaking. Abbott promoted the concept of the parkway as a chain of parks and recreation areas, each a destination in itself. He also proposed preserving the viewshed beyond the parkway corridor through the use of scenic easements. Today, Abbott is considered "the father of the Blue Ridge Parkway."

The parkway's authorization specified that the states would purchase the land for the right-of-way, and the federal government would build the road and recreation areas. Construction of the first 12.5-mile segment began near Cumberland Knob in North Carolina on September 11, 1935; roadway work started in Virginia the following February. On June 30, 1936, Congress formally authorized the establishment of the Blue Ridge Parkway and placed it under the jurisdiction of the National Park Service.

While most of the construction was completed by private contractors, a variety of New Deal public works programs, including the Civilian Conservation Corps, played vital roles in the BRP's development.

World War II brought most parkway work to a sudden halt. Most public works relief programs were disbanded, construction funds were impounded, and many employees left their jobs to join the armed services. Work resumed in 1946, but insufficient appropriations hampered the pace of the effort. By the mid-1950s, only about half of the massive project had been finished. The driving force for the completion of most of the remaining mileage came from a ten-year NPS development program: Mission 66. By the end of the mission in 1966, only the "missing link" remained unfinished.

Completion of the mountain byway would take another two decades because of the unsuccessful attempts to acquire right-of-way for the final 7.7-mile section at North Carolina's Grandfather Mountain. After lengthy negotiations and a creative solution, the innovative Linn Cove Viaduct was completed in 1983. Four years later, on September 11, 1987, the entire 469-mile parkway, from Shenandoah all the way to the Great Smoky Mountains, was opened to public travel. Today, the BRP remains the longest parkway in the National Park system and the longest, uninterrupted—no stop lights, no stop signs—low-speed, scenic drive in the country.

The Blue Ridge Parkway offers magnificent scenery, exceptional roadside wildflower displays, frequent opportunities to observe wildlife, hiking trails, picnic areas, campgrounds, lodges, visitor centers, cultural exhibits, and interpretive programs. With so much to see and do along its 469-mile length of Southern Appalachian ridgecrest and slope, it should come as no surprise that "America's favorite drive" is the most visited unit in the National Park system.

Like large jewels on a slender necklace, fourteen backcountry areas, ranging from 1,000 to 5,000 acres, greatly broaden the scenic byway's linear boundaries (which average 800 feet in width) at irregular intervals. The BRP rises to its highest point (6,053 feet on the overlook sign, 6,047 feet on the parkway map) on the upper slope of North Carolina's Richland Balsam and dips to its lowest point (649 feet) where it crosses Virginia's James River.

America's favorite drive offers trail networks of its own in the backcountry areas. The parkway also provides access to numerous short-to-medium-length trails, many of which leave the parkway corridor and enter FS land. You can even access two of the longest trails in eastern North America: the famed Appalachian and North Carolina's Mountains to Sea.

The BRP's long north-south geographic and geologic reach—along with its inherent range of elevations, aspects, soil types, slope heights and angles, etc.—spans a wealth of environments both large and small. Many of the numerous microhabitats, a Southern Appalachian specialty, are uncommon or rare. Northern plants dip deep into Dixie within the peninsula of high Southern Appalachian peaks. Many essentially southern plants find congenial habitats in the sheltered, lower-elevation river valleys.

The parkway's mostly linear lands pass through parts of four national forests and portions of fourteen major vegetation types. They also contain seventy-five distinct plant communities, twenty-four of which have been designated as globally rare. As expected, this high number of plant communities provides habitat for a bewildering variety of vascular plant and vertebrate species. The fourth highest total of vascular plants in the NPS system—1,633 and counting—has been identified within parkway boundaries. The parkway's relatively small area—82,301 acres and slowly growing—provides living room for 108 types of native trees (more than in all of northern Europe).

The BRP is home to 67 mammal species (elk included), 30 types of reptiles, 130 breeding birds, and 93 different kinds of fish. The wild lands of the parkway host 45 species of amphibians, more than any other unit in the NPS system. A network of 47 Natural Heritage Areas helps preserve this rich diversity within parkway boundaries.

Hiking Club and Trail Histories

The Carolina Mountain Club

Founded by a small group of Asheville naturalists, the Carolina Mountain Club began its existence as a private nonprofit organization on July 16, 1923. Today's Tennent Mountain, the 6,000 footer the Art Loeb Trail passes over, was named in honor of the club's first president, Dr. Gaillard Stoney Tennent. Early on, the membership held social events, hiked in the mountains of western North Carolina, and maintained forest cabins. The CMC merged with the newer Carolina Appalachian Trail Club in 1931. The CATC disbanded, and its members were welcomed into the CMC. The now larger group retained the Carolina Mountain Club name, but it adopted the core mission of the former CATC: hiking, trail building and maintenance, plus vigorous advocacy for local conservation issues such as the creation of the GSMNP.

George Masa and Horace Kephart were among the most colorful and well known of the early CMC members. A major figure in the early history of the organization, Masa was a professional photographer whose striking black-and-white photographs of the Southern Appalachians greatly aided the movement to preserve the Great Smoky Mountains. Club legend Kephart was a nationally recognized writer who specialized in camping and woodcraft articles. Both men worked hard to establish the GSMNP, and both men were honored for their efforts with memorial mountains in the park.

The CMC's highest priority project in the 1930s focused upon constructing, measuring, and maintaining most of North Carolina's share of the Appalachian Trail. World War II suspended the group's meetings for more than three years. After the war, the AT was grown over with thick, sun-gap vegetation and in poor condition. Throughout the late 40s and 50s, the organization's hard-working volunteers battled to keep "the long green tunnel" open and blazed.

Starting in the early 1960s, the CMC intensified its efforts to help protect several of the most scenic areas in western North Carolina. The club strongly supported the successful designation of Linville Gorge and Shining Rock as charter members of the National Wilderness Preservation System. In 1997, the membership mounted a letter-writing and arm-twisting campaign urging the governor and state legislators to protect available land on the NC side of the Jocassee Gorges area.

As always, the group worked on the AT—maintaining the treadway, planning and constructing reroutes, building shelters, sidehilling slopes, etc. Today, another generation of CMC volunteers maintains the 93-mile stretch of the AT between Davenport and Spivey Gaps.

The organization became involved in the initial planning phase for the Mountains to Sea Trail in the late 1970s. CMC members began MST treadway work in 1983. And they have continued their work on the long-march trail, in one often sweaty way or another, ever since. When the last link of their stretch is finished, the group will be responsible for maintaining more than 140 miles of MST tread.

The CMC currently maintains a little over 400 miles of trail, and the mileage and effort keeps increasing. In addition to its extensive maintenance commitments on the AT and MST, the beaver-busy hiking club maintains most of the ALT, trails along the BRP, and trails in the Pisgah National Forest (including routes in the Shining Rock and Middle Prong Wildernesses), among many others. The CMC contributes more volunteer hours to parkway projects than any other group.

For more information about the Carolina Mountain Club go to **www.carolinamountainclub.org**.

Note: The facts concerning the origin and early days of the CMC came from "History of the Carolina Mountain Club" by Peter M. Steurer.

The Art Loeb Trail

Described as an industrialist, Art Loeb rose through the ranks to become vice president and general manager of a division of the Olin Mathieson Chemical Corporation in Brevard, North Carolina. While still in his forties, Loeb suffered a heart attack. His doctors encouraged him to walk as part of his rehabilitation therapy; their advice became his passion. Loeb walked and walked. Soon he was able to hike up fire roads. After gaining more strength and stamina, he joined the Carolina Mountain Club and became a conservationist, club leader, and avid hiker back when Southern Appalachian

ART LOEB TRAIL
A TRIBUTE
ARTHUR J. LOEB
1914 - 1968
INDUSTRIALIST,
CONSERVATIONIST,
AND HIKER WHO DEEPLY
LOVED THESE MOUNTAINS.

Page Luttrell

hiking often led to confusion, spatial disorientation—getting lost—and bushwhacking. Slender, strong-legged, and long-stride tall, Art Loeb lived to hike and hiked to live. Unfortunately, his days afield in the Southern Appalachians were cut unseasonably short. He died of a brain tumor in December 1968, at age fifty-four, with way too much tread left on his boots.

His hiking club comrades went to work on a fitting memorial almost immediately. By the late 1960s, the Forest Service was no longer willing to change the names of mountains, so the CMC proposed a memorial trail stitched together from old roads and railways, existing trails and herd paths, many of which Loeb had explored. The club submitted its proposal for a memorial trail to the FS in June of 1969. The proposal called for a high-ridge footpath through the Great Balsam Mountains Loeb had loved so much. The idea of honoring Art Loeb with a namesake trail found quick traction with both the FS and long-time western North Carolina congressman Roy Taylor, who had known Loeb as a community business leader. Five months later, in November of 1969, hundreds of people attended the dedication of the new Art Loeb Trail.

Primarily a ridgeline and upper-slope route, the Art Loeb winds through the Pisgah NF from a camp at one end to a camp at the other end. The trail's southeastern terminus is located just inside the Davidson River Campground in Transylvania County near Brevard, and its northwestern terminus is located at the Daniel Boone Boy Scout Camp in Haywood County. The ALT is a highly scenic footpath, and parts of it—especially the high-elevation stretch from FS 816 to Shining Rock—are also highly popular.

The ALT is divided into four sections from southeast to northwest. Starting at its trailhead beside the Davidson River, Section 1 rises to the route's first low mountain, High Knob, then travels west atop Shut-in Ridge. The track makes a gap-to-gap half loop around scenic Cedar Rock Mountain before Section 1 ends at Gloucester Gap. Section 2 climbs sharply to Pilot Mountain's views and the trail's first 5,000-foot elevation. Turning north, it then descends to Deep Gap, ascends Sassafras Knob, and ramps down to Farlow Gap.

From Farlow, this National Recreation Trail gains nearly 1,000 feet of elevation to where it crosses the BRP. Across the parkway, the line of march continues to climb Shuck Ridge to its junction with the MST on Silvermine Bald, a near 6,000-foot knob on Pisgah Ridge. Here the newcomer MST piggybacks on the Art Loeb treadway for the easily walked remainder of Section 2 to FS 816.

Section 3 and Section 4 of the ALT correspond exactly to Section 3 and Section 4 in this guide. (See ALT-3, page 77, and ALT-4, page 98, for detailed descriptions of those sections.)

My measuring wheel rolled 31.4 miles for the entire Art Loeb Trail.

The Mountains to Sea Trail

The State of North Carolina Trails System Act of 1973 became the legislative genesis of the Mountains to Sea Trail. That act authorized the creation of the North Carolina Trails Committee, a seven-member citizen council. During a speech at the 1977 National Trails Symposium, Natural Resources and Community Development Secretary Howard Lee first proposed a continuous trail spanning North Carolina from the mountains to the seashore. Lee envisioned a long-distance trail that would traverse public property—federal, state, county, community—as much as possible. Where public lands were unavailable, the MST would be routed through private property whose owners would be willing to grant right-of-way easements.

The idea quickly gained statewide interest, sparking a can-do spirit to build a footpath that would connect and showcase North Carolina's wild lands and beauty spots. The three primary public agencies involved—the NPS, the USFS, and the state of NC—signed a Memorandum of Understanding pledging cooperation in 1979. This pledge served as the official go-ahead, the green light. The ambitious and formidable task of building a trail stretching from mountains to sea now had traction and momentum. Thousands of people from hiking clubs, local communities, support groups, task forces, and land trusts joined with public-agency professionals, private landowners, and other dedicated volunteers from across the state in a creative and collaborative effort that continues today.

In 1982, the 76-mile Cape Hatteras Beach Trail became the first treadway, long or short, to be designated as an official link in the MST. The CMC began construction in the Pisgah NF the following year. Sixty-three miles of footpath in the mountainous South Pisgah section officially joined the MST system in 1987. After a period of sagging interest, Friends of the Mountains-to-Sea Trail incorporated in 1997, giving the long-term project a quick and much needed boost.

By 2000, many segments of the MST were open for hiking, including long sections in the Pisgah NF. North Carolina added the MST to its state park system in that same year. This milestone was immensely important; it allowed state money to be spent for land acquisition and signaled ongoing support for the long-distance trail. Most of the mountain section of the MST, 193 miles, received National Recreation Trail designation in 2005. The MST reached its approximate halfway point of 500 miles in 2008. The projected distance of the completed trail is over 1,000 miles.

Today, by taking temporary connectors on rural roads and state bike paths, adventurous hikers can trek from the MST's western terminus atop Clingmans Dome in the GSMNP all the way to its eastern terminus atop Jockey's Ridge within its namesake state park in the Outer Banks. Along the way, the MST's 3-inch diameter white dot leads foot travelers through two more units in the national park system (BRP and Cape Hatteras National Seashore), three national forests (Nantahala, Pisgah, and Croatan), two national forest wildernesses (Middle Prong and Linville Gorge), two national wildlife refuges (Pea Island and Cedar Island), and seven state parks. Along the way, the trail reveals the diverse landscapes of the Blue Ridge, Piedmont, and Coastal Plain physiographic provinces.

North Carolina's state trail is not afraid of heights; it climbs both the highest peak, Mount Mitchell, and the highest sand dune, Jockey's Ridge, in the eastern United States.

This labor of generations links the observation tower atop Clingmans Dome, where the MST ties into the famed Appalachian Trail, to the lighthouses standing sentry beside the Atlantic Ocean. Between tower and beacon, the MST's winding treadway beckons you to explore and experience the land's many faces: high mountains, hardwood forests, waterfalls, gorges, and overlooks; rolling hills, small rural communities, slow-moving rivers, and tobacco barns; swamps, piney woods, ferry rides, beach walking, breaking waves, and so much more.

The continuing quest is to complete a primarily foot-travel-only path across the state—a journey linking past vision to future pride, linking boreal mountaintop to sand beach and salt water sea, linking brook trout to bluefish, black-throated blue warbler to brown pelican, and Fraser fir to bald cypress. *For more information*, or to find out how you can help, visit this website: **www.ncmst.org**.

Note: Much of the information in this brief history came from Friends of the Mountains-to-Sea Trail, *Hiking North Carolina's Mountains-to-Sea Trail* by Allen de Hart, and *The Mountains-to-Sea Trail: Western North Carolina's Majestic Rival to the Appalachian Trail* by Dossey and Hillyer.

Things to Know Before You Go

Blazes and Signs

The blazes and signs important to hikers along the trail system described in this guide are governed by two agencies: the National Park Service and the National Forest Service. Blazing and signage decisions are governed by management objectives and land classifications, as well as the priorities and wishes of the agencies tempered by budgetary constraints. For hikers, the primary land classifications include the wilderness and nonwilderness lands within the Pisgah and Nantahala National Forests plus the Blue Ridge Parkway's preserved, de facto wilderness corridor.

Blazes are prohibited within the combined wildernesses. You can still occasionally find a few of the old cut-bark blazes, but these relics of early management are becoming fewer and farther between as the blaze trees topple to ground.

The two long trails that pass through the general Shining Rock–Middle Prong area—the Art Loeb and Mountains to Sea—are well blazed with their respective geometric forms except where they traverse designated wilderness. In addition to its regular on-tree blazes, the MST frequently employs low trailposts at road crossings and at nonwilderness trail junctions. Trailposts also mark both sides of the road where the ALT crosses the parkway. The posted access trails leading from the parkway to the MST, such as Bearpen Gap and others too short for names, are all blue blazed.

The named and signed nonwilderness Forest Service trails are usually blazed minimally or not at all. Many of these trails have their blaze colors on their carsonite signs and occasional or no blazing along their lengths. Dead-end routes such as Sam

Knob Summit and Upper Falls are unblazed. All of these trails have treadways that are so well defined and so easily followed that regular-interval blazing is unnecessary.

Interior junctions are not signed within the wilderness. A large gray wooden sign or small green metal sign, or both, frequently indicate where a trail enters and exits the combined wildernesses. Of the four wilderness trailheads, where you leave your vehicle at an obvious parking area and immediately enter wilderness, three of them have at least a kiosk. The fourth, the Fork Mountain–Green Mountain trailhead, is completely unsigned. If you drive by or use that trailhead during a hot summer weekend, you will appreciate the reluctance to place kiosk or trail signs front and center.

Most of the nonwilderness trails and trails with one nonwilderness end are signed or posted at their trailheads and nonwilderness junctions. The Forest Service frequently deploys carsonite signs, narrow and brown, with trail name, sample circle of blaze color if needed, and difficulty rating.

In light of recurring vandalism and slashed budgets, don't expect all of the signs to be up all of the time. Take a map or written directions to help find trailheads, then take a map and compass so you can be sure of the correct direction of travel at junctions. Hiking in general, and wilderness hiking in particular, requires a modest level of common sense and preparation. Policies regarding signage and blazing are subject to change.

Blooming Dates

Most of the "recent year" blooming-date notations encompass the years from 2003 through 2010. Warm weather came and remained extremely early in the springs of 2011 and 2012. During those two springs, many wildflowers bloomed a week to two weeks earlier than during the cooler springs in the previous eight-year span. Only time and the rising CO2 levels will tell if the last two springs were statistical anomalies or a significant spike in the ongoing warming trend.

There are no drive-through windows for wildflowers. If an upcoming spring is unusually warm—or what was recently considered unusually warm—you will know that the wildflowers will be blooming earlier than during the eight-year period I used for my sample.

Camping Areas

Sunburst, Davidson River, and Mount Pisgah offer car-camping opportunities near the Shining Rock–Middle Prong Wildernesses. Sunburst is off NC 215 a little over 8.0 miles north of that highway's junction with the parkway. Davidson River is off US 276 a little less than 14.0 miles south (toward Brevard) of the parkway. Mount Pisgah is located off the parkway approximately 0.4 mile to the north (toward Asheville) of milepost 409.

Sunburst is a small Pisgah National Forest campground with ten sites, all first come, first served. At present, Sunburst remains open from the first weekend in April through the last weekend in October.

Davidson River is a large Pisgah National Forest campground offering 161 sites. Open all year, Davidson River's campsites are available on both a first come, first served and reservation basis.

Mount Pisgah is a large NPS campground with 140 sites plus campfire and interpretive programs. Campsites are available on both a first come, first served and reservation basis. The campground is usually open from mid-May through late October. The exact dates are subject to change.

Campsites at both Davidson River and Mount Pisgah may be reserved online at **www.recreation.gov** or by calling 1-877-444-6777. *For further information* concerning Sunburst Campground, call the Pisgah Ranger Station at 828-877-3265.

Elevations

Elevations were determined primarily from GPS readings, topo maps, and trail maps. If the elevations derived from topo maps (or topo maps and GPS readings) were close to the ones enumerated on the overlook signs—whether for the mountain in view or the overlook itself—the elevations from those signs were cited as is or rounded off to the nearest 5 feet. In the case of Rough Butt Bald Overlook, however, where both GPS and topo indicated an elevation over 100 feet higher than the sign's stated figure for the overlook, the elevation generated from those two sources took precedence.

The plaque atop Tennent gives the mountain's elevation as 6,040 feet. The topo map, however, suggests that this sharp-sloped peak is at least 6,060 feet, and the GPS—calibrated then tested to within 2-foot accuracy at the nearby Black Balsam Knob benchmark—provided a reading of at least 6,070 feet. Mount Hardy's elevation is often listed as 6,110 feet, which is the elevation of its benchmark not its highpoint. Contour lines and GPS readings indicate Hardy's highpoint is nearly a tenth-mile further south from the benchmark.

Where the GPS could not receive a strong satellite signal—such as in a fairly deep gap—the gap's stated elevation is usually a 20-foot split down the middle between the two nearest 40-foot contours. In figuring the elevation of a mountain with no highpoint benchmark—such as a named knob a trail half-circles around—the elevation given is usually 20 feet higher than the last 40-foot contour line.

Global Positioning System

The GPS coordinates in this guide follow the Garmin default format of degrees, minutes, and decimal minutes. The GPS-display coordinates appear in the following format: N 35°18.270' over W082°56.556'. The numbers with north and west in full notation are degrees of latitude and longitude. The second set of two numbers indicates minutes, and the three numbers to the right of the decimal represent what is known as decimal minutes. A single hash mark at the end of the reading means your GPS is using the minutes format; a double hash mark means your format ends in seconds.

All of the GPS coordinates used in this guide started with N 35 and W082, so latitude and longitude have been omitted from the readings. By convention, the final number from the decimal minutes is omitted from the coordinates because it is such a fine pinpointing that it would most often not match yours. All of the GPS readings given in this guide omit the final digit from decimal minutes except for the coordinates accompanying the map of Shining Rock Gap. And with the exception of the just-mentioned map, all of the GPS coordinates provided in this guide represent just minutes and decimal minutes to the second digit: N 18 41, W 52 87—no degrees, just minutes and two decimal minutes without decimal or hash mark.

Hunting Seasons

Hunting is a legal and popular pastime within the Shining Rock–Middle Prong Wildernesses and the nonwilderness land to either side of the parkway. As a hiker, you may want to be aware of bear season. This split season—the Monday on or nearest October 15 through the Saturday before Thanksgiving, and again the third Monday after Thanksgiving through January 1—

brings bear hunters and their hounds to the roads and forests in and around the Shining Rock and Middle Prong Wildernesses.

Modern bear hunting is a fairly sophisticated endeavor. The hounds are wired to transmit signals, which the hunters receive in order to keep track of their baying pack and the bear in front of them. The hunters and their trucks are allowed along the parkway, NC 215, and FS 816 all the way to Ivestor Gap. The men often hunt during the week so that they and their dogs won't get tangled up with hikers. The last time I hiked from the Black Balsam Trailhead during the week in early November, hunters were at the trailhead, more were along the Ivestor Gap Trail, and some were posted on ATVs along Black Balsam Knob's ridgeline.

If it is a busy bear-hunting day, you may want to avoid the ALT from FS 816 to Ivestor Gap, the IGT from the paved end of FS 816 to Ivestor Gap, and the Graveyard Ridge Trail from Ivestor Gap to Dark Prong Gap. *For more information* concerning hunting dates and regulations, check **www.ncwildlife.org**.

Measurement of Big Trees

Some of the old-growth trees mentioned in this guide, the ones tape measured and mileage noted, will no doubt be dead and down before your first hike past their location. That is to be expected. All of the circumference notations featuring lunker hemlocks have already been deleted from the narrative because of their mass death at the almost microscopic jaws of the hemlock woolly adelgid.

Foresters standardized tree measurement long ago. A tree's diameter or circumference is measured at dbh—diameter at breast height, 4 feet 6 inches from the ground. When a tree is standing on a slope, and has a pronounced high side and low side, you must measure from the upslope side, which is often difficult.

Parkway Closures

Wintry weather arrives early and remains late on the high-elevation sections of the parkway. When it comes, the NPS closes those portions of the road that are either impassable or dangerous from frozen precipitation or storm debris. Tunnels are problematic; they frequently remain iced and treacherous when the rest of the sunlit road appears clear. The high-elevation stretch of the parkway from NC 215 to US 276 often closes during late November to early December and reopens during late March to mid-April.

The severity of winter weather is the key factor determining when the parkway will reopen. I witnessed the condition of the still-closed road between NC 215 and US 276 during mid-March of the 2010 winter, the worst in the last twenty years according to a BRP maintenance engineer. The amount of storm debris—including minor landslides—requiring chainsaws and heavy equipment was extensive and would clearly require significant time, money, and effort to clean up.

Landslides and unstable conditions can close short sections of the parkway at any time of the year. If in doubt, call 828-298-0398 for a detailed list of all parkway closures in North Carolina.

Section Numbers

The section numbers assigned to the MST and ALT were employed solely for the purposes of this guide. For the most part, these numbers do not correspond with the official MST section numbers. MST sections 1 and 2 in this guide span all of the whole-trail Section 5 of the MST. Sections 3, 4, and 5 comprise the first two-thirds of the whole-trail Section 6, which ends at the Pisgah Inn. The CMC maintains a long stretch of the MST in the mountains; the club utilizes its own subset of section numbers to help facilitate maintenance.

For the ALT, this guide's sections 1 and 2 are part of the official Section 2. Sections 3 and 4 in this guide correspond exactly to the standardized sections 3 and 4.

Spelling of Place Names

The USGS, 1:24,000 topographic maps are my guides and final arbiters for the spelling, punctuation, and word formation of place names. Examples include Bearpen Gap (Bearpen one word instead of two) and Devils Courthouse (no possessive apostrophe in Devils).

Trail Measurement

I rolled and pushed an incessantly clicking, orange measuring wheel up and down all of the trails in this guide at least twice. By using this tool, I was able to record all distances in feet—such as 1,957 feet to Fork Mountain's Turnpike Creek crossing and 38,081 feet for the entire trail—then easily convert the numbers to the nearest tenth of a mile. If a measurement fell exactly between tenths, 4.85 miles for example, the figure was rounded upward to the nearest tenth.

Green Mountain's lowermost mile proved to be the steepest grade I have ever pushed a wheel up. It was challenging and, when there were loose leaves and acorn windrows across the toughest stretches, sometimes comical.

Tree Diseases

Hemlock Woolly Adelgid

Millions of eastern hemlocks have already died up and down the Appalachians. In 2005, the hemlock was still the most abundant conifer in the Shining Rock region. But in that year death was already clinging to the undersides of their branches, sucking their lifeblood sap away. Only two years later the white plague had disrobed thousands upon thousands of eastern hemlocks in North Carolina's Haywood, Jackson, and Transylvania Counties.

The culprit is the hemlock woolly adelgid (HWA), a tiny aphidlike insect accidentally introduced from southern Japan. In the eastern United States, the HWA was first discovered near Richmond, Virginia, in 1951. This exotic pest spread slowly at first, but in the last twenty years it has burgeoned into a rapidly advancing, perfect-storm pestilence. Since 2000, HWA population levels have reached epidemic numbers as wind, birds, and mammals including humans have quickly spread this invasive scourge at a rate of 15 to 20 miles per year. Since that time, the adelgid has entered the oldest and largest stands of eastern hemlock (*Tsuga canadensis*) in the Southern Appalachians.

By 2008, the HWA had become established in portions of sixteen states stretching from Maine to Georgia—nearly the length of the Appalachian Trail—infesting approximately half of the eastern hemlock's extensive range. Because this insect is cold-adapted to high elevations in Japan, it will probably continue to spread northward and westward until it has invaded the hemlock's entire contiguous range in eastern North America.

The hemlock is a late successional climax forest tree that exhibits extreme shade tolerance. Botanists sometimes refer to this graceful evergreen as the redwood of the East because it is tall and long lived. *T. canadensis* attains its greatest dimensions in the warm and rain-wealthy Southern Appalachians, where the very tallest recently lifted water over 170 feet into the sky. This short-needled conifer reaches the greatest age (rings counted record age is 988 years) and the greatest girth—the very thickest have slowly grown 5 to 6 feet in diameter—of any native spruce, fir, pine, or hemlock in eastern North America.

The hemlock woolly adelgid is parthenogenic in eastern

North America: it reproduces asexually, females cloning females cloning females (a mature adelgid deposits up to 300 eggs twice per year). After developing from an egg, the crawler inserts its mouth parts into woody tissue at the base of a needle and begins to siphon off sap and nutrients. The crawler, the first and only mobile immature life stage, secretes a waxy covering of fluffy white wool soon after it begins feeding. The adelgid's subsequent life stages remain hidden under the wool blanket. Heavily infested trees are easily identified by this dingy white wool on the undersides of their small twigs.

In sufficient numbers the HWA desiccates a hemlock's needles, forcing it into a kind of shock that precipitates needle drop, giving the tree a threadbare appearance. The tree rallies with a new growth of needles the next spring only to have the crawlers feed again. The conifer goes into shock again and most of its needles fall off again. This cycle of steadily weakening shock and substantial defoliation continues until the tree dies.

The aesthetically and ecologically important eastern hemlock has exhibited little or no resistance to HWA attack. Hemlock decline and death typically occur within four to eight years of infestation in the conifer's northern range and within two to five years in its southern range. Once infested, more than 95 percent of the mature hemlocks in a given Southern Appalachian stand will be dead within six years with no chemical or biological controls. Forest ecologists have coined the terms "functional extinction" and "ecological extinction" to describe the tree's status over much of its HWA-infested range. These terms mean the species will survive, but that it has now become such a minor component its numbers and role in the forest are negligible.

While *T. canadensis* will probably suffer high mortality rates throughout much or all of its contiguous range, there is realistic hope that this ecologically important species will not be all but wiped out like the American chestnut. At present, the incredibly prolific adelgid is being fought by a one-two combination of counterpunches, one chemical and the other biological. The NPS has been the clear leader in the use of chemical treatment in the Southern Appalachians. In the GSMNP, crews have worked for a decade, saving stands of old-growth hemlock (for now) by injecting systemic insecticides into the soil at the bases of the trees. These injections have proved effective in reducing HWA populations for up to five years per treatment. Recently, the national forests in NC and a coalition of partners, The Hemlock Woolly Adelgid Working Group, have begun a renewed effort to treat as many surviving hemlocks in the Pisgah and Nantahala National Forests as is practical. Both forests now have a crew treating stands of beleaguered hemlocks, tree by tree.

Although expensive and only a holding-pattern measure, protecting stands of hemlock with chemical treatment serves important functions. Most immediately, treatment protects the two hemlock species (HWA also kills the Carolina hemlock, a highly localized Southern Appalachian endemic) from quick annihilation over large swaths of their ranges, and keeps them alive until the biological-control cavalry comes on tiny wings. When that happens, the treated stands will serve as reservoirs of genetic diversity and sources for future dispersal.

Biological control is the only hope for a widespread and self-sustaining solution to the HWA blight. To that end, predator insects known to feed exclusively on adelgids have been imported from China, Japan, and western North America. These adelgid-munching beetles are currently being mass reared in labs at the University of Georgia, the University of Tennessee, Clemson University, Virginia Tech, NC State, and the NC Department of Agriculture. Thus far, four species of predatory beetles have been released in HWA infested areas. Experts believe it will require time and an efficient complex of four or more beetle species to reduce adelgid populations below hemlock-damaging levels.

To learn about the ecological importance of the eastern hemlock and the efforts to save the species, consult these websites:

- **www.na.fs.fed.us/fhp/hwa**,
- **www.fs.fed.us/r8/foresthealth**, or
- **www.saveourhemlocks.org**.

Beech Bark Disease

As many Shining Rock region hikers have already noticed, entire stands of relatively young, high-elevation beech—most of their boles ranging from 4 to 14 inches at dbh—have been decimated by some bark-crinkling malady in recent years. The culprit is beech bark disease: a two-punch combination of exotic pest and native fungi. The invasive exotic is the European beech scale, a minute sap-feeding insect. The actual pathogens are two native, very closely related, canker-causing fungi.

The bark-cankering dynamic is as simple as it is insidious. Beech scales bore numerous tiny holes in their namesake tree's smooth, smoke-gray bark. The fungus then enters through the holes and attacks, colonizing and killing the scale-modified bark. American beech did not host either of these fungi until the scales hitched a ride across the Atlantic and started drilling holes into the North American version of the species. The erupting cankers are caused by the tree's reaction to the invading fungus. When these cankers expand and coalesce to cover the trunk, they effectively kill the above-ground portion of this broadleaf.

When a stand of beech dies back above ground, a dense stubble of root-sucker saplings quickly takes its place. When these saplings become 1 to 2 inches thick, BBD hits the stand again. This second wave of the disease can kill the saplings above and below ground, graveyard dead.

The scale was accidentally introduced to Nova Scotia around 1890. By 1932, the scale-fungus combination was killing beech throughout the mature forest areas of the Maritime Provinces and as far south as northern Maine. Since that time the scale has been slowly working its way southward down the Appalachian cordillera, dispersing with the wind in an unbroken front at a pace of approximately 5 miles per year. Migrating birds and people transporting beech firewood have enabled this aphidlike exotic species to leapfrog far further south of its solid line of advance. This pest first appeared deep in Blue Ridge Dixie in the mid-1980s, a jump to the GSMNP hundreds of miles ahead of its slow-moving march.

In the mountains of North Carolina, Tennessee, and Virginia, BBD primarily attacks dense stands where the beech is a component of the northern hardwood forest above 4,600 feet. Ninety-five percent of the damage is done above that elevation. At present, the scale survives in low numbers below 4,000 feet in the Southern Appalachians, and the disease exists very sporadically below 3,000 feet.

Thus far, it appears that only 1 to 3 percent of the beech above 4,600 feet have a natural defense mechanism against the scale. The surviving trees and their seedlings and root suckers will form small islands of immunity. The severe competition from the root suckers of all the beech with no immunity, however, will greatly slow the spread of these small islands. Without active human management or the complete BBD death of most of the susceptible trees, passive recolonization by the few resistant specimens would take place very slowly, if at all. In the meantime, do not move beech wood from its dead and down site, and root for the few remaining highcountry beech to tip the balance against the scale.

For more information concerning BBD, consult these websites:

- www.na.fs.fed.us/fhp/bbd or
- www.fs.fed.us/r8/foresthealth.

Weather

Today, now that pinpoint forecasts are literally at your finger-tips—a couple of mouse clicks or finger swipes away—much of the former uncertainty concerning potential weather conditions has dissipated like valley fog under bright sunlight. But these forecasts do not explain the highly synergistic factors governing highcountry weather. And they do not inform the inexperienced hiker that all of these factors conspire to make the highest peaks dramatically colder than the large urban areas in the Piedmont to the east, and significantly colder than the nearby towns of Brevard and Waynesville.

Mountain weather has its own interconnected ecology. Average wind speed and annual precipitation increase with altitude, and temperature decreases 3.0 degrees for every rise of 1,000 feet. This temperature gradient, however, is not a straight-line, linear progression unless all of the conditions are equal at all elevations. And that is the catch; unless the region is blanketed in a stationary high-pressure system, the conditions are rarely equal. As you climb higher up the mountain, not only will you encounter, on average, more rain and stronger winds, but also more cloud cover and fewer hours of clothes-drying, body-warming sunshine per day.

Statistics from nearby GSMNP will give you an idea how mountain weather really works. During July, the warmest month of the year, the town of Gatlinburg (1,460 feet) on the northern perimeter of the park has an average high of 88 degrees, an average low of 59 degrees, and an average precipitation of 5.7 inches. By comparison, Clingmans Dome—the park's highest peak at 6,643 feet—has an average high of 65 degrees, an average low of 53 degrees, and an average precipitation of 8.3 inches. Using the standard 3.0-degree decrease per 1,000-foot rise, you would expect the average daytime temperature difference between the two sites to be 15.5 degrees. The difference, however, is actually 23 degrees, a chilly 4.4-degree change per 1,000-foot rise.

To a substantial and measureable extent, the higher the mountains, the more they create their own weather. The higher the peak, the longer it shades its north slope in the morning. The higher the mountains, the more likely they are to create clouds as they force moisture-laden air to rise over their ridges. And the higher the mountains, the more likely they are to wring highly localized rain from those newly created clouds.

The higher the mountains, the more often they become cloudscrapers, their summits shrouded in blowing mist while a low-elevation trailhead 5 miles away glints in bright sunlight. The highest peaks along the trails in this guide, particularly those in the 5,600- to 6,200-foot range, frequently plow upside-down furrows across the bellies of low-scudding clouds. The 6,000-foot summits in the Shining Rock area produce weather that is the climatic equivalent of a low-elevation, inland site in New England, except the southern mountaintops will generate stronger winds and more rain.

A word about that wind: ridgelines are the windiest places in the mountains, and the wind-funnel gaps are the windiest places on the ridgelines. In general, the higher the mountain and its ridges, the higher the wind speed when it crosses those ridges. Think of this wind as a reverse waterfall, flowing up with increased speed and momentum instead of down. The higher and steeper the slope, the faster the stream of air moves as it gains upward thrust, until it strafes horizontally across the crest when it's really blowing. During the colder months, but especially in winter, powerful cold-front winds regularly whistle through the high gaps at 40 to 60 miles per hour.

Note: Thanks to the GSMNP for the Gatlinburg–Clingmans Dome weather statistics.

How to Use This Guide

This guidebook covers thirty-four trails within or near the Shining Rock and Middle Prong Wildernesses. The trails are grouped by area and interconnectedness; a list of trails and a basic map highlighting those trails in the specific area are provided at the beginning of each chapter.

Trail Descriptions

A concise, at-a-glance summary of essential information is provided at the beginning of each trail description. You can quickly refer to the trail number as it is listed on the map, its length, and its difficulty rating for both dayhiking and backpacking. Also provided here are the starting and ending points of the trail, a list of junctions with other trails, topographic quadrangle names, blaze information, usage, and a brief listing of some of the trail's outstanding features.

Following this information listing, you will find a complete description of the trail with special attention given to the difficulty of grade, terrain and forest type, trail junctions, large trailside trees, water sources, stream crossings, views, and other features such as benchmarks and plaques you will see along the route. GPS coordinates have been provided for some of the harder-to-locate big trees and trail junctions. At the conclusion of the trail narrative, a nature notes section provides wildflower lists, bloom dates, and species profiles of some of the more obvious and interesting flora and fauna.

Finally, the driving or hiking directions will lead you—sometimes with a reference to another trail's directions—to the exact trailhead or interior junction you need. Compass headings in degrees or a more general direction (north, northeast, etc.) are given for the entrances of most interior trails.

When using this guidebook, keep in mind that conditions along wilderness trails are constantly changing and that trails are occasionally rerouted. If you have particular concerns, contact the appropriate Forest Service office.

Trail Ratings

Non-numerical difficulty ratings are inherently subjective and relative; there are no standardized norms that fit all the possibilities. Useful systems, however, are those that achieve consistency by limiting this subjectivity and relativity to a single source and a single region. The ratings in this guide are Southern Appalachian ratings. Easy to moderate means easy to moderate for the Southern Appalachians. The bar for easy to moderate is raised higher than it would be for Florida trails, and the bar for rugged is set lower than it would be for Colorado trails. To this end, I have hiked and rated all of the trails described in this guide. Even if you do not agree with my ratings, I hope you will find them consistent and, after a trip or two, useful.

The trail ratings in this book were based upon the usual criteria: the rate of elevation change, the way that elevation change is accomplished, the difficulty of a route compared to others described in this guide, and the length of the trail. In general, to reflect the cumulative effect of the grade, longer trails were usually rated more difficult than shorter trails with roughly the same elevation change per mile.

This rating system is also based on two assumptions. The first is that this or any other scheme does not apply to people at either end of the fitness-spectrum bell curve—those in excellent condition and those in poor condition. Hikers who are able to run long distances with little effort already know that difficulty ratings are meaningless for them. Conversely, people who become winded while searching for their remotes would find difficulty classifications equally inaccurate, although much harder to ignore.

The other assumption is that a very high percentage of the people who hike or want to hike in the mountains exercise, at least occasionally. After all, if you rarely exercise, it probably would be wise to choose a wilderness route ranked no more difficult than easy to moderate on your first trip. This approach is designed to accommodate those who work out, at least sporadically, and who fall somewhere in that broad, general category between slightly below fair condition and slightly better than good condition.

Four categories of difficulty are employed in this guide: Easy, Moderate, Strenuous, and Rugged. As you will notice, many trails have been assigned two designations. These split designations are used to help bridge fitness levels when trail difficulty falls between obvious gradations. For instance, a trail may be rated "Dayhiking In: Moderate to Strenuous." A hiker in good cardiovascular condition would consider this trail to be about moderate. A hiker in fair shape would probably rate the route moderate to strenuous, and a person with a poor fitness level would probably find it at least strenuous, if not even harder.

The decision to hike a certain trail is a personal judgment. Common sense, however, suggests that beginners who are not sure of their strength and endurance should err on the side of easy until they learn their capabilities. When planning a trip, you should be aware of a trail's difficulty, not intimidated by it; you should think of the rating as a recommendation, not a warning. If you prepare physically, keep the intended mileage reasonable, walk at a comfortable pace, take frequent rest stops, and are energized by mountain beauty, you will often be surprised at what you can accomplish.

Note: The trails within the Shining Rock–Middle Prong Wildernesses and their adjacent lands are rougher, have more of the three *r*'s—rocks, ruts, and roots, plus more step-ups and downs—than the trail systems of the other large (for the east) national forest wildernesses in the Southern Appalachians. This is neither complaint nor criticism, just a simple statement of fact. Shining Creek Trail and ALT-4 are far and away the two rockiest footpaths in this guide. These two routes are frequently very rocky—boulder-jumble rocky. By definition, wilderness trails are maintained to a more primitive standard than non-wilderness trails. In general, except where they follow old railroad grades, wilderness trails are rougher, narrower, and have more obstacles, such as deadfalls, per mile.

Shining Rock Gap

The area in and around the small opening in Shining Rock Gap can be very confusing, especially for inexperienced or first-time Shining Rock hikers. Here in the opening, the ALT makes a quick and frequently unexpected diagonal zigzag from one side of the opening to the other and from one side of the ridge to the other.

At present, the only bare-dirt tread in the opening skirts its high side, the side at 125 degrees, the far right side if you have entered the opening from the south. As you can see from the map, if you are hiking the ALT from south to north and continue straight ahead through the opening on the only track you see, you will be heading in roughly the right direction on the wrong trail—Old Butt Knob. And if you are trekking the ALT from the north, and miss the slot through the strip of vegetation 90 degrees to the left and a few yards away, you will tie into the similarly wide grade of the IGT 33 yards beyond the turn you should have taken. If you are entering Shining Rock Gap from the north, start paying attention after the long spill of white boulders on the upslope side of the ALT. From those boulders it is 0.15 mile to the left turn into the opening as shown on the map.

The best way to reach Shining Rock from the opening in Shining Rock Gap is via Old Butt Knob Trail. After passing near the low bluff line of white rock, you will arrive at the first of two short sidepaths (to the left and up, this one wider and closer to where you want to be than the other) after 0.17 mile. A quick scramble takes you close to the viewing gallery atop the iconic rock. From that first sidepath, Old Butt Knob climbs on its wide and deep treadway for a little less than 150 yards to a bare-spot junction. The path to the left (and nearly north) leads to campsites. The route to the right (entrance southeast) is Old Butt Knob heading toward its low-end junction with Shining Creek Trail.

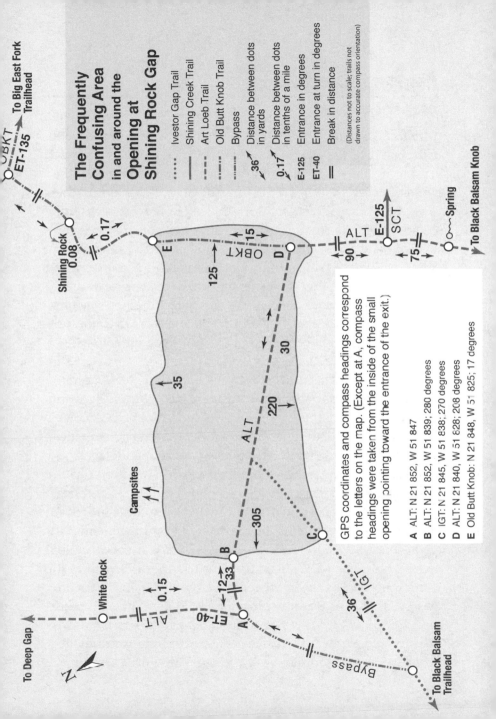

The Frequently Confusing Area in and around the Opening at Shining Rock Gap

⋯⋯⋯ Ivestor Gap Trail
——— Shining Creek Trail
– – – Art Loeb Trail
-·-·- Old Butt Knob Trail
▪▪▪▪▪ Bypass
36 → Distance between dots in yards
0.17 → Distance between dots in tenths of a mile
E-125 Entrance in degrees
ET-40 Entrance at turn in degrees
═══ Break in distance

(Distances not to scale; trails not drawn to accurate compass orientation)

GPS coordinates and compass headings correspond to the letters on the map. (Except at A, compass headings were taken from the inside of the small opening pointing toward the entrance of the exit.)

A ALT: N 21 852, W 51 847
B ALT: N 21 852, W 51 839; 280 degrees
C IGT: N 21 845, W 51 838; 270 degrees
D ALT: N 21 840, W 51 828; 208 degrees
E Old Butt Knob: N 21 848, W 51 825; 17 degrees

To Big East Fork Trailhead
OBKT ET-135
Shining Rock 0.08
0.17
To Black Balsam Knob
Spring
E-125 SCT
ALT
90
75
OBKT
15
D
125
35
30
220
ALT
Campsites
White Rock
0.15
ALT
To Deep Gap
B
33
12
ET-40
305
A
36
IGT
C
Bypass
To Black Balsam Trailhead
N

Regional Directions

Over its full length, the BRP travels from the Great Smoky Mountains National Park to Shenandoah National Park, from southwest to northeast. In the Shining Rock–Middle Prong area, the parkway travels southeast then northeast as it half-loops toward Asheville. Travel directions along the parkway have been simplified to generic north or south. North means you are traveling toward Asheville; south means you are heading toward the Smokies. Overlooks, parking areas, and pull-off parking for trailheads are all either on the generic north or south side of the parkway. Looking at a map, north is everything above the parkway. Directions for traveling on US 276 and NC 215 follow the signage. Traveling south on NC 215 means you are following NC 215 South whichever way it winds.

The directions begin with a short description of the location of the trailhead, or trailheads if the route has vehicular access at or near either end. If the trail or trail section is directly off the parkway or FS 816, the specific name of the overlook, parking area, or trailhead is frequently included along with milepost numbers. (Parkway milepost numbers increase toward the south.)

Next, directions are provided from two directions of travel: all of the approaches begin from the north and the south in this guide. Three access points are utilized along this segment of the parkway—US 276, NC 215, and US 74. US 276 is always used, if needed, as the approach from the north, and US 74 is always used, if needed, as the approach from the south. In the middle, NC 215 is used as either approach point. When the directions say, "From the BRP–access road from NC 215 junction," they mean you have already traveled NC 215 and the access road from 215 to the stop sign beside the parkway.

All the trailheads beside or off of US 276 and NC 215 share the same approach from the north: the four-way NC 215– NC 110–US 276 intersection north of the Shining Rock Wilderness. The southern approaches begin at the respective highway's junction with the parkway. "From the NC 215–access road from BRP junction" means you have already traveled the parkway and the access road from the parkway to the stop sign beside NC 215. This system leaves out specific directions for those traveling US 276 North from Brevard or NC 215 North from the Rosman area. All you have to do, however, is set your mileage count at the entrance to the access road to the parkway as you travel to the trailhead. After the approach from the north and south segment, additional directions, if needed, lead you to the exact trailhead parking area.

Sometimes duplicate directions, or very close to duplicate directions, have already been provided for another trail or trail section. When this is the case, a page-number reference leads you to those directions.

The mileage was set back to zero at each junction to obtain a more accurate and consistent reading.

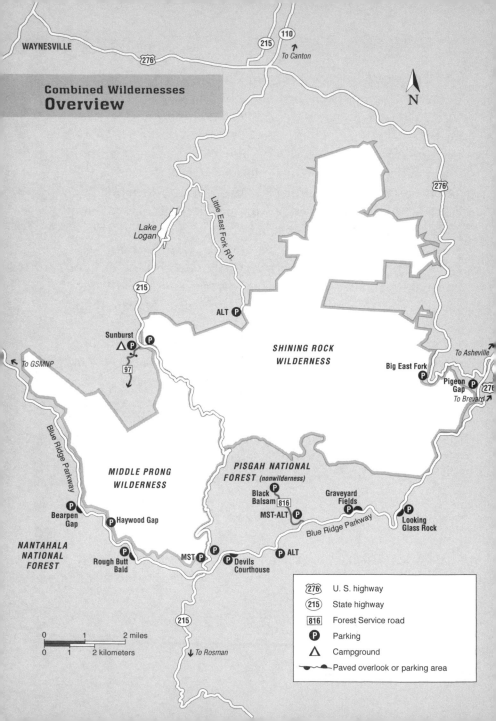

WAYNESVILLE

276

215 110
To Canton

Combined Wildernesses
Overview

N

276

Little East Fork Rd

Lake
Logan

215

ALT P

Sunburst
△ P P

To GSMNP

97

*SHINING ROCK
WILDERNESS*

Big East Fork P

To Asheville

Pigeon
Gap
To Brevard

276

Blue Ridge Parkway

*MIDDLE PRONG
WILDERNESS*

*PISGAH NATIONAL
FOREST (nonwilderness)*

Black
Balsam P
816
MST-ALT P

Graveyard
Fields P

Looking
Glass Rock P

Bearpen
Gap P

Haywood Gap P

Blue Ridge Parkway

*NANTAHALA
NATIONAL
FOREST*

Rough Butt
Bald P

MST P P ALT P

P Devils
Courthouse

215

To Rosman

| 0 | 1 | 2 miles |
| 0 | 1 | 2 kilometers |

276	U. S. highway
215	State highway
816	Forest Service road
P	Parking
△	Campground
●︵●︵	Paved overlook or parking area

Part 1

Shining Rock Wilderness

Eastern Region
Western Region
Northern Region

Roger Nielsen

Shining Rock

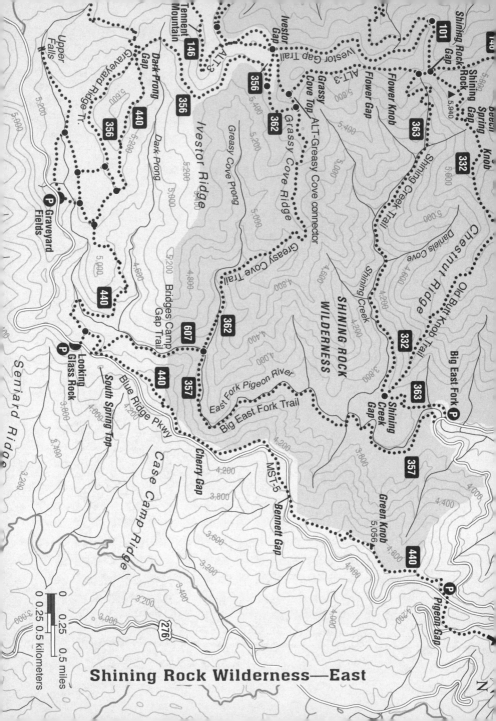

Shining Rock Wilderness—East

Shining Rock Wilderness—East

Gary Crider

Cascade on Greasy Prong

Trails

Old Butt Knob

Shining Creek

Big East Fork

Greasy Cove

Bridges Camp Gap

Mountains to Sea, Section 5

Old Butt Knob Trail

Forest Service Trail 332   **4.0 miles**

Dayhiking (low to high) Strenuous
Dayhiking (high to low) Moderate
Backpacking (low to high) Strenuous to Rugged
Backpacking (high to low) Moderate to Strenuous
Interior Trail Eastern (lower elevation) terminus on
    Shining Creek Trail at Shining Creek Gap, 3,660 feet;
    western (higher elevation) terminus at its junction
    with Art Loeb and Ivestor Gap Trails at Shining Rock
    Gap, 5,755 feet
Trail Junctions Shining Creek, ALT-3, IGT,
    upper-elevation end of Shining Creek nearby
Topographic Quadrangle Shining Rock
Blaze None (wilderness)
Usage Foot travel only
Features Wilderness; Shining Rock lead-in route;
    year-round views from rock outcrops, including
    Shining Rock; late spring–early summer flowering
    shrub display; occasional old-growth trees

A ridgeline and upper-slope route, Old Butt Knob is the most
difficult trail in the Shining Rock Wilderness and the second
toughest hike in this guide. Trekked low to high its first mile—
contour lines bunched tightly on the topo—gains roughly 1,400
feet of elevation. Hikers frequently tackle Old Butt's full length
as the first or last leg of the three-trail near loop (90 yards of the

ALT plus the Shining Creek Trail) beginning and ending at the Big East Fork Trailhead.

One of four routes that pass through or end at Shining Rock Gap, Old Butt is the only trail that ventures just below the two shortest scrambles to Shining Rock's open perch. Most hikers who make the pilgrimage to the high white outcrop walk other treadways to Shining Rock Gap, then follow Old Butt Knob's westernmost 0.2 mile to reach the rocks. This short stretch is heavily tramped; the rest of the track is lightly used in comparison. Old Butt Knob is described as it is most easily accessed—low to high, east to west, Shining Creek Gap to Shining Rock Gap.

Starting at the obvious junction in Shining Creek Gap, the trail forges ahead to the northwest on Chestnut Ridge. Here the hardwood-over-heath forest is dominated by red maple and four kinds of oak—northern red, scarlet, white, and the abundant chestnut. The ridge's namesake tree, now reduced by blight to short-lived root-sucker saplings, remains common along the steep first mile. The understory is ruled by evergreen heath, primarily the abundant mountain laurel and three species of rhododendron—rosebay, Catawba, and dwarf.

The course ascends the lowermost mile in an uneven manner; there are no sustained, gut-buster grades of even 100 yards in length, but rather a constant shifting from easy or easy to moderate to much harder, shorter pulls and back again. Beyond the first mile, the rest of the tread is a cakewalk in comparison.

Old Butt starts its upridge run right away. The first tenth of a mile is moderate to strenuous overall. The next 0.4 mile is somewhat less difficult, moderate overall. But even the easier grades have plenty of step-ups to roots or rocks.

At 0.5 mile you arrive at the first abrupt pitch of ridgetop rock. At the small pocket of Table Mountain pine 65 yards further, a short sidepath to the left leads to a rock outcrop overlook open to the south. Here the land falls away at your feet to the Shining Creek cove far below. Straight out in front of you, Raven Cliff Ridge is the closest crest on the other side of the cove's rim. Raven Cliff Ridge drops off sharply to the left at around 186 degrees. From this drop-off, Raven Cliff rises to the southwest to meet Nobreeches Ridge (blocked from view) at the top of an unnamed knob (5,260 feet) on Grassy Cove Ridge at around 216 degrees. At the right edge of the view, the broad and symmetrically rounded dome of Grassy Cove Top thrusts the land to 6,055 feet on Shining Rock Ledge at around 246 degrees.

South Spring Top, a named knob in the long string of peaks known as Pisgah Ridge, is close to due south immediately to the left of Raven Cliff Ridge's drop-off and just across the parkway. Further to the left of South Spring Top, two unnamed knobs on Pisgah Ridge stand side by side across the East Fork Pigeon River. The parkway runs in front of the peak to the left (the one west of Bennett Gap) and behind the peak to the right (the one at around 153 degrees).

The segment from 0.6 to 0.9 mile, with its repeated surges up ridgecrest rock, is strenuous to rugged and by far the trail's hardest pull. These rocky jump-ups are short but steep; a few of them really get on the elevator. The first of the switchbacks begins at a little more than 0.6 mile. The track slips to the left below the ridgeline at 0.8 mile and passes near a wall of rock outcrop before switchbacking up to the top of the crest again. The final tenth of this memorable grunt is easy to moderate to an overused ridgeline campsite at mile 1.0.

This wilderness footpath now alternates easy uphill grades with nearly level walking as it advances on or near the top of the fold. At mile 1.1 the first red spruce begin to mingle with the oaks, and serviceberry and mountain winterberry become more common components of the understory. At mile 1.6, just beyond a small stand of mature spruce, the route travels past a flat campsite to the right.

A sidepath to the left at mile 1.8 guides you to a rock outcrop overlook open to the southwest. This vantage point gives you a good view of the steep-sided upper drainage of Shining Creek—the high, Southern Appalachian splay of spur ridges ribbing down from the crests, each spur alternating with the concave hollows to either side. The following are the most prominent peaks looking from northwest to southwest along the boundary rim of the basin: Old Butt Knob 0.2 mile away to the northwest; Dog Loser Knob, the next knuckle beyond Old Butt, at around 276 degrees; Shining Rock, with its telltale gleam of white showing through the conifers, at around 268 degrees; the wide dome of Grassy Cove Top at around 228 degrees. Further away than the others but still nearby, the broad top of Black Balsam Knob (6,214 feet) is visible over the high end of Grassy Cove Ridge at around 220 degrees.

Beyond the look-off, the trail rises to the high southern side of Old Butt Knob's peak (5,520 feet) at mile 2.0 before descending to the flat of Spanish Oak Gap (5,380 feet) at mile 2.2. The gap is wide enough that you can camp to the right well away from the trail. Spanish oak is another, older name for the southern red oak, which does not currently occur in its namesake gap. This essentially southern species rarely roots above 3,600 feet even in today's warming climate.

As you ascend to the west toward the next knob, three factors—a substantial increase in elevation, a slightly moister exposure, and a much wider ridgecrest—combine to create a significantly cooler and moister environment than the one along Old Butt's lowermost half mile. Here the forest is a high-elevation northern hardwood/spruce-fir mix: red spruce and Fraser fir mingle with yellow birch, beech, and yellow buckeye, plus red and mountain maple. Early on, the track roams past a few old-growth northern red oaks; the thickest—11 feet 4 inches in circumference—stands a stride to the left of the tread at mile 2.3. Higher up, the forest alternates between pockets of conifers and recently open areas now grown up with early succession hardwoods such as pin cherry and mountain ash.

The upgrade gains the far southern edge of Dog Loser Knob's small crown (5,730 feet) at mile 2.7. Following a descent through small hardwoods and tread-lining thickets of evergreen heath, the trail bottoms out in Beech Spring Gap (5,620 feet, mile 3.0), which is rapidly returning to forest. Beech Spring to the left (southeast) of the trail is intermittent—definitely not reliable at the springhead during drought when the trees are drawing water skyward. The most prominent sidepath leading to the spring is located in the flat of the gap; its entrance (N 22 14, W 51 41) is east. After 35 yards this sidepath reaches a small campsite. Take the continuing path that leads to the right (entrance about south) from the camp. Follow this fainter track (curves to the right and up at its end) 50 yards to the spring bed just downhill from its rise when it flows (N 22 11, W 51 40 at the springhead).

At mile 3.1 Old Butt loser begins a series of switchbacks as it snakes its winding way up Shining Rock's eastern lead. Much of the easy ascent's final 0.4 mile pushes through trail-rubbing heath shrubs, including fetterbush, shaded by low northern hardwoods and red spruce.

Sixty yards before a fork, Old Butt reaches its highpoint (5,970 feet) where a very short sidepath to the left leads to an over-the-vegetation view (for now) open to the south. At mile 3.7, high on the southeastern rim of Shining Rock's summit, the course comes to the small bare spot of a potentially confusing fork. The path to the right, nearly north, heads to campsites;

the trail turns left and down onto the heavily used segment that leads to the highly sought rock. Eroded and rutted (it may be rerouted in the future), the track descends moderately with short lurches and numerous high step-downs. There are two sidepaths that veer back up and to the right toward the top of the rocks. Fifty yards beyond the first, the second sidepath's short scramble ushers you closer to the viewing gallery atop the open rock.

A very low-ranking member of the 6,000-footer club (6,010 feet), Shining Rock is, nevertheless, a pinnacle of Southern Appalachian hiking. Although its obdurately erosion-resistant crest is quartz, Shining Rock is a magnetic mountain. Sooner or later, most serious Southern Appalachian hikers are drawn to the vantage point of its peak. Dayhikers revel in the novelty of the smooth white rock and the views—the ancient symmetries of the worn and weathered Appalachians rearing up into rowed ridges, summer green and forever. But backpackers have it better. They can watch as the dying embers of the day spread fire and free glory over the near horizon of high mountains to the west, tinting the white rock pale rose. Then they can watch as the moon scales the sky, bright and full, lighting up the rock until it almost glows.

With 0.2 mile remaining, the tread skirts Shining Rock's cliff face before bending down and away from the wall. The final grade loses elevation through spruce and rhododendron to the shrinking opening in Shining Rock Gap. Here Old Butt ties seamlessly into the ALT, which makes a sharp turn in the opening with no hint of a junction. Two trails—Old Butt Knob and Ivestor Gap—end here; one trail, ALT-3, travels through the opening, and a fourth route, Shining Creek, ends nearby. An easily located and usually reliable spring is also close at hand. (See page liii for the description and drawing of the Shining Rock Gap area.)

Nature Notes

Although ridge-running Old Butt does not wind through the best wildflower sites—moist, deep-soiled hardwood forests—it still leads hikers past a wide variety of herbaceous species, most of which bloom in relatively small numbers. Painted trillium and lousewort (or wood betony) usually start flowering by May 12. Beginning in late June and early July, the fly poison's dense cylindrical clusters of small white blossoms are held aloft on stems usually rising from 1 to 3½ feet. Asters enliven the ridgecrests from the last half of August into early October. On a recent September 21 the striped gentian (or mountain gentian) bloomed steadily in small numbers beside the trail.

Dwarf rhododendron, also known as Carolina or Piedmont rhododendron, bloomed along much of the first mile's climb on a recent May 9. Catawba rhododendron, mountain laurel, and flame azalea usually peak sometime between June 8 and 22. Mountain laurel was nearly finished and bush honeysuckle was just beginning to bloom on June 27.

American chestnut

The American chestnut (*Castanea dentata*) was the most massive, most numerous, and most important tree—to wildlife and humans alike—in the Southern Appalachian forest. Its destruction by fungal blight was an ecological disaster. This keystone species once crowned as the queen of the eastern forest ranged from 80 to 125 feet tall, with a large, spreading crown easily recognized from a distance in winter. The chestnut grew to an incredible thickness for an eastern tree: a maximum of 10 to 13 feet in diameter. Two primary growth giants in the Smokies measured 33 feet and 33 feet 4 inches in circumference. Now after the four-punch knockout of industrial logging, blight, massive air pollution, and the explosion of exotic insect pests and diseases, a southern mountain hardwood over 30 feet around is hardly imaginable—more a mythological symbol of former fertility than a future pos-sibility.

American chestnut

Mature chestnuts grew in a variety of habitats, from near riverside to dry ridges. In some areas of the Southern Appalachi-ans, this member of the Beech family made up 25 to 40 percent of the forest. It often occurred in nearly pure stands on ridgetops up to approximately 5,200 feet in elevation. Regarded as hardy and disease resistant before the imported blight, these eastern forest monarchs were capable of lifting water from soil to sky for six centuries. (The fungus invaded nearby GSMNP around 1925; by 1938, 85 percent of the park's chestnuts had been killed or affected by the blight.)

Before the blight, wildlife fattened upon the bountiful mast crop of large chestnuts that rained to the forest floor. Deer, bear, raccoon, turkey, squirrel, and other animals, including free-range hogs, gorged on this bonanza every year without fail. Bear and the now extinct passenger pigeon preferred the nutritious nuts above all other foods. Today, the wildlife that is left copes as best it can with the cyclical hard mast production of oak, hickory, and beech.

Thus far, *C. dentata* has refused to die out completely. Ever since the blight, root sprouts have grown into small saplings, only to be mown down in turn by the fungus. Since these root-sprout saplings are genetic clones, they offer the species no chance to develop selective resistance to the fungus. Occasionally, a sapling will reach 4 to 7 inches in diameter before succumbing to the bark-ripping blight.

By the autumn of 1728, the Virginia commissioners had surveyed their state line from the Dismal Swamp all the way to the foothills of the Southern Appalachians. Over all that distance, their hunters had bagged no bears—the most sought after sustenance—until they approached the mountains and their chestnuts. Their stock of biscuits low and their horses weak, the terrain becoming steeper and the nights growing colder, the exhausted survey team pronounced their work done for the year and headed home on October 26. The following accounts come from William Byrd's *Histories of the Dividing Line betwixt Virginia and North Carolina.*

> *Oct 12*...We judg'd by the great number of Chestnut Trees we approach't the mountains, which several of our Men discover'd very plainly. The Bears are great Lovers of Chestnuts...Our men kill'd a bear of 2 years old which was very fat.
>
> *Oct 16*...the men knock't down no less than 4 bears and 2 Turkeys.
>
> *Oct 20*...kill a monstrous fat Bear
>
> *Oct 21*...shot a Bear so prodigiously fat, that there was no way to kill Him but by fireing in at his Ear.
>
> *Oct 22*...we found no less than 3 Bears...had thrown in our course...they brought in no less than six Bears, exceedingly fat.

Note: On this day two parties of hunters (the group that shot six usually not very skillful) killed nine bears by fireing flintlock muskets, a testimony to the former abundance of bears in the chestnut-dominated primary growth forests.

Fetterbush

The fetterbush, a dense evergreen shrub usually 3 to 10 feet in height, is common where the trail tunnels through heath thickets on the high ridgelines. Endemic to the Southern Highlands, this heath prefers sunny, high-elevation sites—exposed ridges and upper slopes, the edges of balds and rock outcrops.

This species is most common above 4,400 feet in the Shining Rock area.

Also called mountain andromeda and mountain pieris, fetterbush is readily identified when leaf and flower are seen in combination. The dark green and glossy leaves are alternate,

fetterbush

narrow, and about 2 inches long. Fetterbush foliage is noticeably narrower, darker green, and more sharply pointed than the similarly sized leaves of the mountain laurel.

Numerous small, urn-shaped blossoms cluster along the bottoms and sides of the terminal and axillary flower stalks. The cream-colored blooms are sometimes tinged with a light pink color. Old Butt's fetterbushes were open for pollination on April 22, May 7, and May 18 during three recent years.

Directions

Old Butt Knob is an interior trail that has its eastern end on Shining Creek Trail and its western end at Shining Rock Gap, where it ties into the ALT (Section 3) and IGT.

To reach the lower-elevation end of Old Butt Knob, walk 0.8 mile on Shining Creek Trail starting from its Big East Fork Trailhead. Located at Shining Creek Gap, the junction (N 21 50, W 49 27) is readily recognized by its scuffed loafing place, erosion bars, and forking trails. Shining Creek continues straight ahead, nearly west, and slightly downhill from the junction; Old Butt Knob heads sharply up the ridgeline to the right and nearly north. (See Shining Creek, the following trail, for further information.)

Notes

Shining Creek Trail

Forest Service Trail 363 **4.2 miles**

Dayhiking In Moderate to Strenuous
Dayhiking Out Moderate
Backpacking In Strenuous
Backpacking Out Moderate to Strenuous
Start The prominently signed Big East Fork Trailhead,
3,410 feet
End Junction with Art Loeb Trail close to Shining Rock
Gap, 5,760 feet
Trail Junctions Big East Fork (near trailhead),
Old Butt Knob (lower-elevation end), ALT-3, IGT and
the upper-elevation end of Old Butt Knob at the
nearby opening in Shining Rock Gap
Topographic Quadrangle Shining Rock
Blaze None (wilderness)
Usage Foot travel only
Features Wilderness; East Fork Pigeon River; Shining
Creek; spring and summer wildflower display;
waterfall (see description); occasional old-growth
trees; Shining Rock lead-in route; boulder fields

As you walk this scenic track up the watershed from river to ridge,
many things tug at your attention, from wildflowers and old-
growth trees to cascades and rocky footing. Beyond the Old Butt
Knob junction, this slope-and-streamside path closely parallels
the flash and flow of Shining Creek's wilderness-clear water. The

rollicking beauty of this small-volume watercourse is at its sliding and sluicing best in winter or early spring after substantial rainfall.

This heavily used Shining Rock lead-in route rises from east to west, from the East Fork Pigeon River to Shining Rock Gap. Hikers most often walk it in and out, to Shining Rock and back, or as the longest leg of a three-trail loop—Shining Creek, ALT-3 (only 90 yards), and Old Butt Knob—beginning and ending at the Big East Fork Trailhead.

Shining Creek gains its considerable elevation, 2,350 feet, steadily rather than by sharp ascent. There are no long strenuous grades, but this route, occasionally boulder-jumble rocky, is one of the two rockiest trails in this guide.

Shining Creek begins with easy walking on a former roadbed through a young, species-rich mesophytic forest, the canopy all hardwood, the tallest trees pole-timber yellow poplar. Looks to your left give you partial views of the East Fork Pigeon River, its cascades a white lather when the river is up and rolling. The tread enters a thicket-growth of evergreen heath and quickly crosses the rocky and usually summer-parched bed of Dry Branch.

The old road comes to a fork at 0.3 mile; Shining Creek continues up and to the right on wide sidehill path. At 0.4 mile the trail switchbacks up and to the right, then rises on a moderate pull before downshifting to easier grades. It continues to switchback up the slope through a forest of tall, straight trees—now second-growth with no disturbance since the first bout of logging—that includes black cherry, sweet birch, cucumbertree, silverbell, and Fraser magnolia. After gaining the top of a spur, the boot-worn treadway quickly slants to the left of the rising ridge, then dips to and rounds a rich hardwood hollow. The course heads uphill on an easy-to-moderate grade to the obvious junction and small pack-drop spot at Shining Creek Gap (0.8 mile;

3,660 feet; N 21 50, W 49 27) near the foot of Chestnut Ridge. Here Old Butt Knob Trail climbs the ridgeline to the right and nearly north, and Shining Creek proceeds straight ahead across Chestnut Ridge before dipping slightly to accompany its namesake stream.

All of the sustained grades for the next 1.1 miles are easy. A diverse hardwood forest remains in control of the canopy. Some of the species not already mentioned include northern red, chestnut, and white oaks; red and sugar maples; yellow birch, white basswood, white ash, and yellow buckeye. Living in deciduous shade, the evergreen heaths thoroughly dominate the shrub layer.

By mile 1.0 the footpath closely parallels and provides frequent good views of the boulder-bedded creek, either from alongside it or from further up the slope. The difference between a rainy spring and a drought-ridden summer is dramatic. It is the difference between the surging power of cascades flying into foam, lit and alive with sunsparkle, and the listless spills and slow weavings of low water. At mile 1.2 you pass a room-sized boulder (a room with a very high ceiling) crowned with alumroot. By mile 1.5 the track follows an obvious railroad bed left over from the timber rush days.

Seventy-five yards past a high bedrock cascade, the trail comes to and crosses an unnamed feeder branch flowing down from Daniels Cove (mile 1.9, 4,050 feet). Before and after the crossing, sidepaths lead sharply uphill for approximately 0.1 mile to Daniels Cove Falls, a small volume, 15- to 20-foot freefall followed by a longer slide canted at a 25- to 30-degree angle.

At mile 2.1 the line of march slants up and away from the cascading stream onto a sidehill treadway where the railroad cut continues straight ahead. The next mile is memorably scenic. Here the hiking ascends onto the lower flank of Bearpen Ridge before shadowing a much smaller stream, the North Prong. Where the trail rises high above the prong, it frequently wanders through a woods of well-spaced trees with a ground cover of grasses, ferns (primarily hay-scented and New York), and wildflowers amid the many gray rocks. At mile 2.2 you pass the first of occasional old-growth sugar maples and northern red oaks.

By mile 2.4 the track roughly parallels the branch-sized North Prong to the northwest. The rock-bound trail provides a close and clear view of several low cascades at mile 2.6 before rising higher up and away from the stream. At mile 2.8 you pass above a high cascade skimming over a bank-to-bank bedrock ledge, a slanting fall of perhaps 15 feet. Thirty-five yards beyond a miniature pour and pool (mile 3.0), a northern red oak 4 paces upslope measured 11 feet 3 inches in circumference.

At mile 3.1 (4,880 feet) the course crosses a small side branch that arises just south of Beech Spring Gap, then continues to work its way up the North Prong watershed. Steeper grades, ramping up to short moderate-to-strenuous ascents, lift the treadway higher above what's left of the prong. Two-tenths mile further, the hike zigzags through a double switchback that leads up and away from the stream's notch. Hobblebush (an opposite-leaved viburnum shrub) is now conspicuous, and tall red spruce, conical and dark green, mix with the cove and northern hardwoods. Small boulders and lichen-splotched rock jumbles continue to enhance the trail corridor.

The footpath comes to a rock-lumpy campsite and resting place appointed with a small cube-shaped boulder at mile 3.5. Much of the tenth-mile above the boulder climbs sharply on very short rocky pitches mixed in with longer moderate grades. Above the switchback to the right at mile 3.6, the overall easy-going gradient winds up a moist seepage slope frequently lush with tall forbs—white snakeroot, black cohosh, and nettles among them—by late spring. After wending through an area where mature yellow buckeye are common, the course enters a belt of tall red spruce and sapling Fraser fir. Up here, you'll begin to see additional high-elevation species such as mountain maple, mountain ash, and fetterbush, an evergreen heath shrub.

At mile 4.0 the treadway makes a rounded switchback to the right at a huddle of tall spruce, the lower end of a dense stand of mature trees that started dying, from top to bottom, in 2006. The remainder of the route slowly angles upslope toward Shining Rock Ledge. Hay-scented fern is often abundant where living spruce still provide shade. Following one last short, easy-to-moderate upgrade, Shining Creek T's into the ALT 90 yards south of the major junction in the small opening in Shining Rock Gap. Shining Rock and an easily found spring are also nearby. (See page liii for the description and drawing of the Shining Rock Gap area.)

Nature Notes
Shining Creek offers an excellent wildflower display during spring, summer, and early fall. Showy orchis, meadow parsnip, and Vasey's trillium were blooming along the lowermost 0.8 mile on a recent May 9. Vasey's, wakerobin, and painted trilliums; speckled wood and bluebead lilies; and Michaux's saxifrage were in full splendor among many others on May 23. The flowers of numerous other species had already faded and fallen. The creek-screening rosebay rhododendron was beginning to whiten the stream borders on a recent June 28.

Pink turtlehead, crimson bee balm, and two types of jewel-weed were showcasing their come-hither colors on August 15. The moist, high-elevation slopes were packed with black cohosh and members of the Composite family such as white snakeroot, goldenrod, white wood aster and other asters, yellow and lavender on September 6. A grass-of-Parnassus colony was in bloom and bud on September 3 and 6 of consecutive years.

Sugar maple

At mile 2.2 the route enters an open, predominantly northern hardwood forest where old-growth sugar maple, northern red oak, and yellow birch frequently control the canopy. In this scenic pocket, shaggy, gray-barked sugar maples (*Acer saccharum*) from 8 to 11 feet in circumference are common. These old-timers, which escaped last century's holocaust of industrial logging, are now crashing to earth with increasing frequency.

sugar maple

Maples are among the few trees with both opposite leaves and branches in the Shining Rock area. The sugar maple's familiar leaf—the silhouette gracing the Canadian flag—is unmistakable. It develops long, pointed lobes, green stems, and smooth margins. The leaf margins of the other three maples found in the area—mountain, striped, and red—are noticeably toothed.

Generally recognized as the most fiery in eastern North America, this broadleaf's fall foliage is multihued—red, yellow, and orange often occur on the same tree, even on the same branch.

Foresters classify this northern hardwood as tolerant, which means it is able to grow well in shade. Like the beech, hemlock, and buckeye, its saplings can thrive beneath an unbroken canopy without the aid of a light gap.

A. saccharum is one of the larger deciduous trees in the eastern forest. In the Southern Appalachians, mature, forest-grown sugar maples have clear, straight boles and average 75 to 100 feet in height and 2 to 4 feet in diameter. A very large specimen can attain impressive dimensions: 5 feet in diameter and 120 to 130 feet in height. This tree is also long-lived, from 300 to 450 years.

Wakerobin

The wakerobin, also known as red trillium and purple trillium, shows off purplish red flowers over most of its large range. But it also exhibits other color morphs: pink, yellow, white, and greenish. White is by far the most common of the alternate colors.

Trilliums are characterized by plant parts that come in threes and the length of time they take to unfurl their first flower: six years. The wakerobin's solitary blossom, usually 2 to 3 inches wide and nodding, rises above the whorl of leaves on an erect stalk. The sepals are green, the stamens are white, and along this trail, the petals are a dark wine red. The center of the corolla has an exposed brownish maroon ovary with evenly spaced ridges similar to some cake molds.

wakerobin (white)

Usually 6 to 16 inches tall, this member of the Lily family is most common in rich, moist, predominantly deciduous forests. It is particularly common on north slopes and near small streams without rhododendron. One rainy spring May 10, hundreds of wakerobins were in fresh flower along the lower and middle elevations of this trail.

Vasey's trillium

The richly colored Vasey's, usually 10 to 20 inches tall, is the largest North American trillium. Endemic to the Southern

Appalachians, these large-leaved native perennials are most common on moist, fertile slopes at low and middle elevations.

The Vasey's also features the largest flower of any North American trillium, ranging from 2 to slightly over 4 inches wide. Often slightly recurved, the carmine-colored petals nod below the distinctive three-leaved whorl.

Vasey's trillium

This species blooms later than any other Southern Appalachian trillium. On May 24 of a recent rainy spring, the flowers were faded on the lower part of the trail but blooming fresh and by the hundreds higher up.

Directions

Shining Creek begins at the large and prominently signed Big East Fork Trailhead, which is located north of the BRP on the eastern side of the Shining Rock Wilderness off US 276. Overflow parking is available across the highway.

Approach from the south: From the US 276–access road from BRP junction, travel US 276 North approximately 2.7 miles to the trailhead on the left side of the highway.

Approach from the north: From the four-way US 276–NC 215–NC 110 intersection, travel US 276 South (also marked with a Cruso Rd. street sign) approximately 11.4 miles to the trailhead on the right side of the road

Big East Fork Trail

Forest Service Trail 357 **3.6 miles**

Dayhiking Easy to Moderate in either direction
Backpacking In Moderate
Backpacking Out Easy to Moderate
Start Small trailhead 0.1 mile from the prominently
   signed Big East Fork Trailhead, 3,430 feet
End Junction with Bridges Camp Gap and Greasy Cove
   Trails beside the East Fork Pigeon River, 3,985 feet
Trail Junctions Shining Creek (near trailhead),
   Bridges Camp Gap, Greasy Cove
Topographic Quadrangle Shining Rock
Blaze None (wilderness)
Usage Foot travel only
Features Wilderness; cascades, pools, and the cold clear
   water of the East Fork Pigeon River; two riverside
   rock gardens

A streamside and lower-slope route, this trail closely shadows
the East Fork Pigeon River to the south and upstream, almost
always remaining within eyesight or earshot of the fall and
flow of the water. The treadway starts out wide, well worn, and
heavily traveled. But by the time the track narrows to a path
between hedging doghobble, the friction of distance and the
pull of the river have siphoned off many of the fishers, swim-
mers, and close-to-trailhead campers. Even though it often
undulates to match the sloping terrain along the way, this

frequently rocky route is the easiest trail mostly or completely within the combined wildernesses.

During sunny days in April or very early May, before full leaf-out and after substantial rainfall, the East Fork really shows off its churning beauty. Then its surging flow, wild and loud, shatters to white against spray-shined boulders. Then all the alchemy of sunlight and gravity and gradient, clear water and gray rock, glossy rhododendron and the widening wedge of blue sky create one of the earth's many magic shows.

The trail begins on the mild downhill grade of a former road. Sidepaths drop down to floodplain campsites closer to the river. Now, with the remaining mature hemlocks dead or dying, the trailside forest has a solid broadleaf canopy. Especially along the first mile, stands of yellow poplar rise straight and tall with the eye-pleasing symmetry of their species. Southern Appalachian evergreen—mountain laurel, rosebay rhododendron, doghobble—is still exceedingly plentiful in the riparian understory.

By 0.2 mile the walking closely parallels the river, providing steady views of the East Fork's cold pools and beginning the pattern of now you see it, now you don't, with the gin-clear stream. The nearly effortless, frequently aislelike track continues to the forking paths at 0.5 mile. Here, where the lower fork leads straight ahead toward a swimming-hole pool, the course heads up and to the left away from the river. After 60 yards the footpath forks again. For now, these 0.1-mile-long forks form a loop where they tie back into one another. The upper-left fork rises more suddenly through an open forest past wildflowers in season. The lower fork gains elevation more steadily through seepage-slope rhododendron.

The line of march crosses the small, unmapped branch coming out of Rocky Cove at 0.7 mile. Following an easy-to-moderate descent, the railroad-bed treadway frequently undulates beside the stream, close enough so you can spot trout holding, heads upstream, in the pools. At mile 1.1 the trail leaves the old logging grade and ventures onto a long slab of water-worn bedrock on the outside bend of a fast glide of curving water. The high side of the slab is a wet rock garden during the warm-weather months.

Now, and for the remainder of the route, the former railway is often hemmed in to single-file footpath by thicket-growths of doghobble. Yellow poplar, sweet and yellow birch, chestnut and northern red oak, white ash, sugar maple, black cherry, white basswood, and beech are common in the trail-corridor canopy. The track turns up and to the left from the stream at the obvious fork (mile 1.3) where the fisherman's path proceeds straight ahead. Here the hike rises well up and away from the river before dipping to and crossing the rock-step shallow Bennett Branch a tenth-mile further.

Beyond this East Fork feeder, the trail gently porpoises across a moist wildflower slope before descending harder to mile 1.8, where it begins to follow the straight, easygoing rail-line bed alongside the river again. A tenth-mile further, you reach a trailside beauty spot with boulders to sit on above a pool and cascade. To the left across the river, a slender, wet-weather falls makes a quick slanting slide down bankside rock before spreading out into fingerlike ribbons. The tread, occasionally an aisle lined with mountain laurel and rhododendron, continues to gain elevation slowly as it provides steady views of a particularly scenic stretch of the East Fork.

At mile 2.9 you drop down and skirt the river again on flood-smoothed slabs of bedrock. Back above the mountain stream, the footpath turns toward the west as it continues to work its way up the watershed. Here the combination of higher elevation and moister, north-slope exposure contributes to the increased abundance of yellow birch.

The route levels out above the river before reaching its three-way junction with Bridges Camp Gap and Greasy Cove Trails. Two nearby and plainly visible campsites—the first immediately below the trail junction (N 20 22, W 49 61) and the second across the river from the first—mark this often confusing connection. If you follow the railroad grade on the same side of the river, straight ahead and upstream from above the first camp, you will be traveling south on Bridges Camp Gap Trail parallel to the East Fork. If you ford the river to the second campsite, you will be walking on Greasy Cove Trail.

Nature Notes

Primarily a riparian-zone route, which is another way of saying it is often flanked by evergreen heath shrubs, the Big East Fork rates only a fair spring wildflower display. The first half of the trail occasionally enters pockets of good wildflower habitat where it rises onto moist hardwood slopes above the river. But along the second half, where the treadway more closely parallels the cascading stream, the forest floor is often shaded by rosebay rhododendron (usually begins blooming in mid to late June) and doghobble-tangled thickets.

During one May 2 trip, showy orchis, foamflower, lousewort, Michaux's saxifrage, and wakerobin (both white and red color morphs) were blooming among others. Vasey's trillium, speckled wood lily, and false Solomon's seal were still flowering three weeks later.

The trail skirts the rock-slab bank of the river at mile 1.1 and again at mile 2.9. These two spots, both sunny and wet, are natural rock gardens. Michaux's saxifrage, mountain lettuce, umbrella-leaf, and bluets embellished the first wild garden on a recent May 21. Fragrant and white flowered, the swamp azalea decorated the same bank the first week in June. Pink turtlehead, monkshood, spotted jewelweed, several asters, plus bottle gentian and a lobelia species bloomed at one or the other of the sites on a recent September 17.

Doghobble

Beyond mile 1.6 the route is frequently flanked by a low, slope-blanketing, trail-narrowing evergreen shrub. That shrub is doghobble, a prolific heath often forming dense thickets in moist, shaded, acidic soils next to or near Southern Appalachian streams. Shiny and pointed at the tips, doghobble leaves alternate along arching, slightly zigzag branches. New growth is usually a reddish color in the spring. In winter the uppermost leaves frequently turn reddish purple. Pendent clusters of small white, urn-shaped flowers bloom beneath the branches as early as late April along the East Fork.

doghobble

This riparian species received its colorful common name from mountaineer bear hunters. The powerful black bears could barge their way through the tangled mesh; the dogs sometimes couldn't.

Tiger swallowtail

If you walk this trail during the warm weather of late spring and summer, you will probably observe the doddering flight of tiger swallowtails as they sail up and down the river. The swallowtails fluttering over the East Fork are definitely males, and they are not flitting about as aimlessly as you might assume. Males patrol particular routes or territories, usually along streams, in search of mates. The beautiful winged stage of this butterfly is characteristically brief: the males search for and mate with the females for a maximum span of approximately twelve days. The biological clock ticks even faster for females; they must mate and lay eggs within a mere seventy-two hours.

This large (3⅛ to 5½ inches across), black-striped yellow butterfly with swallow-tailed hindwings is one of the most familiar and widespread insects in North America. One of the few butterflies capable of hanging upside down on a flower, this species favors largely deciduous forests along streams. From north to south across its vast range, the tiger produces from one to three flights per year. In the Southern Appalachians, caterpillars resulting from the third flight bundle up in chrysalises and wait for spring.

Slightly larger than the male, the female comes in two color phases—a yellow form, like all the males, and a mimetic black form. The black phase is an assumed Batesian mimic of the foul-tasting pipevine swallowtail. The males prefer to mate with the blonds, but birds attack the black mimics at a significantly lower rate. Thus the female tiger teeters on a genetic fence, and both forms are maintained in the population by different selective advantages.

Directions

The much smaller trailhead parking area for the Big East Fork is 0.1 mile further south on US 276 and across the river from the much larger and prominently signed Big East Fork Trailhead. (See Shining Creek, the preceding trail, for directions to its trailhead.)

Greasy Cove Trail

Forest Service Trail 362 — **3.3 miles**

Dayhiking (low to high) Moderate
Dayhiking (high to low) Easy to Moderate
Backpacking (low to high) Moderate to Strenuous
Backpacking (high to low) Moderate
Interior Trail Eastern (lower elevation) terminus
at the junction of Big East Fork and Bridges Camp
Gap Trails beside the East Fork Pigeon River, 3,985
feet; western (higher elevation) terminus at its
junction with Graveyard Ridge Trail east of Ivestor
Gap, 5,650 feet
Trail Junctions Big East Fork, Bridges Camp Gap,
ALT–Greasy Cove connector, Graveyard Ridge
Topographic Quadrangle Shining Rock
Blaze None (wilderness)
Usage Foot travel only
Features Wilderness; late spring–early summer Catawba
rhododendron display; Greasy Cove Prong; open
hardwood forest; occasional old-growth trees

Three landforms—a top, a ridge, a gap—all bear the name Grassy
Cove on the Shining Rock Quad. But, for some reason, the
stream that drains the cove south of the ridge is labeled Greasy
Cove Prong. The only explanation I have heard for this came
from a stout man I met in Ivestor Gap. His last name was
Inman; he handed me his business card as proof. The first time I

encountered this man, he delivered a proprietary harangue against the inaccuracies of the Cold Mountain movie. The second time I met him, again at Ivestor Gap, I asked him what he knew about the grassy-greasy question.

He said he heard the story when he was young. "The name came from the logging days. Logs were so easy to skid down the grassy slopes—it was like they were greased. I don't know if that's the truth, but that's the story I heard a long time ago."

Lightly used by Shining Rock standards, this route traverses a succession of habitats, each with its own appeal. Hiked bottom to top, the path accompanies Greasy Cove Prong, rises up a hollow, follows the crest of Grassy Cove Ridge, then swings onto the slopes of Grassy Cove Top. The prong features cascades; the hollow, an eye-pleasing mix of ferns, grasses, and wildflowers beneath large, widely spaced hardwoods. The ridgeline and upper slope offer evergreen heath thickets and open views until the recovering forest takes them away.

This trail is described as it is most quickly accessed and most often intentionally trekked end to end—from low to high, from east to west, from the East Fork Pigeon River to the upper-south slope of Grassy Cove Top. From its three-way junction with Big East Fork and Bridges Camp Gap, Greasy Cove dips to and fords the East Fork, skirts the right side of the camp across the river, then bears to the right and uphill. The track slants upslope, then quickly shadows Greasy Cove Prong. The treadway passes above the first cascade visible from the trail at 0.1 mile as it closely parallels the brook upstream on a rocky footpath of overall moderate difficulty before leveling near the crossing. At 0.3 mile the course drops to and makes a narrow crossing of the prong just downstream from a shallow-angle slide and catch pool.

Once across, the sidehill path escorts two streams, first the prong and then a small unmapped branch, for the next 1.2 miles.

Here the hiking roughly parallels the prong while gradually angling higher above and further away from its bouldery bed. After switching streams, the route closely tags alongside the branch to the north-northwest. This segment, which steadily gains elevation, remains on the flank of Nobreeches Ridge, a Grassy Cove Ridge spur. Only one of the often rocky grades is more difficult than moderate.

Most of this 1.2-mile stretch passes through an open hardwood forest with occasional old-growth northern red oak, yellow birch, sugar maple, and yellow buckeye. On the upslope side of the trail, much of this open forest is underlain with ferns, grass, and wildflowers, with few shrubs or saplings to block the views or memorable beauty of the savannah-like landscape we humans seem to find so appealing. During spring, after the ferns unfurl, the ground cover is often a combination of velvety grass and extensive colonies of evenly spaced and symmetrical New York and hay-scented ferns, both of them exquisitely wrought.

When the prong is up and running during a rainy spring before full leaf-out, you can see the white flash and pour of cascades until the trail switches streams.

The sidehill path pulls up to its first nearby old-growth tree, a lunker yellow birch, just to the left at 0.4 mile. After rising through a boulder jumble, you will pass a large yellow buckeye standing uphill at 0.6 mile. The tread makes a short, moderate-to-strenuous climb through another boulder jumble at mile 0.9. A tenth-mile further the line of march switches streams and runs abreast of the spilling branch—the low-volume flow of the unmapped sidestream. The track ascends into cooler red spruce habitat and reaches a graybeard sugar maple (10 feet 7 inches in circumference above the burls) 3 paces to the left at mile 1.1. The route continues to work its way up the small watershed, past the first of the Fraser firs.

At mile 1.5 follow the right fork up and away from the stream and its ravine. The sidepath that continues straight ahead leads to a spring less than 35 yards away. This spring is intermittent where it emerges, but you can find water downstream even in drought. Here Greasy Cove rises the rest of the way to Grassy Cove Ridge through acres of grass and fern covering the mountainside all the way to the crest. The upgrade gains the top of the tectonic fold at Grassy Cove Gap (5,150 feet, mile 1.6) before turning left to climb the ridgetop to the west. Silverbells are abundant on this first ascending segment; northern red oaks are the thickest of the ridgetop trees.

Following a steep 55-yard surge, the hike returns to easy walking before passing over a low knuckle of a knob. It then slowly descends for 0.1 mile to the flat of the next saddle (5,220 feet, mile 1.9) and two impressively thick trees. Here the track travels to the right of a huge northern red oak, its nonstandard trunk—it looks like three boles grown together—measuring 16 feet 10 inches in circumference. The low-branched red maple to the right of the route in the bottom of the gap has a girth of 12 feet 5 inches.

After an easy-to-moderate grade from the gap, the treadway gradually gains elevation through a grove of mountain winterberry where the crest is flat across its width. At mile 2.0 the narrow path enters a tunnel of heath dominated by Catawba rhododendron, then rolls gently down to the next shallow saddle (5,300 feet) at mile 2.2.

The course continues to ride Grassy Cove Ridge, a Grassy Cove Top spur, as it rises 470 feet to the crown of the next knob. Now the uphill hiking makes headway through short hardwoods and deciduous heath shrubs as it slips to the left of the rearing ridgeline. At mile 2.3 the ascent switchbacks twice before climbing sharply for 65 yards. The wilderness track gains elevation steadily as it slants back and forth across the top of the fold through forest still in various stages of recovery. The route makes an end run around the southern rim of the last knob's cap, leveling off at the trail's highest point (5,770 feet) before starting an easy descent at mile 2.7.

At mile 2.9 Greasy Cove ramps down to a small opening on the southern edge of a saddle (5,720 feet; opening N 20 91, W 51 51). The ALT–Greasy Cove connector that ties into the Art Loeb northeast of Ivestor Gap is located along the high side of this opening. Wending roughly west-southwest, this connector is a shortcut for hikers wanting to head north toward Shining Rock on the ALT. This bypass is 0.2 mile long, easy to moderate for dayhikers, and shortens the way by a mile.

The course advances straight ahead along the lower side of the opening. The remainder of the route is easygoing on a former railroad grade narrowed to path by the recovering forest. (A wet-weather spring crosses the tread a short distance beyond the opening.) From the final gap, the track heads south off the ridge and holds its course for 0.2 mile before bending back toward the west. Greasy Cove's upper-elevation terminus ties into the Graveyard Ridge Trail, which at this end is a single-track road still occasionally used, in season, by high-clearance vehicles.

Greasy Cove has no drought-proof trailside water beyond mile 1.4.

Nature Notes

Traversing riparian, moist slope, and ridgeline habitats in succession, Greasy Cove features good spring wildflower and shrub displays, then another round of color in late summer and early fall. On a recent May 29, two of this trail's largest and most beautiful spring wildflowers—painted trilliums (hundreds of them grow under the high-elevation rhododendron) and wakerobin trilliums—were already finished blooming, while a third, the Vasey's, was still fresh and richly colored. The shrubs, primarily mountain laurel and Catawba rhododendron, were just beginning to break bud on that same date. The rhododendron was in peak bloom along the trail's highest elevations on a recent June 10. Fly poison and bush honeysuckle were in fresh flower on a recent July 3. Pink turtlehead and crimson bee balm blossomed on a recent August 21 as the asters began to advertise their colorful and conspicuous diversity.

Catawba rhododendron

Catawba rhododendron

Once the route gains Grassy Cove Ridge, it often tunnels through dark green thickets of evergreen heath, where Catawba rhododendron is the dominant shrub. Many people rank the Catawba as the best-of-show flowering shrub in the Southern Appalachians. It's easy to see why. The deep pink to rose-lavender blossoms, bell shaped and about 2 inches across, are striking. In the good years when flowering is heavy, this heath produces numerous ornate clusters of up to twenty or more of the upright blossoms. The dark magenta buds are even more richly colored than the open corollas. This 4- to 15-foot-high Southern Appalachian endemic usually reaches peak color atop Grassy Cove Ridge between June 6 and 18.

Catawba rhododendron bears lustrous evergreen leaves 3 to 8 inches long and about two times longer than wide. The undersides are generally hairless. This species is most often found at higher elevations (above 3,600 feet) on upper slopes and narrow, rocky, thin-soiled ridges. It often occurs in extensive understory stands beneath open ridgetop forests or in heath balds—also known as "slicks," "woollyheads," or "hells"—almost pure thickets that exclude or nearly exclude trees. The Catawba is the predominant shrub of the Southern Appalachian heath bald.

Blue cohosh

A member of the Barberry family along with umbrella-leaf and mayapple, the blue cohosh is common along the trail segment north of Greasy Cove Prong up to Grassy Cove Ridge. This rhizomatous perennial is easily identified by its large size, its distinctively shaped leaflets, its small flowers, and its berries. Growing up to 3 feet tall, the blue cohosh generates only two alternate compound leaves, a larger lower one and a smaller upper one. Each of the two leaves is divided and redivided so that the resulting leaflets resemble small leaves. The leaves have a waxy, bluish white tinge when they first appear in the spring.

blue cohosh

The inconspicuously colored blossoms, star shaped and occurring in loosely branched clusters, are purplish brown to yellow green. The ½-inch-wide flowers are replaced by more conspicuous clusters of deep blue berries (poisonous) in late summer.

Primarily a northern species, this herb prefers the rich, moist soils of hardwood slopes, coves, and hollows in the Southern Appalachians. Blue cohosh was in bloom beside a nearby trail of similar elevation on a recent May 3. Nearly all of the berries have finished turning from green to blue by the end of the first week in September.

Pink turtlehead

The pink turtlehead (*Chelone lyonii*), a native perennial, occurs sporadically in small colonies along this forest path from its lower-elevation end to Grassy Cove Gap at mile 1.6. This species sinks its roots into wet habitats—seeps and the margins of spring runs at middle-to-high elevations—within the Southern Appalachians. Turtlehead colonies are easily identified in season by their wet situations and by their large (up to 1½ inches long) and attention-grabbing flowers atop the usually 1- to 3-foot-tall plants.

The pink to rose-pink corollas, two lipped and tubular, resemble their common name (*Chelone* is Greek for tortoise). If you press the sides of the flower, the turtle's mouth pops open. Five fused petals form the tube; the upper, two-lobed lip arches over the lower, three-lobed lip. This member of the Snapdragon family was blooming along the lower reaches of this route on a recent August 21.

Directions

Greasy Cove is an interior trail that has its eastern end at the junction of Big East Fork and Bridges Camp Gap Trails and its western end at its junction with Graveyard Ridge Trail.

The Greasy Cove–Bridges Camp Gap–Big East Fork junction looks like it should be easy to locate after a quick glance at the wilderness map. But that is definitely not the case. Bridges Camp Gap and Big East Fork Trails, both of which closely parallel the East Fork Pigeon River from different directions, flow seamlessly into one another.

If you approach this junction via Bridges Camp Gap Trail, the shortest way, you will enter the wilderness at the large sign at 0.94 mile. Slightly over 0.3 mile beyond the sign, you will come to a prominent campsite (the first one since the wilderness sign) to the left of the treadway. The three-way junction (N 20 22, W 49 61) is right above this camp. You will also see another camp just across the river. If you turn left and ford the river to the second camp, you will already be on the eastern end of Greasy Cove Trail. (See Bridges Camp Gap, the following trail, for further information.)

If you approach this junction by way of Big East Fork Trail, you will see the prominent camp to your right and the second camp across the river at the end of the trail. If you turn right and ford the East Fork at the camp, you will come out of the river at the second camp. Greasy Cove Trail continues uphill and to the right from this campsite. (See Big East Fork, the preceding trail, for further information.)

Greasy Cove's western end at its junction with the Graveyard Ridge Trail is much easier to find. Art Loeb and Ivestor Gap Trails pass through Ivestor Gap. The northwestern end of Graveyard Ridge Trail is also located at the gap: a can't-miss junction and resting spot (wilderness sign, vehicle-blocking boulders) located on the southern boundary of the Shining Rock Wilderness. To reach Greasy Cove Trail from Ivestor Gap, follow Graveyard Ridge Trail, the old road, generally east from Ivestor Gap (to the right if you have walked either IGT or ALT-3 from their FS 816 trailheads) for 0.3 mile to the Greasy Cove–Graveyard Ridge junction (N 20 70, W 51 73). Here Graveyard Ridge's single-track road curls downhill to the right, and Greasy Cove's narrow treadway continues straight ahead to the east.

Bridges Camp Gap Trail

Forest Service Trail 607 **1.3 miles**

Dayhiking In Easy
Dayhiking Out Easy to Moderate
Backpacking In Easy to Moderate
Backpacking Out Moderate
Start Bridges Camp Gap off the parkway, 4,480 feet
End Junction with Big East Fork and Greasy Cove Trails
   beside the East Fork Pigeon River, 3,985 feet
Trail Junctions MST-5 (see description), Big East Fork,
   Greasy Cove
Topographic Quadrangle Shining Rock
Blaze Yellow until it enters wilderness, no blazing
   beyond wilderness boundary
Usage Foot travel only
Features East Fork Pigeon River; diverse forest;
   occasional old-growth trees; spring wildflower
   display

Short, relatively easy, and well constructed, this scenic trail
descends northward to the East Fork Pigeon River before closely
accompanying its quick current downstream. During a rainy
spring the East Fork's full flow is a noisy succession of froth-
white cascades where it runs through boulders, light green
pools where reduced gradient gives the river rest, and clear glide
water where it shallows. The East Fork is so clear it creates the

same illusion as rock-bound streams out West: the goose-pimple-cold pools are deeper than they look.

Starting at its namesake gap on the southwestern shoulder of South Spring Top, the footpath's first 0.1 mile follows a gentle downgrade alongside the parkway. After 80 yards the white-blazed MST turns onto the tread. The two trails share the same track to their usually signed junction at 0.1 mile. Bridges Camp Gap heads downhill on the left fork into a diverse, largely hardwood forest. Fifty-five yards beyond the split, an old-growth, hollowed-out black cherry—11 feet 2 inches in circumference, the thickest trailside cherry in this guide—stands just to the right of the route.

One-tenth mile past the cherry, the trail passes an old-growth northern red oak rooted next to the lower end of a rock outcrop nearly 40 feet long but only 6 feet tall at its highest point. The sidehill path continues to steadily lose elevation toward the river. Following a sharp switchback into the riparian belt of rosebay rhododendron, the line of march makes a short moderate dip to the former logging grade beside the East Fork at mile 0.5 (4,210 feet).

Here the course curves to the right and closely parallels the river downstream to the north. The easy but often rocky downhill hiking, which affords numerous good views of the stream below, gradually rises higher above the sharply descending East Fork. Now too low for red spruce, the route threads through a forest of yellow buckeye, white basswood, black cherry, yellow birch, sugar maple, white ash, northern red oak, and other hardwoods. Some of the yellow birch are old-growth, usually poor-form specimens that escaped last century's logging.

After passing below a moss-furred boulder jumble, another legacy from the last glaciation, the treadway reaches the usually signed Shining Rock Wilderness boundary at 0.9 mile. Thicket-growths of doghobble now occasionally narrow the passage to single-file footpath. The steady views of the river through rhododendron continue as the track ramps closer to the white chutes and narrow sluices over bedrock and around boulders. If you want to see the East Fork at its surging and sun-bright best, hike when the water and sun are high and the hardwood branches are bare.

Bridges Camp Gap ends at a potentially confusing three-trail junction located above the first campsite it comes to within the wilderness (N 20 22, W 49 61). If you keep hiking straight ahead and downstream from just above this camp, you will almost seamlessly tie into the Big East Fork Trail and soon begin traveling to the east. If you ford the river slightly upstream from the campsite and enter a second campsite across the Big East Fork, you will be walking on the Greasy Cove Trail.

Greasy Cove Prong's final run—a long series of cascades, loud and white when the water is up—ends straight across the river from the right side of the first camp.

Nature Notes

On the nineteenth of a recent cool and rainy April, the densely colonial trout lily covered large swaths of the forest floor with spring's first widespread flourish of deciduous green. On that same day, this spring ephemeral's flower line had yet to rise above the river. A week later the slopes well above the stream were brightened with blooming trout lily. Once the route enters riparian habitat, the herb layer is no longer as lush, but there are small numbers of a surprising variety of species. A partial roll call of other common or conspicuous wildflowers that bloom before May 23 includes squawroot, blue cohosh, false

Solomon's seal, Solomon's seal, wakerobin, foamflower, yellow mandarin, wood anemone, mountain meadow rue, speckled wood lily, Canada mayflower, jack-in-the-pulpit, umbrella-leaf, and mountain lettuce. The best time to see the most species in bloom is between April 20 and May 10.

Red squirrel

The red squirrel is often the only mammal hikers encounter in the Shining Rock–Middle Prong area during daylight. Common, curious, and noisy—all twitch and chatter—this rust-red rodent is the smallest diurnal tree squirrel in its vast range. The red's head and body measure a mere 7 to 8 inches; its expressive, reddish brown tail adds another 4 to 6 inches. Easily recognized, this feisty little creature is colored dull red to grayish red on its back and sides, white on its belly. During summer a black strip separates white from red; a white ring encircles the dark eyes year-round.

A decidedly northern species, the red squirrel is one of the most widespread mammals in North America. It enters the deep south of eastern United States only down the narrow peninsula of the Southern Appalachians. The southern limit of the eastern portion of its range dips to the mountains in northernmost Georgia. This inquisitive animal is often called "boomer" or "mountain boomer" in the Southern Highlands.

Unlike gray squirrels, boomers are intensely territorial, chattering at and chasing away all grays and other reds. This fierce defense of home ensures a solitary life, at least until mating season. Territorial adaptations have also given the boomer a wide range of vocalizations and a spirited boldness lacking in many larger squirrels.

Occasionally, when you sit down for a break, one of these

compulsively curious critters will sidle up for a closer look from a low perch, then scold you with an insistent, ratchetlike *chirr* while waving its tail forward in quick twitches. Except for the chirr, most of this rodent's extensive repertoire of sounds—squeaks and trills, chucks and chirps—could pass for bird noise.

Mountain lettuce

Mountain lettuce, a saxifrage species also known as brook lettuce, is endemic to central and Southern Appalachia. This

mountain lettuce

infrequent native perennial requires the continuously wet conditions of seepages and the rocky beginnings of rivulets, where it sometimes forms long, linear colonies following the flow downslope. Well adapted to shade, mountain lettuce does not cling to sunny clefts up high in rock outcrops like the Michaux's saxifrage, which thrives in more exposed and less saturated habitats.

The coarsely toothed leaves of the mountain lettuce are large and distinctive, often 8 to 12 inches long and up to 3 inches wide. The light green foliage does not have any of the red coloration characteristic of the leaves of the more common Michaux's saxifrage.

Usually 12 to 26 inches tall, the flowering stalk is topped by open clusters of tiny white corollas less than ¼ inch wide and accented with a single yellow spot at the base of each petal. This forb was starting to blossom beside this trail on a recent May 12; the next year it was in flower on May 29.

Directions

Bridges Camp Gap begins near the Looking Glass Rock Overlook at BRP milepost 417. (See MST-5, the following trail section, for directions to its southwestern access at the overlook.)

Starting from the parking area, angle to the right across the BRP and follow that shoulder to the right, downhill to the northeast, for 0.1 mile. Just beyond the overlook sign, you'll see a long, maintained grassy area to the left of the road. Look for the trail's beginning yellow blaze or narrow treadway near where the far end of the grassy area arcs back toward the parkway.

Notes

Mountains to Sea Trail, Section 5

(Junction with the access trail leading from Looking Glass Rock Overlook to the power tower beside the parkway in Pigeon Gap)

Forest Service Trail 440   4.8 miles Mountains to Sea only, 4.9 miles including access trail

Dayhiking Moderate in either direction

Backpacking Moderate to Strenuous in either direction

Vehicular Access at or near Either End Southwestern (slightly lower elevation) access at Looking Glass Rock Overlook, 4,495 feet; northeastern (slightly higher elevation) terminus off the parkway at the power tower in Pigeon Gap, 4,530 feet

Trail Junctions Access trail from Looking Glass Rock Overlook, MST-4, Bridges Camp Gap (see description), access trail from Wagon Road Gap Parking Area, MST continuing to the sea

Topographic Quadrangle Shining Rock

Blazes White circle, possibly a yellow rectangle or two for Bridges Camp Gap

Usage Foot travel only

Features Year-round vista at Cherry Cove Overlook; hardwood forests; extensive fern colonies; rock outcrops

Section 5 is the second longest (access trails added), the second most difficult, and the least hiked of the five MST sections described in this guide. With one exception, all of its sustained grades are either easy or easy to moderate.

Walked as described, this upper-slope and ridgetop route closely parallels and crosses the parkway from southwest to northeast, ranging over part of a long string of knobs known as Pisgah Ridge from near Bridges Camp Gap to Pigeon Gap. As it follows Pisgah Ridge and the parkway along the slopes and crests of Chestnut Ridge and Green Knob, the treadway is often within or on the NPS boundary.

While the first three MST sections never descend below 5,000 feet, and the western end of the fourth begins at 5,900 feet, this section rises above 5,000 feet only once, atop Green Knob's small crown. Here the warmer and drier trail corridor is completely forested, and the canopy is almost totally controlled by the hardwoods, the oaks numerically dominant among them.

Heading to the right (north-northeast) from its T-junction with the access trail, MST-5 gently descends through a diverse forest featuring witch-hazel, Fraser magnolia, red maple, beech, and black locust, among others. The round leaves of the galax, a highly colonial wildflower, shine on the forest floor. (Galax produces the sweet, skunky scent that many have long associated with the mountains.) The track turns left onto an old road at 0.3 mile and runs alongside the parkway as it shares the tread with Bridges Camp Gap Trail. The two paths split apart at their usually signed junction on the upper-west slope of South Spring Top at 0.4 mile. The white-blazed MST follows the right fork uphill.

Here the hiking gradually rises past cucumbertree, silverbell, striped maple, and small red spruce. After the quick zigzag of a double switchback, the route gains the backbone of Chestnut Ridge at 0.6 mile and continues the easy march up the oak-grown crest. The wide ridgetop is scenic in mid-May when the unblemished green of ferns, grasses, and wildflowers underlies the hardwood canopy. At 0.9 mile the footpath slabs to the right of the quickly climbing keel before beginning a downhill run that bypasses a 4,810-foot unnamed knob on Chestnut Ridge.

The course returns to the ridgeline at mile 1.2, then continues the downgrade on or near the top of the fold. Section 5 dips to the MST post beside the parkway at mile 1.5, then turns left and proceeds along the grassy shoulder (the trail does not cross the road here) for 0.1 mile to the next trailpost. The roadside walking in Cherry Gap (elevation listed as 4,327 feet on the Cherry Cove Overlook sign) affords an open view straight out to the southeast from the paved overlook. Both Looking Glass Rock and Cedar Rock Mountain with its double band of cliffs are close and conspicuous.

The route re-enters the forest at the slot in the thicket of dark rhododendron. Above the double switchback, the path works its way up to the top of the spine (mile 1.7) through drier woods where chestnut oak and American chestnut saplings are common. Here the uphill hiking ascends a short, rock-step steep grade before passing through a narrow aisle lined with mountain laurel. At mile 1.8 the long tread of the MST reaches the crown of a slight knob with a NPS boundary marker (a low, metal-capped, concrete cylinder) immediately to the right of the track.

After slowly slanting toward the crest, the trail rides the ridgetop again, finishing the undemanding upgrade to the narrow backbone of a 4,600-foot knob at mile 2.1. After losing elevation for slightly less than 0.1 mile, you ramp down to a saddle and cross the parkway from trailpost to trailpost at mile 2.2 (4,525 feet, near BRP milepost 415). Quickly regaining and rising with the keel, the MST makes an easy-to-moderate ascent to the next speed bump on Pisgah Ridge—a small, unnamed knuckle (mile 2.4, 4,620 feet)—before heading downhill to the parkway again. Here the easygoing grade slants onto upper north-facing slope where wildflowers bloom and ferns uncurl their crosiers in spring. After regaining the top of the fold for a few yards, the treadway swerves off the crest and loses elevation more sharply as it twists and turns its way down toward the BRP.

The route crosses the parkway at mile 2.7, then follows the shoulder to the east through Bennett Gap (4,410 feet) for 0.1 mile before returning to the forest beyond the MST post. Here the hike starts the slow and steady climb (a mile long and easy to moderate overall) to Section 5's highpoint: Green Knob. The way through the woods remains on or near the rising ridge-line as it travels beneath a canopy numerically dominated by three oak species—northern red, chestnut, and white. Sweet birch, black cherry, red maple, and pignut hickory are all minor components compared to the oaks. Mountain laurel is frequently the only evergreen in sight.

You reach the top of Pisgah Ridge again at mile 2.9. The course veers to the left at mile 3.5, angling up and across the keel in order to swing around and below the lower of Green Knob's two peaks. After horseshoe-curving over a spur, the gradual upgrade forges ahead atop the rock-rugged crest again at mile 3.6.

Where the highest reach of the ridge levels atop Green Knob at mile 3.8, you can find a small square NPS boundary marker a pace to the left of the track 25 yards before the benchmark (5,056 feet), which is set in low rock a stride to the right of the treadway. From Green Knob, the MST descends to a shallow saddle and rises over the next knuckle before accompanying the crest to the bottom of a more pronounced saddle at mile 4.0. It then slips to the west of the slowly lifting spine, skirting below the next top before dipping to another shallow saddle and gaining elevation to the next highpoint (4,960 feet) at mile 4.3. Here, where the path drops off to the right of the ridge, the downgrade to Pigeon Gap begins in earnest.

After a moderate downhill run of 0.1 mile, the rest of the descent is easy to moderate as the trail remains on or near the ridge through a series of switchbacks. Below the last switchback in the set at mile 4.4, the track advances steadily down the spine, frequently winding around rock outcrops Mohawked atop the scenic crest. Yellow birch inhabit the moist upper slopes, and Catawba rhododendron form roached clumps of evergreen growth where the top of the fold narrows to rock.

Where the ridgeline forks at mile 4.6, the route bends to the right onto nearly north-facing slope before passing beside a 12-foot-high rockface. After rejoining the right-fork spur, the trail dips to and crosses the parkway at Pigeon Gap. Across the road, the long brown tread quickly comes to a junction just past the power tower. If you want to add 0.4 mile to your hike, turn left (entrance 65 degrees) and head uphill onto the access trail leading to Wagon Road Gap Parking Area. The MST continues straight ahead and downhill toward its US 276 crossing.

Section 5 has no reliable trailside water.

Nature Notes

MST-5 is lower, drier, and warmer than the other MST sections detailed in this guide. The loss of elevation and its attendant decrease in rainfall (and increase in temperature) produces a noticeable change in the flora. Here the forest canopy is frequently dominated by several types of oak, not the northern hardwood/spruce-fir mix typical of higher elevations. And mountain laurel is now the dominant heath shrub, not the Catawba rhododendron.

Walked as described, this ridgeline and upper-slope route runs generally southwest to northeast. Thus the uphill grades often face the drier southwestern exposure while the downhills frequently face the moister northeastern exposure. The longer the grade, the greater the difference in the flora from one side of a knob or peak to the other. As you will notice, the forest tends to be more open and oak-canopied on the climbs.

Section 5's spring wildflower display offers only moderate diversity coupled with low numbers of most species. On May 19 and 27 of recent years, wildflowers not commonly found at higher elevations or on moist slopes included—in leaf or blossom—squawroot, yellow star-grass, pink lady's-slipper, bellwort, and dwarf iris. The abundant mountain laurel was in peak and profuse bloom on June 13. The occasional small colonies of fire pink were also in red flower on that same date.

New York fern

New York fern

The New York is not only the most abundant fern along this stretch of trail, but it is also the most abundant fern in the Shining Rock area and the entire Southern Appalachian region. These ancient spore-producing plants often occur in dense, nearly monocultural beds—extensive colonies that sometimes cover the forest floor for a tenth-mile or more of trail. Growing at even intervals beneath an unusually open forest, the New York is similar in uniformity of size and spacing to an agricultural crop. There are two reasons for this homogeneity. This pteridophyte spreads from perennial underground rhizomes that often generate evenly spaced, cloned colonies. And this fern also applies its own herbicide; it prevents many would-be competitors from gaining a roothold with poison—all natural, all organic, no multinational corporations involved.

The New York fern is exceedingly prolific and unusually distinctive. The mostly alternate pinnae (leafy foliage) of this species gradually taper to nearly nothing at either end, creating a very narrow tip and base. The lowermost pinnae of this deciduous, 12- to 24-inch-tall vascular plant resemble tiny wings.

Squawroot

The squawroot is a member of the Broomrape family, a group of parasitic flowering plants that lack chlorophyll. This species is an obligate parasite: its roots penetrate those of trees

squawroot

and shrubs, especially oaks, and siphon off necessary sustenance. Because it no longer supplies its own food, the squawroot has no need for chlorophyll or green leaves. Over time its leaves have evolved into vestigial afterthoughts: a scaly covering of overlapping bracts.

The stalks of this fleshy, unbranched perennial are usually 3 to 8 inches tall. Yellow or brownish yellow when they first break ground, the small, closely crowded clusters resemble slender, spiky ears of corn in the spring. This strange-looking parasite quickly begins to dry out and turn brown. By fall the stiff and shriveled stalks have darkened to blackish brown.

The squawroot's inconspicuous pale yellow or brownish yellow blossoms are not readily recognized as such unless your eyes are near plant level. These flowers—very thin, tightly two lipped, and only half an inch long—bloom between the bracts. From normal eye level the flowers look like evenly spaced short spikes protruding from the stem.

Primarily a mountain species, this parasite is most often occasional in predominately deciduous forests where oaks are plentiful. Here, along this stretch of the MST, this pallid herb is common. On a recent May 22, pale yellow islands of squawroot poked up through the fresh green of fern and grass. Bears avidly seek and eat the fleshy clusters as soon as they emerge. Where both bear and squawroot are common, you can sometimes follow where a foraging bruin has walked a trail, grubbing up nearby squawroots (sometimes called bear corn in the mountains) along the way.

Chestnut oak

Rare to absent above 5,300 feet in the Shining Rock area, the chestnut oak (*Quercus prinus*) is especially common along this section's lower elevations. Primarily an Appalachian species, this hardwood greatly increased its share of the canopy after the chestnut blight and is now a major component of several forest types.

The chestnut oak's common name reflects the superficial resemblance of its leaves to those of the American chestnut, which is no longer able to survive beyond

chestnut oak

sapling stage in most of its range. The foliage of these two Beech family trees, however, is easy to differentiate. Much narrower than those of the chestnut oak, American chestnut leaves have numerous sharp-pointed teeth. *Q. prinus* leaves— solar panels 4 to 9 inches long—have margins with noticeably rounded, wavy lobes with no points and no bristles.

This oak lives to grow thick and old. It averages 2 to 4 feet in diameter at maturity, but like many other eastern hardwoods, this tree reaches its largest dimensions in the Southern Appalachians. A survivor from the primary forest rooted beside Shining Rock's Fork Mountain Trail recently measured 13 feet 8 inches in circumference. A massive specimen in the Cades Cove area of the GSMNP grew to a girth of 16 feet 9 inches a few decades ago. Slow-growing even on good sites, this member of the white oak group holds heartwood and bole together for up to half a millennium.

Directions

Section 5 has vehicular access at or near either end. Its southwestern access is located at the Looking Glass Rock Overlook at BRP milepost 417, and its northeastern end is located at the power tower in Pigeon Gap between BRP mileposts 412 and 413.

Southwestern access at the Looking Glass Rock Overlook

Approach from the south: From the BRP–access road from NC 215 junction, turn left onto the parkway and travel approximately 6.2 miles to the overlook on the right side of the road.

Approach from the north: From the BRP–access road from US 276 junction, turn left onto the parkway and travel approximately 5.1 miles to the overlook on the left side of the road.

The short access trail leading to the southwestern end of Section 5 begins across the parkway from the overlook. Turn right onto the MST and you will be walking Section 5 toward the power tower in Pigeon Gap. Turn left and you will be on the eastern end of Section 4 heading toward FS 816.

Northeastern end at Pigeon Gap

Approach from the south: From the BRP–access road from NC 215 junction, turn left onto the parkway and travel approximately 10.7 miles to the power tower in Pigeon Gap.

Approach from the north: From the BRP–access road from US 276 junction, turn left onto the parkway and travel 0.6 mile to the power tower in Pigeon Gap.

The MST crosses the parkway at the tower in usually signed Pigeon Gap. Most of the on-the-grass parking is on the tower side of the road. If you hike the MST from its trailpost on the northern side of the parkway, the side opposite the tower, you will be on the northeastern end of Section 5 hiking toward the access trail to the Looking Glass Rock Overlook.

Notes

Shining Rock Wilderness—West

Shining Rock Wilderness—West

Gary Crider

The rise to the rocky topknot of Tennent

Trails

Fork Mountain
Ivestor Gap
Art Loeb Spur
Art Loeb, Section 3
Little East Fork

Fork Mountain Trail

Forest Service Trail 109   **7.2 miles**

Dayhiking In Moderate to Strenuous
Dayhiking Out Moderate
Backpacking In Strenuous
Backpacking Out Moderate to Strenuous
Start West Fork Pigeon River Trailhead, 3,125 feet
End Junction with Ivestor Gap Trail north of Tennent
   Mountain, 5,760 feet
Trail Junctions Green Mountain (at trailhead), IGT
Topographic Quadrangles Sam Knob, Waynesville,
   Shining Rock
Blaze None (wilderness)
Usage Foot travel only
Features Wilderness; year-round view from the highest
   gap until the forest returns; diverse flora; occasional
   old-growth trees; Fork Mountain ridgeline

Long and remote, Fork Mountain rises from northwest to south-east, from its trailhead beside the West Fork Pigeon River to its junction with the IGT on the upper-north slope of Tennent Mountain. This route is the second longest trail continuously within the combined wildernesses, and it also offers the longest stretch of walking without a junction. After immediately fording the West Fork, this footpath gains 1,545 feet of elevation in its first 2.2 miles. This trail's length (which includes another 1.7 miles on the IGT for the shortest one-way trek), its perceived difficulty, its remoteness, its beginning ford—plus its fairly long shuttle—combine to produce a predictable outcome: Fork Mountain is the loneliest trail in this guide. Most of the relatively few people who hike this route start from its IGT junction and walk the easy 1.2 miles to the steadily disappearing opening at the obvious gap.

This scenic trail features a wide range of elevations, exposures, and environments. Except after significant rainfall, the ford is usually not difficult or dangerous from spring's leaf-out in the highcountry to late October. The switchbacks leading to the Fork Mountain spur are well designed; all of the sustained grades along this footpath's first 2.2 miles are easy or easy to moderate.

Drop down to the river, follow the bank upstream from the room-sized boulder to the faster and shallower water, then ford the West Fork. Haul out, scramble up the bank, turn right onto the treadway, and quickly enter the wilderness. No big deal, unless the river is high and potentially dangerous. Then, as always, it is your call.

The easy walking on old roadbed generally parallels the West Fork through a tall, straight, second-growth forest. Look for the old-growth white oak (circumference 11 feet 2 inches) approximately 25 feet up the slope from the edge of the track at 0.2 mile. At 0.4 mile the path dips to and rock-steps Turnpike Creek, then turns east-northeast to accompany this small tributary branch up its steep-sided valley. Now you begin the climb from river to ridge on a nearly north-facing slope lush with wildflowers and ferns in the spring. Downslope, the forest in this rich, moist habitat has quickly regenerated from logging. Here the highest hardwood canopy along the route includes sweet birch, white basswood, yellow buckeye, sugar maple, white ash, and yellow poplar (the fastest growing of them all, some already lifting their uppermost leaves above 130 feet).

At mile 0.8, where the course closes to within a dozen feet of the creek's south fork, the tread switchbacks sharply to the right, up and away from the stream. This branch-sized fork is the last drought-proof source of trailside water. The next 1.4-mile segment slowly slants upslope to the ridge of a Fork Mountain spur through a series of thirteen more switchbacks. At mile 1.1 the grade rounds the notch of a hardwood hollow. Six-tenths mile further it crosses an intermittent rivulet that bisects rich wildflower habitat in spring.

As the treadway winds up the slope on exposures ranging from west to northwest, both tree size and herb-layer height and density decrease above Turnpike Creek's rich cove. The predominantly deciduous forest (some hemlocks may still be alive) includes striped maple, sourwood, silverbell, blackgum, cucumbertree, black cherry, Fraser magnolia, pignut hickory, and sassafras, among others.

Beyond the final switchback, the footpath angles onto the crest of a Fork Mountain spur at mile 2.2 (4,670 feet). Occasional old-growth, mostly northern red oak, still stands strong on this flat-topped section of the spur. Look for the thickest standard-growth tree beside the trails in this guide—a low-limbed chestnut oak 13 feet 8 inches in circumference—just to the right of the route at mile 2.3.

At mile 2.4 the track slips to the left of the rising spur onto west-facing slope. The line of march makes a double switchback up to an obvious roadbed at mile 2.7. One hundred fifty yards further, it bends to the right onto another wide grade and continues the nearly effortless walking.

You crest Fork Mountain and turn to the right onto an old roadbed at mile 3.0. From here, all but the final 1.1 miles remain on or near the trail's namesake ridgeline—a long and prominent Tennent Mountain lead—as it gradually ascends to the southeast. Evergreen heath shrubs—primarily mountain laurel plus rosebay, Catawba, and dwarf rhododendron—frequently hedge the tread along its remaining mileage. Just beyond where it reaches the top of the fold, the trail bears to the left onto path where the roadbed proceeds straight ahead. The track follows the rocky keel to the heath-topped highpoint of a knob at mile 3.1 (5,130 feet), where the course abruptly changes character. The next half mile becomes more rugged and scenic as it descends Fork Mountain's dry and often narrow ridgetop. This stretch enlivens the trek with short rocky pitches, Table Mountain pines, partial views of nearby peaks, occasional rock slabs, and frequent slots through shoulder-rubbing heath shrubs. Chestnut oaks and American chestnut saplings are common in the low-crowned forest.

After the short downgrade off the knob, the line of march eases up in a slender aisle lined with mountain laurel, then maintains course down the backbone of the ridge to a rock slab at mile 3.3. Beyond the rock-paved opening, the treadway passes small knots of short and contorted Table Mountain pine before coming to a much wider crest and leveling in the flat of a gap (4,870 feet) at mile 3.6.

The route rises with the ridgecrest through a more open forest of larger broadleafs for a tenth-mile before angling onto the sunrise sidehill. It then slants back onto the descending keel, ramps down to a shallow saddle, and gains elevation to the crown of a slight knuckle at mile 4.0. The footpath crosses a boulder jumble on a rich, moist mountainside flush with wildflowers and ferns at mile 4.2.

The track forges ahead on a gradual upgrade as it works its way around the upper-east flank of Birdstand Mountain well below its highpoint. The trail ascends to Birdstand's spine before dipping to the next saddle at mile 4.5 (5,100 feet). Here, where the ridge rears up again, the course curves to the left onto an old railroad line. The trek regains the keel, then quickly arrives at a confusing wrong-way fork at mile 4.6. Where hikers often stray nearly straight ahead on a steep, bare-dirt pitch, the route swerves to the right on rock before heading downhill on the very top of the fold.

At mile 4.8 the path swings down and to the left off the ridgetop onto a nearby logging grade, where it turns right and rises slowly in the same southeasterly direction. After rolling through the next gap (mile 5.2, 5,150 feet), the tread heads up its first and only sustained climb of consequence—a quarter-mile long, solid moderate overall—since gaining the Fork Mountain crest. On the way up the ridge, the track enters an open broadleaf forest (occasional red spruce and short Fraser firs) with a ground cover of grass, ferns (primarily New York), and herbaceous wildflowers. The upridge run slacks off to easy by mile 5.4; a tenth-mile further, the hike descends on the mild grade of a former railway through more open forest, the canopy largely controlled by mature northern red oaks.

At mile 5.6 the rail-to-trail treadway slants to the right onto the uppermost southwestern slope of a relatively long and flat-topped knob. Here, as the no-strain walking nears the next gap, the young forest increasingly exhibits signs of recent resurgence. At mile 6.0 the footpath regains the ridgeline as it bottoms out in the gap's steadily shrinking opening (5,460 feet), where black locust and serviceberry saplings are currently leading the charge of the light brigade.

The opening will offer views to either side of Fork Mountain until the forest returns. From the left side of the gap, you have a good look at the nearby ridgeline of Shining Rock Ledge as it rises to nearby Shining Rock (6,010 feet) at around 44 degrees and Stairs Mountain at around 30 degrees. A little farther out, you can trace the long ascent of Cold Mountain's northwestern ridgeline to where it disappears just short of the summit behind Stairs Mountain's left shoulder at around 25 degrees.

To the right you can easily locate a trio of local 6,000 footers: grassy-pated Black Balsam Knob (6,214 feet) at around 163 degrees, double-knuckled and unmistakable Sam Knob (6,060 feet) at around 210 degrees, and conifer-topped Mount Hardy (6,125 feet) further away than the other two at around 224 degrees.

Now on the other side of the crest, the wide corridor of the former railroad gently gains elevation on the moister and cooler north and northeast-facing slopes well below the top of the next knob. The largely hardwood forest features yellow birch and four maple species—red, sugar, striped, and mountain. Red spruce and Fraser fir become more common as the course ascends above 5,600 feet.

The route crosses a clear-water spring and several muddy seeps, all intermittent, with 0.1 mile remaining. Forty yards beyond the wilderness sign, Fork Mountain Trail ends at its junction with the road-wide IGT. A right turn onto the IGT will lead you to the Black Balsam Trailhead and the usually reliable spring on the left side of that trail after 135 yards.

Nature Notes

Because of Fork Mountain's length, its half-mile elevation differential, its numerous aspects and habitat types—from riverine to narrow, rock-slab ridgeline—it boasts the most diverse flora of any trail or section of trail in this guide. The wild richness of the Southern Appalachians filled up pages and pages of my notebooks, ran ink pens dry. Without making a special effort for a high count, I noted forty-one types of trees standing within easy eyesight of the treadway—a total much higher than in all of Yellowstone National Park's 2.2 million acres.

The Southern Appalachians—never glaciated from the north, never flooded from the south—provide sanctuary to one of the earth's most diverse temperate zone forests. The finest remaining North American expression of this forest, the half-million acres of the GSMNP harbors over 100 native tree species (more kinds of native trees than in any other nonlinear North American national park) and provides refuge for 1,673 (and counting) vascular plants.

On five dates over a recent eight-year period, I noted eighty-one types of wildflowers in leaf, bloom, or bud. No doubt I missed many more. A partial roll call includes fly poison and featherbells; three kinds of orchids; three different trilliums; and bluebead, speckled wood, and Turk's-cap lilies. I also frequently recorded crimson bee balm, bloodroot, starry campion, pink turtlehead, wild sarsaparilla, rose twisted-stalk, wild geranium, mountain mint, plus a profusion of asters.

Late May through June 15 is usually the window for the big-three heath-shrub show: flame azalea, mountain laurel, and Catawba rhododendron.

Table Mountain pine

Starting at mile 3.3 and continuing to mile 4.6, the treadway passes occasional pockets of Table Mountain pine where the ridgeline is especially dry, narrow, and rocky. This small, rather uncommon conifer becomes increasingly gnarled and picturesque as it thickens through the years. Endemic to the central and Southern Appalachians, the Table Mountain remains small, usually only reaching 25 to 40 feet in height and 12 to 20 inches in diameter.

This fire-born pine can be readily identified by its stiff needles, its menacing-looking cones, and its preferred habitat. The Table Mountain's sharp-pointed, dark bluish green needles are 1½ to 3 inches long and occur in often-twisted bundles of two.

There is no mistaking the weaponlike look or feel of this conifer's cones. The closed and heavy cones, which can persist for up to twenty years on the tree, are 2½ to 3½ inches long and usually occur in whorls of three or four wrapped around a branch. They are thickly armed with stout, upwardly curving spines; if a branch were to end at a whorl of cones, it would resemble a mace. This pine competes best on fire-prone sites—dry, rocky, south-facing slopes and dry, exposed, rocky ridgelines.

Table Mountain pine

Experts believe this evergreen requires a scorched-earth fire for regeneration. Its cones explode during blazing crown fires, dispersing their seeds on newly cleared soil.

Dwarf rhododendron

Much more dwarf rhododendron grows beside this trail than along any other route described in this guide. Three rhododendrons grace the Southern Highland forest: the stream-flanking rosebay, the colorful Catawba, and the often overlooked but distinctive dwarf. *Rhododendron minus* is the only one with the combination of rhododendron flowers and short leaves. Its leaves, usually 2 to 4 inches long and rust-colored beneath, are approximately the same size and shape as those of the mountain laurel.

Although its leaf size remains roughly the same, this heath's height and blossom color vary throughout the southern mountains. When rooted in the open, on dry rocky soils, this species is frequently only 3 to 6 feet tall. But where it inhabits moist, shady slopes, as it does on this trail, it reaches heights of 8 to 12 feet. This shrub bears smaller and fewer flowers per cluster (usually only seven to ten blossoms) than its showier cousins.

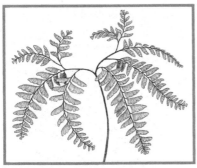

Corolla colors range from pinkish red to dull white, often accented with a small freckling of greenish spots. All of the specimens blooming in the Shining Rock region were light colored—dull white to pale pink. Fork Mountain's dwarf rhododendron were past their peak on a recent June 5 and May 29.

northern maidenhair fern

Northern maidenhair fern

The finely wrought northern maidenhair fern is common on the moist slope above Turnpike Creek. The maidenhair's stems are glossy dark brown or black. Its main stem forks, and the branches curve horizontally back toward each other until they form a horseshoe-shaped semicircle or sometimes a fully recurved circle. Those that bend into a full whorl have a delicate, double-circle symmetry. The fan-shaped foliage radiates out and away from the empty inner circle.

This fern is deciduous; it unfurls from its crosier in spring and withers to a brown crumple with the first frosts of fall.

Directions

Fork Mountain's trailhead is located between the West Fork Pigeon River and NC 215 just to the south of Sunburst Campground. The long, heavily used (not by hikers) parking area is especially obvious during summer weekends.

Approach from the south: From the NC 215–access road from BRP junction, turn left onto NC 215 North toward Canton and travel approximately 8.1 miles to the long pull-off parking area on the right side of the highway immediately before the bridge over the Middle Prong, which joins the West Fork at the bridge. Sunburst Campground is on the left side of the highway a short distance beyond the bridge.

Approach from the north: From the four-way NC 215–NC 110–US 276 intersection, travel NC 215 South (also marked with a Love Joy Rd. street sign) approximately 9.5 miles to the long, pull-off parking area to the left of the road immediately after the bridge over the Middle Prong. Look for this bridge just after you pass Sunburst Campground.

Notes

Ivestor Gap Trail

Forest Service Trail 101   **4.3 miles**

Dayhiking Easy in either direction
Backpacking Easy to Moderate in either direction
Start The Black Balsam Trailhead at the paved end
    of FS 816, 5,815 feet
End Junction with Art Loeb and Old Butt Knob Trails
    in Shining Rock Gap, 5,755 feet
Trail Junctions Flat Laurel Creek, Sam Knob, and Art
    Loeb Spur at the Black Balsam Trailhead; IGT–ALT
    connector; Fork Mountain; ALT-3 (four junctions,
    see description); Graveyard Ridge; Little East Fork;
    Old Butt Knob
Topographic Quadrangles Sam Knob, Shining Rock
Blaze None
Usage See description
Features Wilderness; Shining Rock lead-in route;
    year-round views, especially in the Ivestor Gap area;
    three-season wildflower display

Primarily an upper-slope route, Ivestor Gap runs south to north, from the end of the pavement on FS 816 to Shining Rock Gap. This heavily used trail serves at least four different functions. It is by far the easiest Shining Rock lead-in hike. It is a major artery, leading directly to eight trails (the Black Balsam Trailhead junctions included) and one connector. It is an easily walked way to enjoy beauty: three seasons of wildflowers and year-round views (until the nonwilderness, downslope forest recovers). And in late summer and autumn the southern, nonwilderness half of the track provides a challenge for high-clearance vehicles and their drivers.

The hike, bike, and horse sign at the trailhead does not tell Ivestor Gap's entire usage story. Bikes are not allowed in the wilderness north of Ivestor Gap. Horses and other pack stock such as llamas are not allowed beyond the Little East Fork Trail junction west of Shining Rock Gap. From mid-August through January 2, the trailhead gate remains open for the high-clearance vehicles of blueberry pickers, hunters, and campers. During this time of year, it is legal for vehicles to travel the trail/road south of the wilderness boundary at Ivestor Gap.

Ivestor Gap's upslope side—the right and generally eastern side—is now the western boundary of a controlled burn unit for the 2.2-mile length from its trailhead to Ivestor Gap. A series of low-intensity burns within the roughly 600-acre unit will soon reset succession's clock to an earlier year.

Beginning on the western slope of Black Balsam Knob, the IGT winds to the north on the easygoing grades of old roads and railroads. From the trailhead to Ivestor Gap, where the treadway enters the Shining Rock Wilderness, the route follows the wide and rocky bed of former FS 816, almost all of it wider than a single track for vehicles. North of the prominent gap and within the wilderness, the vehicle ban and resurgent forest have narrowed the former road to footpath.

The eroded and rock-humped road passes a usually reliable pipe spring to the right at slightly less than 0.1 mile. Here the boot-and-tire-worn track closely follows the 5,800-foot contour on the western and northwestern slopes of Black Balsam Knob. South of Ivestor Gap, much of the forest along the western, downslope edge of the trail is still recovering, still in the early stages of woody plant succession. Pioneer tree species such as mountain ash, pin cherry, and serviceberry are rapidly rising along the downhill margin of the grade, screening the views and shading the shrubs. Where the roadway travels to the east and the slope faces north, the forest has regenerated to young hardwoods, yellow birch by far the most numerous.

The sidehill trek gradually pulls up and away from the 5,800-foot contour as it rises toward a Tennent Mountain spur, which it crosses in a shallow saddle at mile 1.0. Here the ridge-line—trail highpoint at 5,870 feet—is picketed with planted red pines, many already dead or dying. Native much further north, red pines were formerly used in high-elevation reforestation projects in the Southern Appalachians. This conifer is identified in the Shining Rock highcountry by its bark's reddish brown scales and its 4- to 6-inch-long needles, which occur two per bundle. Now heading downhill, the roadbed quickly comes to the wide entrance of the IGT–ALT connector, located up and to the right (southeast) approximately 50 yards beyond the crest of the spur. Overall easy up and 0.2-mile long, the connector ties into the ALT in the small gap between Black Balsam Knob and Tennent Mountain.

The course slowly descends to and crosses over the notch of Wash Hollow at mile 1.2. Beyond this point all of the land to the left of the tread (generally to the west or north) lies within the Shining Rock Wilderness. The IGT passes over another ridge planted in red pine at mile 1.4—Fork Mountain, a major Tennent Mountain lead. Now on a very gradual downgrade again (a usually reliable spring to the right at mile 1.6), the rough road reaches its junction with the Fork Mountain Trail to the left (entrance 310 degrees; N 20 37, W 52 13) at mile 1.7. The occasionally cairned entrance to Fork Mountain is often a narrow, easily missed gap in the vegetation. The spring is 135 yards before the Fork Mountain junction.

One hundred thirty-five yards past the Fork Mountain junction, the usually signed ALT ties into the IGT from the right. The ALT shares the route for 55 yards before splitting away at the small open area located in the first gap north of Tennent Mountain. On its own again at mile 1.8, the roadbed trail makes a gap-to-gap half loop around the sunset side of an unnamed knob. At mile 2.2 you enter the open flat of Ivestor Gap (5,690 feet), a busy trail junction and loafing spot on the southern perimeter of the Shining Rock Wilderness.

Ivestor is a gateway gap. Its wilderness sign, its vehicle-blocking boulders, its various paths and roads radiating away in different directions, and the view of the broad dome of Grassy Cove Top nearby to the northeast make Ivestor unmistakable. The IGT makes a sudden transition—one totally unexpected by many first-time hikers—from wide roadway to narrow path at the gap. From the left side of the first boulder you come to in the gap, continue straight ahead along the left (northwestern) side of the open area and pick up the tread (entrance approximately 50 degrees) immediately to the right of the wooden wilderness sign and the boulder right in front of it.

Graveyard Ridge Trail's northwestern, upper-elevation end ties into the IGT here at its namesake saddle, and Section 3 of the ALT also passes through the gap. If you turn right with the single-track road and proceed generally eastward, you will be walking the Graveyard Ridge Trail. If you turn right with the road from the right side of the first boulder you come to in the gap, then follow the right edge of the road for less than 15 yards before bending right and up through the vehicle-blocking wooden railing, you will be on the ALT heading south toward

Black Balsam Knob. If you curl to the right with the road from the right side of that same boulder, then follow the road for a little less than 50 yards before turning left onto the usually signed footpath (entrance north), you will be hiking to the north on the ALT toward Shining Rock.

Now in wilderness, most of the IGT's remaining distance travels along the western pitch of Shining Rock Ledge, a north-south-running string of prominent peaks. Here on the western slant of Grassy Cove Top (a 6,055 footer) the vegetation has often narrowed the formerly wide bed to single-file footpath. As the track advances further north, it passes through forest that has regenerated to an older successional stage—a forest where the trailside trees stand much taller and thicker than they do south of the wilderness.

At mile 3.0 the line of march crosses over the spur ridge descending to the northwest from Grassy Cove Top's northern knob. Here the forest is most often a mix of highcountry conifers and cold-tolerant hardwoods shading an undergrowth layer of evergreen and deciduous heath shrubs—mountain laurel, Catawba and rosebay rhododendron, and blueberry bushes. All of the tallest conifers are red spruce. The curly-barked yellow birch is by far the most abundant of the larger hardwoods.

Mature red spruce are especially common (for now) from mile 3.4 to 3.5. Beyond mile 3.5 the forest, which includes sugar maple, yellow buckeye, and black cherry, is often underlain with herbaceous wildflowers, grasses, and ferns. The long stand of young beech that ends before the Little East Fork junction is currently under attack by beech bark disease. At mile 3.9 Ivestor Gap arrives at its obvious junction with the Little East Fork Trail, which ties in from a bend-back angle to the left (nearly west) at a small loafing spot where Ivestor Gap bends to the right and east.

After curving to the right over the Flower Knob spur, the remainder of the route heads east to finish the half loop to Shining Rock Gap. The small opening in the gap is the most confusing trail junction in the combined wildernesses. Here hikers routinely head the wrong direction on the wrong trail. Two trails (Ivestor Gap and Old Butt Knob) end in the opening. A third trail (Art Loeb) crosses through the opening diagonally, and a fourth trail (Shining Creek) ends nearby. An easily found spring, numerous campsites, and Shining Rock—the area's most popular destination—are also close at hand. (See page liii for the description and drawing of the Shining Rock Gap area.)

Nature Notes

Ivestor Gap, especially along its wide and sunny southern half, features an excellent late spring and early summer flowering shrub display. June is the best month, and June 1 through 20 is the best time for peak color. Dwarf rhododendron is often past prime by June 1. Goat's beard, bush honeysuckle, mountain laurel, flame azalea, and Catawba rhododendron all bloom or begin blooming in June. Rosebay rhododendron starts to whiten the trailside forest in late June, when most of the others are either finished or fading.

Ivestor Gap also offers a good late-spring-through-early-fall herbaceous wildflower show that includes galax, Michaux's saxifrage, St. John's-wort, pink turtlehead, bluets (abundant and blooming on a recent May 23), crimson bee balm, stiff and bottle gentians, rose twisted-stalk, a phlox species, and more than a dozen kinds of brightly colored asters.

Virgin's bower, a native perennial vine with showy white flowers and three maplelike leaflets per leaf, is abundant and blooms in July and August. If you look closely, you might spot the glue-tipped reddish leaves of the round-leaved sundew, a diminutive predatory plant that grows along the seeping bases of the upslope road banks along the first half of the trail.

Cranberry (*Vaccinium macrocarpon*)—the commercial cranberry—blossomed along the high side of the trail on a recent June 26 and July 3. Usually less than 6 inches high, this low, trailing heath with wire-slender woody stems is inconspicuous when not in bloom or berry. The cold-hardy cranberry's elfin leaves are evergreen and leathery. The small white petals of the flowers recurve sharply to reveal long orange stamens. The buds resemble miniature pink popsicles.

bush honeysuckle

Bush honeysuckle

The bush honeysuckle (*Diervilla sessilifolia*), a Southern Appalachian endemic, is a low-growing shrub inhabiting forest openings, balds, and exposed ridges at high elevations, most often from 4,000 to 6,200 feet. Usually only 3 to 5 feet tall, this soft-wooded, sun-loving species is currently abundant where succession has reached the low shrub and sapling stage in the Shining Rock area. It is particularly numerous along the sunny margins of old, high-elevation roads. For now, dense thicket-growths of this honeysuckle frequently hedge the downslope edge of this route from its beginning to Ivestor Gap. This highcountry shrub becomes much less common as saplings grow taller and block its sun. The Forest Service, however, may be giving this woody plant a reprieve by turning back the successional sequence with fire.

This shrub's deciduous leaves, opposite and finely toothed,

are either stemless (sessile) or very short stemmed. Lance shaped and usually 2 to 5 inches in length, the long-pointed leaves feature a prominent midvein. The pale yellow blooms, which occur in clusters of three to seven flowers, are tubular, ¾ inch long, and flare into five star-shaped lobes. Bush honeysuckle was in bud and bloom on June 27 and July 4 of recent years. The corollas turn a darker orangish red with age.

Mourning cloak

On a recent May 14 and 30, both warm and sunny days, mourning cloaks flitted along the road-wide treadway of this trail's southernmost 2.2 miles. This unusual butterfly is large, widespread, long-lived, and remains dormant—its colorful wings in the hangar—for much of its long life. The mourning cloak, which has a wingspan of 2¾ to 3⅜ inches, lives almost everywhere throughout temperate and subarctic North America. The adult of this species is the Methuselah of North American butterflies, often surviving to the ripe old age of more than ten months. Since most butterflies are dead and down in two weeks or less, ten months is truly a long time to hold onto your wings.

The mourning cloak's unique life cycle helps it avoid predation and greatly aids its longevity. This winged insect also actively aids its longevity by emitting an audible click just as it takes flight away from would-be predators. The mourning cloak both estivates and hibernates: it holes up during both summer and winter. Overwintering adults occasionally become active on warm late winter or early spring days, even when snow lingers in the mountains.

This butterfly is easily identified by the distinctive color patterns covering the top side of its wings. A broad and irregular band of yellow borders the wings except along the leading edge of the forewing. A single row of bright purple-blue spots border the inside edge of the yellow, separating the band from the rest of the velvety, purplish black wings.

Directions

Ivestor Gap begins at the Black Balsam Trailhead at the paved end of FS 816 (Black Balsam Road) to the north of the parkway. The entrance to FS 816 is located between BRP mileposts 420 and 421. FS 816 is usually marked with some combination of signs large and small: Black Balsam Trailhead, Black Balsam Road, FS 816–Black Balsam Road.

Approach from the south: From the BRP–access road from NC 215 junction, turn left onto the parkway and travel approximately 3.0 miles before turning left onto FS 816.

Approach from the north: From the BRP–access road from US 276 junction, turn left onto the parkway and travel approximately 8.3 miles before turning right onto FS 816.

Travel FS 816 1.2 miles to the large parking area at the end of the paved road. Gated except during blueberry picking and hunting seasons, the usually signed IGT is the decidedly unpaved road that continues nearly straight ahead where the pavement curves to the left into the parking area.

Notes

Art Loeb Spur

Forest Service Trail 108	0.4 mile

Dayhiking In Moderate

Dayhiking Out Easy to Moderate

Backpacking In Moderate to Strenuous

Backpacking Out Moderate

Start The Black Balsam Trailhead at the paved end of FS
816, 5,815 feet

End Junction with Art Loeb Trail below the top of Black
Balsam Knob, 6,140 feet

Trail Junctions IGT, Flat Laurel Creek, and Sam Knob at
the Black Balsam Trailhead; ALT-3

Topographic Quadrangle Sam Knob

Blaze Orange

Usage Foot travel only

Features Views; Art Loeb connector

The Art Loeb Spur is a short connector that serves one primary
purpose: it makes the two most popular IGT–ALT loops—from
the Black Balsam Trailhead out to either Ivestor Gap or Shining
Rock Gap and back—complete and closed loops, no paved road
walking necessary. Today's spur (the shortest trail detailed in
this guide, excluding the Graveyard Fields system) is a well-
designed makeover of an old, highly eroded, straight-up-the-
slope route that served the same purpose.

Switchbacking to the east up a high, wind-strafed, west-
facing slope, the trail gains 325 feet of elevation in a little more

than 0.4 mile. All of the bends and switchbacks make the steady ascent surprisingly easy for its nearly 15 percent grade. The treadway currently climbs above the steadily encroaching tree line. If the fire-management policy for the area is implemented as planned, the forest will have to wait while the wind-rippled grass and long distance views remain for years to come.

The spur T's into its usually signed junction with the ALT atop the ridgeline rising toward nearby Black Balsam Knob. To the right, the ALT descends 0.5 mile to its FS 816 crossing. To the left, the ALT continues to the north for 2.5 miles to Ivestor Gap and 4.4 miles to the small opening in Shining Rock Gap, the ALT's northernmost junction with the IGT.

Directions
Art Loeb Spur, Ivestor Gap, Sam Knob, and the northeastern end of Flat Laurel Creek all share the same major trailhead. The spur's wide and usually signed entrance is a couple of paces past the right-hand gatepost at the beginning of the IGT, the dirt-rock road that continues straight ahead from the paved end of FS 816. (See Ivestor Gap, the preceding trail, for directions to the Black Balsam Trailhead at the paved end of FS 816.)

Art Loeb Trail, Section 3

(FS 816 to Deep Gap)

Forest Service Trail 146	7.9 miles

Dayhiking (low to high) Moderate to Strenuous
Dayhiking (high to low) Moderate
Backpacking (low to high) Strenuous
Backpacking (high to low) Moderate to Strenuous
Start Mountains to Sea–Art Loeb Trailhead off FS 816,
    5,900 feet
End Junction with Cold Mountain Trail in Deep Gap,
    5,015 feet (Art Loeb Trail continues to the southwest)
Trail Junctions MST-3, MST-4, and ALT-2 at the MST–ALT
    Trailhead; Art Loeb Spur; IGT–ALT connector; IGT
    (four junctions, see description), Graveyard Ridge;
    ALT–Greasy Cove connector; Shining Creek; Old Butt
    Knob; Cold Mountain; ALT-4
Topographic Quadrangles Sam Knob, Shining Rock, Cruso
Blaze White rectangle south of Ivestor Gap, no blazing
    in the wilderness north of the gap
Usage Foot travel only
Features Wilderness; Black Balsam Knob; Tennent
    Mountain; year-round panoramic views; Shining
    Rock lead-in route; flowering shrub and herbaceous
    wildflower displays

A north-south-running ridgeline and upper-slope route, ALT-3 is
the longest and highest trail or trail section described in this

guide. This treadway remains above 5,000 feet as it follows Shining Rock Ledge, the main divide of the Shining Rock area. It passes near or over the summits of four 6,000-foot peaks— Black Balsam Knob, Tennent Mountain, Grassy Cove Top, Shining Rock—and rises above 6,000 feet twice.

Section 3 is described as it is most easily accessed and most often hiked, from south to north, from FS 816 south of Black Balsam to Deep Gap south of Cold Mountain. This section's features predictably account for its popularity. Relatively few people, however, hike the entire segment. The trail is very heavily trod to the summit of Black Balsam, heavily tramped from Black Balsam to Shining Rock Gap, but comparatively lightly used from Shining Rock Gap to Deep Gap.

The ALT reaches its first signed junction where the MST splits off to the right (east) less than 20 yards in from the road. Continuing straight ahead toward Black Balsam, Section 3 rises easily through spruce, passes above the current tree line, then ascends more briskly to the first outcropping of light gray rock. The track arrives at another usually signed T-junction atop a slight knob (6,140 feet) at 0.5 mile. Here the Art Loeb Spur's deeply cut tread heads downhill to the left and nearly west.

Beyond the shallow saddle, the line of march follows the left fork onto the sidehill (the old straight-uphill route needs time to heal) before finishing the mild grade to the ALT's highest elevation along its full length (6,180 feet, 0.7 mile). Paths cross to the four cardinal points here near the top of Black Balsam Knob. The Art Loeb turns left (north) and downhill on the open ridgecrest; the spur to the right and south leads higher still to the mountain's highpoint benchmark and plaque. You will find the benchmark's small metal disk embedded in low rock just to the right of the sidepath after 110 yards (N 19 67, W 52 47; 6,214 feet—the highest elevation near the trails in this guide). A tribute to Arthur J. Loeb, the plaque is straight ahead another 55 yards to the knot of outcropped rock.

The panoramic view from Black Balsam is a showstopper. The rough, "halfway to heaven" country of the Southern Appalachians surrounds you a full 360 degrees, paling to invisibility toward every horizon save far south. Starting in the north and sweeping around clockwise (while you walk between benchmark and plaque), this short sampler of mostly local peaks begins with movie star Cold Mountain (5.8 miles, 6,030 feet) at around 16 degrees. Shining Rock is the speck of white in the conifer green just to the right of, and half the distance to, Cold Mountain. Conical and tipped with a tower, Mount Pisgah (9.5 miles) is obvious at around 53 degrees, and Mount Mitchell, the highest summit in eastern North America (observation tower, 46.5 miles, 6,684 feet, 396 feet higher than the loftiest presidential peak in New England, Mount Washington) frequently plows upside-down furrows in passing clouds at around 56 degrees. The tour continues with Looking Glass Rock's steeply sloping rockface (4.9 miles) at around 117 degrees, Cedar Rock Mountain's double-banded rockface (6.4 miles) at around 146 degrees, Pilot Mountain's distinctly conical peak (3.8 miles) at nearly south, and Toxaway Mountain's broad and towered top (14.9 miles) at around 214 degrees. The light gray cliffs of Whiteside Mountain (22.8 miles) are visible through clear, cold-front air at around 226 degrees.

Turning toward the west, you will recognize Mount Hardy's high, conifer-clad crown (3.5 miles, 6,125 feet) at around 248 degrees, Rough Butt Bald (5.2 miles—the next major uplift along the parkway to the right of Hardy) at close to west, and swaybacked Sam Knob (1.1 miles, 6,060 feet) at around 280 degrees. Cap dark with Fraser fir, Richland Balsam (7.1 miles, 6,410 feet) boasts the highest reach in the neighborhood at around 300 degrees. The slowly descending and landmark-flat ridge to the left of Richland Balsam (across the parkway) is Piney Mountain, and the long, high crest losing elevation to the right and nearly north from Richland Balsam is Lickstone Ridge. Lickstone Bald's prominent highpoint (8.8 miles) is located on its namesake ridge at around 327 degrees.

At 0.9 mile the trail takes the left fork where the former route runs straight and highly eroded down the ridge. The most recent makeover slips onto the high sunset slope before working its steady and switchbacking way down the frequently wide grade. The course crosses an intermittent rill at mile 1.4. Two-tenths mile further, the ALT ties back into the ridgeline at the gap (5,910 feet) between Black Balsam and Tennent Mountain. The prominent tread back and to the left in the gap (entrance 290 degrees) is the 0.2-mile IGT–ALT connector leading to the IGT.

Your next goal is in clear view from the open gap. This short climb ratchets up to moderate before gaining Tennent's narrow topknot of rock (mile 1.9, 6,070 feet) and another plaque, this one honoring Dr. Gaillard Stoney Tennent. Like Black Balsam, Tennent offers an open look in every direction, the whole encircling horizon ringed with the rolling swell of mountains.

Beyond Tennent's tiny crown, the trek descends the highest reach of Ivestor Ridge, its rugged crest narrow, rocky, and running downhill to the east. At mile 2.2, the footpath switchbacks sharply to the left and down off the top of the fold before steadily losing elevation to the northwest for 0.4 mile to its first junction with the IGT. Here the usually signed ALT turns right onto the IGT, shares its single-track road for 55 yards, then forks away to the right onto footpath again at the shallow saddle.

The track slabs to the right of the ridgetop as it rises toward the mound of the next knuckle, conifer capped and 5,800 feet high. The red pines surrounding the unnamed knob's campsite may soon be eliminated by a controlled burn, but the camp's nearby rock outcrop overlook will still afford the same long-range views. After passing just below the highpoint, the boot-worn treadway crests the ridge and rides it downhill to the north. The grade ends where the ALT ventures through the vehicle-blocking split-rail gate and dips to the road in Ivestor Gap (5,690 feet) at mile 3.0.

Section 3 connects with both the IGT and Graveyard Ridge Trail here at this busy gateway gap. (See IGT, page 66, and Graveyard Ridge Trail, page 129, for further information concerning this potentially confusing junction.)

At Ivestor Gap, the Art Loeb curves to the right onto the road (Graveyard Ridge Trail), advances 35 yards, then bears off 90 degrees to the left onto the usually signed footpath (entrance north). Now within the Shining Rock Wilderness, the ALT's next 0.7 mile makes a half loop around the sunrise slant of Grassy Cove Top, steadily gaining elevation on easy and easy-to-moderate grades along the way. After taking the right fork less than 60 yards in from the road, the route crosses an intermittent spring at mile 3.1. Three-tenths mile further, you pass the sometimes difficult to locate ALT–Greasy Cove connector to the right (N 20 84, W 51 66; 0.2 mile long). The sidehill tread continues its slow ascent through a young forest where early succession hardwoods are increasingly winning rootholds in the often dense growth of heath shrubs.

At mile 3.7 the path curls to the right onto the main divide, Shining Rock Ledge, and strikes out toward Grassy Cove Top's slightly lower northern knob. After the saddle's easy walking, the hike heads up through heath as it skirts the western edge of the knob's crown at mile 4.0 before descending. Here the course makes a moderate downridge run to the seemingly always windy

Flower Gap (5,790 feet) at mile 4.3. The open, grassy portions of the gap lose more and more ground to the willful forest every year.

Just up from the saddle, the track closely follows the contour of the slope on an old railroad bed as it swings around the eastern flank of Flower Knob. At mile 4.4 a slender sidepath to the left quickly leads to the cavelike pit of a former mica mine. Two-tenths mile further, the nearly effortless walking passes above the first and less reliable of the two springs along this stretch. At mile 4.8 the wide track passes closely above the more reliable of the two springs (flowing in September of the drought year 2007). Shining Creek Trail (to the right and down, entrance 125 degrees, still mile 4.8) connects with the Art Loeb 75 yards beyond the spring.

The ALT enters the small, steadily shrinking opening in Shining Rock Gap (5,755 feet, mile 4.9) 90 yards beyond the Shining Creek junction. This opening is a major trail junction and a major cause of confusion. Two routes—Ivestor Gap and Old Butt Knob—end here, and the Art Loeb crosses the opening diagonally. (See page liii for the description and drawing of the Shining Rock Gap area.)

Back on railroad bed and traveling generally north again, the easy-as-pie hiking threads through high-elevation conifers, evergreen heath hedges, and hardwoods such as mountain maple, sugar maple, northern red oak, and the ubiquitous yellow birch. After ranging through the long flat of Crawford Creek Gap (5,770 feet) at mile 5.6, the trail leaves the railroad grade and the top of the fold as it angles to the left of the rising ridgeline. Here the frequently rocky and undulating tread slants up the high western slope of Stairs Mountain. At mile 5.9 the trek crests Stairs just above the peak's second and slightly lower benchmark (5,869 feet at the benchmark), then immediately descends.

From Stairs Mountain most of the next 0.8 mile is a steady downgrade ranging from nearly level to easy-to-moderate. Here the forest remains a mix of short-needled conifers and cold-adapted hardwoods as the route loses elevation to 5,400 feet. Beyond the noticeably wide and flat ridgetop at mile 6.7, the trail becomes progressively steeper until a sharp pitch drops you onto a section of Shining Rock Ledge accurately labeled as The Narrows at mile 6.9. Approximately a half mile in length, the ridgeline along this rugged and scenic stretch is frequently pared down to rock outcrop width.

At mile 7.0 a sidepath leads to a short scramble up to a rock outcrop overlook open from west to north. The course quickly reaches a high road/low road choice of routes, both challenging with a steep rocky pitch or two. The shorter, higher, and rougher path provides another view similar to the one just described. Back on single treadway, the wilderness path travels over a spot where the exact keel of the crest is only a long hiking stick wide at mile 7.2. The forest shading this dry, exposed ridge is dominated by short, low-branched northern red and chestnut oaks.

Two-tenths mile further, you come upon a double-barreled look-off—one to the right of the ridge, another to the left. The view to the right allows you a closer look at Cold Mountain (left edge of the view at around 30 degrees) and Mount Pisgah at around 76 degrees. The deeply entrenched Crawford Creek cove is far below your rocky perch. To the left, the rock outcrop overlook offers a prospect to nearby Fork Mountain and beyond. Over and above the Fork Mountain ridgeline, the nearly flat crest of Piney Mountain slowly rises toward Richland Balsam at around 248 degrees. Just across the parkway from Piney, 6,410-foot Richland Balsam is the highest summit in near view at around 260 degrees. The long horizon line that rolls downhill and to the north away from Richland Balsam is Lickstone Ridge.

At mile 7.6 a steep, 80-yard grade drops you off The Narrows onto a much wider ridgetop with a high herb layer and much taller hardwoods, including black cherry and yellow buckeye, below 5,200 feet. After winding its way down to a slight saddle with 0.1 mile remaining, Section 3 rises over one last bump of a knob before rolling into Deep Gap's thinning stand of black locust. Deep Gap's open junction doubles as a resting and camping spot. Here the Cold Mountain Trail ascends straight ahead (entrance 30 degrees) on Shining Rock Ledge, and the ALT bends to the left and downhill toward its terminus at the scout camp.

There is no drought-proof water near Deep Gap. The closest intermittent wet-weather spring is located 0.2 mile down the ALT toward the scout camp.

Nature Notes

ALT-3's southernmost 3.0 miles, from FS 816 to Ivestor Gap, follow the crest and upper slopes of the high ridge at the heart of an approximately 600-acre controlled burn unit. If this tract is managed as planned, the prescribed fires will reverse the current course of succession. The burns will allow grasses and forbs to spread downslope against the grain, displacing shrubs, saplings, and young trees that had been charging up the hill. In the immediate future, this segment will have many more herbaceous wildflowers and far fewer flowering shrubs than at present. The extent of the change depends on the frequency and intensity of the burns.

After the fires, ALT-3 will feature an excellent diversity of both flowering shrubs and herbaceous wildflowers to complement the views. Seven species of flowering shrubs—fetterbush, flame azalea, mountain laurel, Catawba and rosebay rhododendron, bearberry and bush honeysuckle—are both common and easily identified when in bloom along this section of the ALT. Fetterbush flowers the earliest; it often begins blossoming between the 5,600- to 6,000-foot contours in late April or early May. Bush honeysuckle remains in bloom the longest and latest. In recent years this highly colonial woody plant had just begun to blossom on June 16 and remained in bloom through most of July. The best time slot to admire the attractive heath shrubs—flame azalea, mountain laurel, Catawba rhododendron—is usually between June 10 and 22.

On one June 16, wakerobin, painted trillium, Canada mayflower, and bluebead lily had already faded, while fly poison, wild columbine, fire pink, and whorled loosestrife were still in bloom. Later, on July 4, I spotted fly poison and a herbaceous St. John's-wort blossoming among a few other less conspicuous wildflowers. The tall and flamboyant Turk's-cap lily flowered near Deep Gap on a recent July 21. White wood aster, whorled wood aster, white snakeroot, pale jewelweed, black-eyed susan, and other asters were blooming on August 29. Now that Black Balsam will be burned on a regular rotation, several types of goldenrod will reliably yellow its high slopes from late August well into September.

American mountain ash

The American mountain ash (*Sorbus americana*) toddled southward far in advance of the most recent glaciation. As the towering walls of ice melted and the earth warmed, this cold-adapted tree was forced to march again—to the north and to higher elevations in the South. Still primarily a northern, cold-climate species, the mountain ash is now Dixie's most boreal broadleaf. It is most comfortable above 5,400 feet and grows atop the tallest peaks in eastern North America: the Southern Highland's 6,600 footers.

This hardwood is a short-lived succession species, one of the first trees to invade exposed and disturbed highcountry sites. The pinnately compound leaves of the mountain ash—leaves alternate, leaflets opposite—closely resemble those of the staghorn sumac. Narrow, lance shaped, and toothed, the eleven to eighteen leaflets are 2 to 4 inches long and only ½ to 1 inch wide. The new growth of the thick leaf stem is often pale to deep red in June.

S. americana flaunts 3- to 5-inch-wide, flat-topped clusters of tiny white blossoms in June. By September and October, the five-petaled flowers have been replaced by heavy clusters of shiny orange-red berries. When the local mountain ashes produce an exceptionally heavy berry crop, they emblazon the highcountry's leaf season with another fiery color. Autumn's cold weather slowly turns the berries bright red.

Mountain ash is an ash in common name only. It is a member of the Rose family; the real ashes belong to the Olive family and the *Fraxinus* genus.

This small broadleaf (maximum height 35 to 40 feet) was once widely known as the rowan-tree. According to one explanation, Roan Mountain, a peak straddling the NC-TN border, was named for the rowan-trees found on its summit.

Interrupted fern

Arching fountains of the Shining Rock region's tallest fern, the interrupted, occasionally grace the trailside from Shining Rock north to The Narrows. This distinctive vascular plant requires cool, moist conditions; its huge range—much of eastern North America and eastern Asia—barely extends southward into the mountains of north Georgia.

This fern's descriptive common name aids in identification. On fertile fronds, the regular rows of green pinnae are interrupted by one to five pairs of fertile pinnae laden with clusters of

round spore cases, green at first, then turning dark brown as the spores are released.
Located on the lower blade (the leafy part of
the frond), these stalks are small, dark, and
have no foliage whatsoever. After the spores
disperse, the cases and stems wither away,
leaving the blade with a pronounced gap
between upper and lower pinnae.

Growing in clumps or clusters, this
ancient nonflowering plant is usually 2½ to
5 feet tall. Occasional colonies rise to over
6 feet if you straighten their fronds to full
height. The slightly alternate pinnae are
blunt tipped and deeply divided. The stipe
(the stem from ground to first green pinnae)
is smooth, not fuzzy like the similar cinna-
mon fern. Most fronds are infertile and
uninterrupted.

interrupted fern

Directions

The southern end of ALT-3 shares the exact same trailhead as
the western end of MST-4. The two trails split apart less than 20
yards in from the right (northeast) side of the road. The MST
turns 90 degrees to the right; the ALT continues straight ahead
toward Black Balsam Knob. (See MST-4, page 127, for directions
to its western, MST–ALT Trailhead off FS 816.)

Little East Fork Trail

| Forest Service Trail 107 | 5.0 miles |

Dayhiking In Moderate
Dayhiking Out Easy to Moderate
Backpacking In Moderate to Strenuous
Backpacking Out Moderate
Start Near the parking area for the Art Loeb Trailhead
at Daniel Boone Boy Scout Camp, 3,360 feet
End Junction with Ivestor Gap Trail west of Shining
Rock Gap, 5,730 feet
Trail Junctions ALT-4 at the trailhead parking area, IGT
Topographic Quadrangles Waynesville, Sam Knob,
Shining Rock
Blaze None (wilderness)
Usage Hike and horse (see description)
Features Wilderness; Little East Fork Pigeon River;
Shining Rock lead-in route; diverse forest; diverse
spring wildflower display

Wide and well worn where it parallels its namesake stream, this route is heavily tromped when the Daniel Boone Boy Scout Camp is in full session and lightly trod in comparison much of the rest of the year. This trail, which closely follows the small-volume flow of the Little East Fork Pigeon River for its first 2.5 miles, makes an excellent spring hike.

The best time to walk this old road is during the warming weather of a wet spring after the pulse of a substantial rain. It is then—on a clear day after the wildflowers have quilted the slopes and before scout camp and broadleaf buds open—that the river is a magic show, free for the small effort. Then gravity and gradient and full, sun-bright flow give strong voice and steady Appalachian beauty to this boulder-bedded stream. Then you can revel in the foaming power of fast-falling mountain water—its innately pleasing spill and weave, its unceasing sound and motion.

A riverine and upper-slope route, this hike gains a hard-to-ignore 2,370 feet of elevation, but it accomplishes this rise, for the most part, at an unusually steady pace. There are no sustained grades more difficult than easy to moderate until you cross the Little East Fork. After its initial climb above the crossing, the track settles down again as it winds and switchbacks to the northeast.

One of five Shining Rock lead-in trails—paths that converge at or near Shining Rock Gap—this route is most often walked as a way to the white outcrop, or as the first or last leg of the Little East Fork–Ivestor Gap–Art Loeb loop beginning and ending at the scout camp trailhead.

The camp runs full blast from around June 1 through August 10. The sessions last for a week; newcomers arrive on Sunday and leave the following Saturday. There is no need to call before you arrive—just drive in, park in the proper place, and hike. Cell phone service is problematic in the camp valley; a pay phone is provided outside of the camp office.

The Little East Fork is designated a hiker and horse-rider trail. Thus far, I have never seen horses or any signs of them on the treadway, and the camp director confirmed that horse usage is rare.

The track, which quickly enters the Shining Rock Wilderness, follows the contours of the streamside terrain as it gradually ascends along the rhododendron-edged Little East Fork. The usually wide bed of the former road alternates between good, close-range views of the stream and no views at all from further up the slope. Here at this relatively low elevation, the tall, straight forest includes red maple, yellow poplar, sweet birch, white ash, white basswood, and northern red oak. Today, after the adelgid-driven demise of all the larger hemlocks, hardwoods totally control the canopy.

There is a good upstream view during the bare-limb season just before Hemlock Branch adds its flow to the Little East Fork at mile 0.9. Continuing generally southward, the sometimes rocky and eroded grade passes above long cascading runs, loud and white when the water is up and lively. The cascades at mile 1.3 and 1.6 are probably high enough to be called waterfalls. The first one—a long, sliding sheet of froth after substantial rain, with much more run than rise—drops 25 to 30 feet. The second is 12 to 15 feet high and nearly vertical.

The course continues to work its way up the scenic watershed. Several room-sized boulders have come to rest—and to slow resistless erosion—in the streambed. Trees that have an affinity for cooler and moister habitat—such as yellow buckeye, black cherry, yellow birch, silverbell, and sugar maple—become more common and conspicuous beyond the second high cascade.

At mile 2.5 (4,440 feet) you cross the Little East Fork just downstream from a horseshoe-shaped slab of bedrock deflecting the river's flow through a narrow channel. This high up, above the tributary waters from Shining Rock Creek and the river's northern prong, the Little East Fork is a small stream usually easily crossed.

Once across, the uphill hiking doglegs to the left onto the rocky bed of an old woods road, then quickly bends back to the right above a large and heavily used campsite. Here the first sustained grade worth mentioning (overall moderate) climbs for 250 yards before crossing a spring run at mile 2.7. This step-over rivulet marks the beginning of a pattern that lasts the next 0.8 mile. Steadily ascending, the trail curls over the crest of a spur before half-looping around one or more steep-sided ravines, crossing the small watercourses flowing down their notches along the way.

This over-spur-and-around-hollow stretch winds up the western slope of the master ridge running from Black Balsam Knob to Cold Mountain: Shining Rock Ledge. All of the spring-fed runs feed the Little East Fork, and most of them are dry by July and August during drought.

Beyond where the roadbed tread curves over a spur at mile 3.5, the remainder of the trail rises slowly; all of the sustained grades are mild. The trek gradually angles upslope to this section's first rounded switchback at mile 3.8. It then continues to half-loop up the mountainside with the help of three more switchbacks, which average a little more than 0.1 mile apart. Above the final switchback at mile 4.1 (5,390 feet), the rest of the route heads east for a few tenths of a mile before bearing to the north and slowly slanting up the sunset pitch of the nearly 5,900-foot-high Flower Knob.

The uppermost 1.5 miles range through a mixed spruce-fir/northern hardwood forest where stands of young beech have recently been decimated by BBD. Now light-gap vegetation and root-sucker beech saplings will crowd the path in places until the forest shades the track again. In the meantime, please carry a lightweight handsaw so you can help keep this trail, and others, clear of all the hemlock and beech that will be falling to ground soon.

Little East Fork ties into the IGT at a pack-drop loafing spot. If you continue nearly straight ahead (east) on Ivestor Gap, you will arrive at its end in Shining Rock Gap's small opening after 0.4 mile. If you bend back to the right (southwest) onto Ivestor Gap, you will be walking toward that route's Black Balsam Trailhead.

A usually reliable spring surfaces near the small opening in Shining Rock Gap. (See page liii for the description and drawing of the Shining Rock Gap area.)

Nature Notes

With its short spills and long sliding cascades, its diverse forest that gains new species with the rise of elevation, and its diverse spring wildflower display (small numbers of many species), Little East Fork tugs at your attention up, down, and sideways. On a recent April 18 it was still too early for most wildflowers. Squirrel corn and bloodroot were already done for the year; trout lily and toothwort were blooming, and wakerobin and lousewort were about to bust out. Nearly two months later, on a recent June 13, it was too late for the flowers of the speckled wood lily, Vasey's trillium, wild geranium, sweet cicely, foamflower, and mayapple, but just the right time for the high-elevation pocket of showy-flowered shrubs—mountain laurel, Catawba rhododendron, and flame azalea.

Rosebay rhododendron was still in the sex-by-proxy business along the river, and a herbaceous St. John's-wort was blossoming in good numbers on a recent July 19. On a recent September 19, black cohosh was almost finished flowering while some of the light gaps created by BBD well above the river crossing had become linear aster gardens.

Eastern hemlock

The recently abundant eastern hemlock *(Tsuga canadensis)* remains the only tiny-needled conifer beside this trail for its first 2.5 miles. (A scatter of small survivors was still alive in

2012.) A few tenths mile further the lowest of the red spruce begin to mingle with the hemlock and hardwoods. Still further and higher, at mile 3.0, a few Fraser firs join the hemlock and spruce. Beyond mile 4.0 and above the 5,200-foot contour, however, the hemlock becomes scarce, then absent (upper-elevation limit is usually listed as 5,700 feet), as the track continues to gain elevation into the colder country at trail's end.

This graceful evergreen was most numerous and reached its best growth on north-facing ridges, moist slopes, stream margins, and in cool ravines. Where abundant, the hemlock's dense, lacy foliage shaded mountain streams and darkened the forest floor.

Three small-needled conifers darken Shining Rock's ridges and slopes—eastern hemlock, Fraser fir, and red spruce. The hemlock, where still extant, is the largest of the three in overall size, but

eastern hemlock

its cones and needles are the smallest. The roughly oval cones of *T. canadensis*, averaging only ¾ of an inch long, are significantly smaller than those of any other native Southern Appalachian pine, fir, or spruce. Its flat, flexible, blunt-tipped needles are ⅓ to ⅔ of an inch long, with two whitish stripes running the length of the undersides. The foliage of the Fraser fir is also flat and striped beneath, but its needles are longer and wider than the hemlock's. The Fraser is balsam scented, and its needles are sessile (stemless). Eastern hemlock needles are not balsam scented and have tiny stems. Red spruce needles are unstriped, ridged rather than flat, and sharp pointed.

In the northern half of its extensive range this species is, or was, a medium-sized tree—60 to 80 feet in height and 2 to

3 feet in diameter. But near the warm, deep-soiled, rain-wealthy southern end of the high Appalachians, this evergreen grew to its most impressive proportions, over 170 feet in height and 5 to 6 feet in diameter. The tallest hemlock on record before the invasion of the adelgid soared 173 feet in the Cataloochee Valley area of the GSMNP. The current national record holder, 165 feet tall and 16 feet 10 inches around, also resides (if it is still alive) in the nearby GSMNP. These impressively large, slow-growing conifers are the Methuselahs of the mountain forests in

the eastern United States. The record age, rings actually counted, is nearly 1,000 years.

This species is facing a sustained and deadly onslaught from the hemlock woolly adelgid, another exotic insect destroying another mountain tree with no immunity. Most of the hemlocks along this trail are already dead or dying. How many will survive, if any, remains to be seen.

white basswood

White basswood

A large and distinctive tree, the white basswood is common beside this trail until the route quickly gains elevation beyond the Little East Fork crossing. Classified as a cove hardwood, this broadleaf competes for the canopy and is often a significant component within its preferred habitat—the rich, moist soils of coves, north-facing slopes, and stream valleys—throughout the Shining Rock region below 4,800 feet.

Basswood is sometimes known as linden, a name German settlers transferred from a *Tilia* species in Europe, and as bee-tree, because honeybees swarm to its fragrant blossoms. The accepted common name comes from the fibers in the tree's inner bark, called bast, which Native Americans stripped to make rope.

The white basswood is identified by its alternate, heart-shaped leaves, which are sharply pointed, finely toothed, and usually 4 to 6 inches long and almost as wide on trees past the sapling stage. The leaf base is frequently asymmetrical; the bottom surface is usually densely coated with whitish hairs. Especially in once- and twice-cut forests, the basswood often occurs in multiboled clumps.

Directions

The driving directions for the Little East Fork Trail are exactly the same as those for ALT-4. (See ALT-4, the following trail section, for directions to the Forest Service kiosk and trailhead.)

Little East Fork's actual trailhead, however, is 0.3 mile beyond the kiosk. If you are not affiliated with the Boy Scouts, you must walk from the designated parking area along the right side of the road past the Forest Service kiosk and Art Loeb Trailhead. After parking in the approved spot, walk the road straight ahead a short distance before turning right (usually signed) and crossing the bridge over the Little East Fork. Once across, turn left (following the arrow at the top of the large camp directory sign) at the T-intersection and follow that road for 0.25 mile as it parallels the stream and passes encampments named for First Nation tribes. Usually identified with wilderness and trail signs, Little East Fork is the narrow old road that continues nearly straight ahead between the last camps to either side of the road.

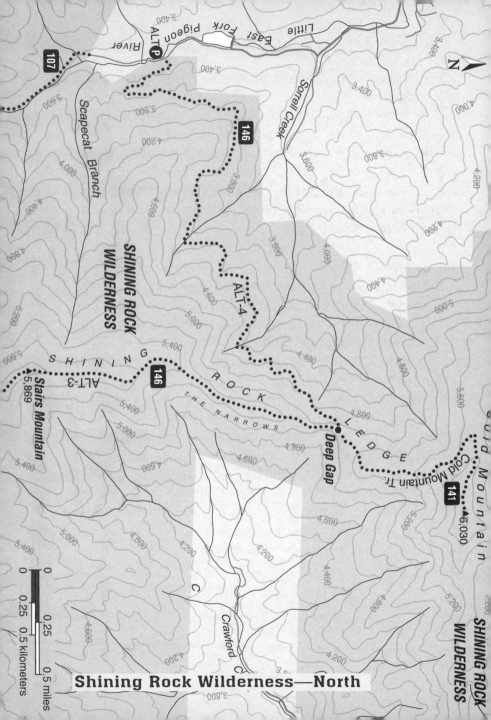

Shining Rock Wilderness—North

Shining Rock Wilderness—North

Roger Nielsen

View of Cold Mountain from near Shining Rock

Trails

Art Loeb, Section 4
Cold Mountain

Art Loeb Trail, Section 4

(Camp Daniel Boone to Deep Gap)

Forest Service Trail 146   **3.8 miles**

Dayhiking In Moderate
Dayhiking Out Easy to Moderate
Backpacking In Moderate to Strenuous
Backpacking Out Moderate
Start Art Loeb Trailhead at Camp Daniel Boone,
    3,260 feet
End Junction with Cold Mountain Trail in Deep Gap,
    (Art Loeb Trail continues south from Deep Gap),
    5,015 feet
Trail Junctions Little East Fork near the trailhead
    parking area, Cold Mountain, ALT-3
Topographic Quadrangles Waynesville, Cruso
Blaze None (wilderness)
Usage Foot travel only
Features Wilderness; diverse forest; impressive rock
    outcrop; shortest Cold Mountain access; excellent
    spring wildflower display

ALT-4 is most often hiked as the shortest way to Deep Gap and
the Cold Mountain Trail, and as the first or last leg of a three-
trail loop—Art Loeb, Ivestor Gap, Little East Fork—beginning
and ending at the scout camp. Section 4's grades are not steep
by Shining Rock and Middle Prong standards, but this ungraded
and sometimes canted footpath is also often very rocky. It is

one of the two most rock-bound trails or trail sections in this guide. As a backpacker with a British accent cheerfully said to me just after he slipped off the downslope edge of this route, "Bit of a challenge, this one, but we don't want sidewalks, now do we?" He was right. Let's hope it remains much as it is today.

Passing beside large rock outcrops, through a diverse forest, and over small headwater streams (all of them Sorrell Creek feeder forks and capillaries), this sidehill hike winds from southwest to northeast, from the Little East Fork Pigeon River to Shining Rock Ledge at Deep Gap. Except where it quickly curls over spurs, this wilderness path travels on sharply slanting slopes all the way from river to master ridge.

Beginning at its trailhead kiosk, the ALT quickly leads uphill into a diverse forest numerically dominated by a tall, straight stand of yellow poplar. The treadway rises into the Shining Rock Wilderness and continues the initial climb to where it curves to the right on a rocked-in switchback. At 0.1 mile the track passes below an impressive rock outcrop 25 to 30 feet high, by far the largest of the many outcrops and boulders beside this section. Now the course slowly angles up the slope on mostly easy and often undulating grades. Here at this low elevation (for the Shining Rock Wilderness), the forest includes species such as blackgum, scarlet oak, sassafras, and sourwood, none of which can accompany you all the way up to Cold Mountain's crown.

At 0.4 mile the route makes a quick double switchback closely followed by the zigzag of a triple switchback. An impressively straight and tall pignut hickory stands on the tread's left edge less than 20 yards past the last dogleg in the series. With a circumference of 9 feet 3 inches, this pignut is the thickest trailside hickory in the combined wildernesses.

Now traveling north on west-facing slope, the sidehill hike steadily gains elevation through forest including white ash, black cherry, white oak, sweet birch (aka black birch), and cucumbertree. After following an old logging bed for a short distance, you slant up to and curl over a prominent, spur-top resting spot at mile 1.1 (3,910 feet).

The next 0.9-mile segment ventures east-southeast; most of its mountainsides are moist, face north to northeast, and are quilted with a profusion of wildflowers in season. The added elevation and northern exposure has spurred the second-growth forest—yellow buckeye, white basswood, northern red oak, and the especially abundant sugar maple, among others—to regenerate tall and straight.

Starting at mile 1.7, the Art Loeb gradually loses elevation on old roadbed for nearly a tenth-mile, by far the longest of Section 4's numerous downgrades, most of which are short dips. The way through the woods swings parallel to a highly variable rivulet before crossing the headwater tributary at mile 2.0 (4,130 feet). Beyond this first water source, the track continues to work its rocky way up through the interlocking splay of hollow and spur. At mile 2.2 an old-growth blackgum—its circumference measurement of 9 feet 2 inches impressive for its species—stands a long stride to the right of the treadway. Mature blackgums are readily identified by their characteristic bark, which is deeply furrowed and cross-checked into blocky squares. After a short sharp pitch, the sidehill route alternates between easy and easy-to-moderate grades to its crossing of an intermittent rivulet at mile 2.4.

The path winds over a pair of spurs before traversing a rich, north-facing wildflower slope. As the trail rises above 4,300 feet, the yellow birch becomes more common in the predominantly hardwood forest. After shadowing the stream's steep-sided ravine, the ALT crosses a usually flowing rivulet (often reduced to a small trickle during a dry summer) at mile 2.9 (4,460 feet).

The line of march hooks around the headwater stream's hollow, then changes direction again—this time to the northeast—as it finishes the ascent to Shining Rock Ledge. The final stretch, which gains roughly 560 feet in 0.9 mile, is ALT-4's most difficult segment. Its steepest pulls, those longer than the very short rocky surges, often top out at moderate to strenuous.

At mile 3.1 the course crosses the rocky furrow of an intermittent spring run above a bouldery slope lush with wildflowers. Fifty feet beyond this notch, the thickest trailside tree along this ALT section—a northern red oak with a girth of 11 feet 8 inches—is rooted about two stretched strides upslope from the trail. After switchbacking onto and following the sharply climbing crest of a spur for 30 yards at mile 3.2, the tread gains elevation on mostly easy grades to a couple of rock outcrops just right for a sit-down break at mile 3.4. Here the uphill hiking pushes forward to the highly intermittent, wet-weather seep at mile 3.6.

The final upslope run, occasionally rising through Catawba rhododendron, is an overall solid moderate grade with a daypack. ALT-4 pops up to Deep Gap's ridgetop opening and stand of black locust. This busy clearing is a multipurpose loafing spot, camping area, and trail junction—the only connection in Shining Rock's narrow northernmost reach. The lower-elevation end of the Cold Mountain Trail, which heads north-northeast toward its namesake peak, is to the left (entrance 30 degrees). The Art Loeb turns to the right and follows the ridgeline south toward the iconic white rock.

Nature Notes

Rising from river to ridge and frequently changing aspects as it winds from southwest to northeast, ALT-4 is a showcase of Southern Appalachian diversity. I identified thirty-four types of trees—including four species of maple and four species of oak—without making a special effort for a high count. On a recent June 10 I noted forty-six kinds of herbaceous wildflowers, many already blown. Fire pink, Vasey's trillium, and whorled loosestrife were blooming among others on that date. On August 14, when pale jewelweed and assorted asters were flowering profusely up at Deep Gap, I noticed nearly twenty more species not on June's list. By October 6 the list of blooming forbs had shrunk to striped gentian (aka mountain gentian, darker blue stripes on the inside of the petals) plus six aster species—goldenrod, white wood aster, and the lavender blossoms of the heart-leaved aster among them.

On June 5 of an unusually early spring, mountain laurel, flame azalea, and Catawba rhododendron colored the slopes along the upper end of ALT-4.

Jack-in-the-pulpit

The jack-in-the-pulpit (*Arisaema triphyllum*), whose huge range includes the Appalachians from northern Alabama to southern Quebec, is one of the most widespread and familiar wildflowers in our eastern mountains. This native perennial received its common name because the erect, club-shaped "jack" (the minister) stands inside the cowled pulpit. Spadix is the botanical term for the jack. A leaf bract called the spathe encloses and canopies the pulpit; it may be solid green or green with varying shades of purple striping.

A. triphyllum usually attains a height of 6 to 24 inches; female jacks rooted in rich habitats occasionally grow much taller. Depending upon their sex, jack-in-the-pulpits bear either one or two compound basal leaves, each palmately divided into three leaflets.

This plant's maroon color and carrion odor indicate that it is probably pollinated by flies. The purple striping of the spathe may also serve as warning coloration: a pattern to reinforce the memory of pain. All parts of this species, from pulpit to corm, contain calcium oxalate crystals. Any hiker or herbivore that takes a bite out of jack is immediately persuaded never to attempt the experiment again. The numerous needlelike crystals cause instant and intense burning as they embed themselves in the soft tissues of tongue and mouth.

This member of the Arum family has the ultra-adaptive ability to change sex from year to year: a rare reproductive strategy known as sequential hermaphroditism. By late summer the witless wildflower has made the developmental decision about what sex to be the following year. This decision is based upon the size of the corm—the bulblike underground portion of the stem used for food storage—the plant's pantry. The better the growing conditions, the larger the corm. And the larger the corm, the more likely the plant will remain or switch to female.

jack-in-the-pulpit

Jacks with large pantries remain or become jills; they grow two leaves, develop female flowers, and display a tight fist of crimson berries after their spathes wither away in late summer. This changeling chooses from three different reproductive options: it bears pollen as a male; it bears fruit as a female; or, much less frequently, it is sexless and bears no flowers at all. Lift the hood to see the flowers deep inside: jack flowers look like threads; jill flowers resemble tiny green berries.

Dutchman's pipe

The twining vine that frequently uses this trailside forest as its tall trellis is the Dutchman's pipe. The woody stems of the mature vines resemble thick gray ropes, self-coiling and knotting as they climb higher and higher into the hardwoods. Young vines often garland the tops of shrubs and saplings, using them for support while stealing their sunlight. An Appalachian endemic, this deciduous species is the signature vine of the rich and rainy Southern Appalachian hardwood forest.

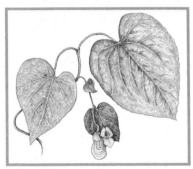

Dutchman's pipe

The Dutchman's pipe is easily recognized. Its large heart-shaped leaves are alternate and untoothed. Leaves well off the ground are normally 4 to 8 inches wide and 5 to 10 inches long. The leaves of young plants near the forest floor occasionally become platter-sized solar panels. Its unique flowers have no petals; their sepals form hooklike, pipe-shaped blossoms approximately 2 inches long. The fleshy, tubular flower flares into three short lobes at the bowl end of the pipe. The blooms, greenish yellow at first, turn brownish purple after the pipe opens for pollination.

The Dutchman's pipe belongs to the Birthwort family. Flowers and roots from this group of plants were formerly used as medicinal aids in childbirth. They were selected, primarily, based upon the Doctrine of Signatures—a medieval theory stating that if any part of a plant resembled a part of the human body, that part was divinely created to contain curative properties for that body part. Since the flower of this species supposedly looked like a fetus, it was administered to ease the pain of delivery.

Yellow mandarin

Considerably more yellow mandarin bloom and berry along this section of the Art Loeb than along any other similar length of treadway in this guide. This native perennial prefers the rich, moist, deep soils of hardwood slopes, hollows, and coves. The yellow mandarin is most often 1 to 2 feet tall with slightly zigzagging stems and two nearly horizontal branches that fork again. Its leaves, which closely resemble those of the Solomon's seal, are alternate, 2 to 4 inches long, and parallel veined (a characteristic of the Lily family).

One to three of the inch-wide flowers, yellow-green and usually obscured by leaves, nod from the tips of their stems. The inconspicuous corollas consist of slender unspotted petals and sepals with long flaring points.

The showiest part of this wildflower is its large berry. As summer deepens, these berries slowly change from light green to bright orange. Most of the fruits have turned to their richest color by late August or early September.

Directions

ALT-4 begins at the Daniel Boone Boy Scout Camp located at the end of Little East Fork Road on the western boundary of the Shining Rock Wilderness.

Approach from the south: From the NC 215–access road from BRP junction, turn left onto NC 215 North toward Canton and travel approximately 12.6 miles before turning right onto signed Little East Fork Road immediately before the bridge over the West Fork Pigeon River.

Approach from the north: From the four-way NC 215–NC 110–US 276 intersection, travel NC 215 South (also marked with a Love Joy Rd. street sign) for approximately 5.0 miles before turning left onto signed Little East Fork Road immediately beyond the bridge over the West Fork Pigeon River.

From Little East Fork Road: Paved Little East Fork Road is additionally indicated with an arrowed Camp Daniel Boone sign. Follow Little East Fork Road and the occasional signs for the scout camp for approximately 3.8 miles to the Art Loeb Trailhead on the left side of the road. The pavement ends at the prominently signed entrance to the camp after approximately 3.2 miles. Continue straight ahead on the gravel road, passing the lake and numerous scout structures. A carsonite sign, an improved treadway entrance, and an information kiosk to the left of the road make the ALT's northwestern terminus difficult to miss. Hikers who are not affiliated with the scout camp are required to park in the signed, pull-off parking strip along the right side of the road beyond the kiosk.

Notes

Cold Mountain Trail

Forest Service Trail 141   **1.5 miles**

Dayhiking Moderate to Strenuous
Backpacking Strenuous
Interior Trail Southern terminus on Art Loeb Trail at
   Deep Gap, 5,015 feet; northern terminus dead-ends
   atop Cold Mountain, 6,030 feet
Trail Junction ALT-3, ALT-4 at Deep Gap
Topographic Quadrangle Cruso
Blaze None (wilderness)
Usage Foot travel only
Features Wilderness; Cold Mountain; unusual rock
   outcrop; year-round views from the summit;
   occasional old-growth oaks

Cold Mountain is Inman's mountain of book and movie fame. A
ridgecrest and upper-slope route leading to rock outcrop overlooks, this boot-worn trail is one of two short interior spurs
included in this guide that dead-end atop a 6,000-foot peak.
Rising up Shining Rock Ledge from south to north, from Deep
Gap to the highpoint of its namesake summit, Cold Mountain
is the shortest trail or trail section totally within the combined
wildernesses.

   This frequently rocky footpath gains 1,015 feet of elevation.
The shortest way to Deep Gap and the Cold Mountain junction
is the 3.8-mile section of the ALT beginning at the scout camp.
Combined, the two routes gain a rock-rugged 2,770 feet of elevation over their one-way distance of 5.3 miles.

Beginning at Deep Gap's open stand of black locust, the track remains on or near Shining Rock Ledge's ridgeline for its first 0.7 mile. The ledge is characterized by a narrow, often rocky crest and steep slopes falling away to either side. The treadway rises on a south-facing ridge through a predominantly broadleaf forest numerically dominated by northern red oak and yellow birch. The occasional old-growth northern red oaks are thick trunked and low branched. Fraser fir, red spruce, and a few white pine saplings near the lower-elevation end comprise the conifer component. The understory is often dominated by mountain laurel and Catawba rhododendron.

Here the hike frequently slips onto the upper-east slope, sometimes to avoid ridgetop rock, before working its way back to the crest again. Most of the sustained grades range from easy to moderate; short, often rocky moderate-to-strenuous surges add to the difficulty.

At 0.7 mile, where the ledge tilts more sharply straight ahead, the route slabs onto the sunset side of the crest and continues the climb on a sidehill path to the northwest. The trail passes an impressively large outcrop with an unusual shape and high slant of rock on the nearby upslope at 0.9 mile. The narrow end of the higher, piggyback piece of rock—fingerlike and pointing skyward—is perhaps 25 to 30 feet above ground.

In recent years there has often been a water pipe to the right of the tread 40 yards beyond the outcrop. This source, the highest headwaters of Sorrell Creek, is intermittent and highly unreliable during drought.

The trek pops up to a gap at mile 1.0 (5,700 feet), then turns to the right onto the high end of the long Cold Mountain lead rising from the northwest. Here the gradual upgrade soon passes flat, grassy campsites. Small, cold-adapted hardwoods—succession species such as mountain ash, pin cherry, and serviceberry—are reclaiming the recently treeless patches. Fetterbush and successional hawthorns have joined the Catawba rhododendron in the understory.

After an overall easy ascent for 0.2 mile, the remaining sustained grades are a mix of easy and easy-to-moderate upridge runs. At mile 1.4 the track passes the first outcrop overlook to the right. Beyond this first view, the path skirts the drop-off edge of Cold Mountain's crown before angling back to the crest. Here the rest of the route dips and rises as it zigzags from one side of the narrow and rocky keel to the other. Seventy yards before the benchmark, a backward-bending sidepath to the right leads to the best rock outcrop overlook. The official trail ends at the rock-embedded benchmark (6,030 feet) to the right of the treadway.

The large rock outcrop look-off near the end of the route—encompassing 180 degrees east to west, with south in the middle—affords excellent views of the local high peaks, many close to or over 6,000 feet. Shining Rock Ledge swoops down to Deep Gap 1,000 feet below before curving up to the next peak, Stairs Mountain. From Stairs, the ridgeline rolls through a series of arched curves—the repetitive, forest-wrapped symmetry of the Southern Appalachians—familiar, ancient, and timeless. Shining Rock rises to barely over 6,000 feet at around 190 degrees. Higher and further south, the broad and gently sloping crown of Black Balsam Knob lifts the land to 6,214 feet at around 196 degrees.

To the right of Black Balsam, slightly double-humped Sam Knob stands 6,060 feet at around 206 degrees. To the right of Sam and further away, Mount Hardy thrusts 6,125 feet into the sky just north of the parkway at around 214 degrees. Still further away, the nearly flat crest of Piney Mountain is unmistakable at around 244 degrees. To the right and across the parkway from Piney, Richland Balsam rears up to 6,410 feet at around 254 degrees. Lickstone Ridge roller-coasters downhill for miles to the right (and nearly north) away from Richland Balsam.

Nearby, two prominent ridges rank up one behind the other, their crests rising higher right to left. The first one, Fork Mountain (ridgeline prominent at 240 degrees) ascends to the southeast through the Shining Rock Wilderness to its high-elevation end atop Tennent Mountain. The second undulating line in the sky, Fork Ridge (tectonic fold prominent at 220 degrees) rolls to the south through the Middle Prong Wilderness, anchoring the horizon to Mount Hardy.

Nature Notes

Succession is rapidly returning the last of the open land atop Cold Mountain to forest. Three-hundred years ago, the outcome of this succession would have been swift and certain: Cold Mountain's crown would have quickly become dark again with spruce-fir forest. But today, the endangered Southern Appalachian spruce-fir community faces major manmade threats—massive air pollution, an exotic insect pest (affecting the Fraser fir), and climate change—in its quest to turn the mountain cold and mossy again beneath the dense shade of conifers.

Increased elevation compresses the blooming season. Up high on the summit, spring comes late and autumn arrives early. On a recent June 18 the large colonies of Canada mayflower were nearly spent. Fire pink, wild columbine, and wild geranium were blossoming on that date. Mountain laurel and Catawba rhododendron were still in the pollination business along the highest ridgeline. The Catawba was in fresh bloom atop Cold Mountain on June 5 of a recent unusually early spring. Turk's-cap lilies, the tallest over 7 feet and still in bud, were waiting for their grand opening in July.

On a recent August 15, half a dozen aster species, pale jewelweed, a phlox species, starry campion, southern harebell, tall bellflower, and a few fire pink and wild columbine were in flower. The very beginning of the trail was an aster garden on a recent September 6. By October 6 the number of blooming species had dwindled to two—both lavender-flowered asters.

Pale jewelweed

A long pocket of pale jewelweed, a few of the yellow-blooming wildflowers over 6 feet tall, brightened the ridgeline at Deep Gap on a recent August 15. (It is especially abundant beside the ALT just south of Deep Gap.) More widely distributed in the northeastern U.S., this species requires the cool, moist conditions of the middle and high elevations in the southern mountains. It usually occurs at higher elevations than its close cousin, the spotted jewelweed—the one with the freckled orange flowers.

pale jewelweed

This member of the Touch-me-not family develops leaves from 1½ to 4 inches long and lemon-yellow blossoms most often 1 to 1½ inches long. Dangling from long stems, the spurred flowers are often sparsely spotted with small reddish brown dots. The ruby-throated hummingbird is a major pollinator for both jewelweed species.

The seeds of this native plant mature within a tightly coiled capsule. When the seeds are ripe and ready, the capsule explodes when touched, broadcasting its contents across the forest floor. This mechanism accounts for the jewelweed's other common names—snapweed and touch-me-not.

As you may have already noticed, water readily beads up on jewelweed leaves. The stories explaining the origin of this annual's name share two elements: morning sunlight and sparkling water.

Northern red oak

Often abundant at middle and high elevations up to approximately 6,100 feet, the northern red (*Quercus rubra*) is the most common oak beside the trails in this guide. This oak greatly benefited from the chestnut blight, ranking second only to the chestnut oak in replacement of the devastated American

northern red oak

chestnut. This broadleaf has the greatest north-south range of any eastern oak, from Nova Scotia down to southern Alabama.

Below 4,800 feet in elevation, northern red and black oaks (whose leaves are very similar) are hard to tell apart without specific taxonomic knowledge. But here on the Cold Mountain Trail and other trails above 5,000–5,200 feet, the northern red can be identified by leaf and elevation alone. So if a *Quercus* species is rooted at or above the mile-high mark and belongs to the red oak group—bark with smooth vertical streaks and leaves with toothed, bristle-tipped lobes— that oak is a northern red.

This mast tree's solar panels, dull green above and dull light green below, are usually 5 to 8 inches long and 3 to 5 inches wide. Their seven- to eleven-toothed and bristle-tipped lobes are separated by regular sinuses extending a little less than halfway to the midrib. Like other members of the red oak group, the northern red's bark is patterned by long, smooth, vertical streaks of lighter color running up bole and branch. These smooth streaks look slick and shiny compared to the rest of the darker, rougher bark.

Q. rubra is one of the largest and fastest growing oaks in the Southern Highlands. Mature trees are often 60 to 90 feet in height and 2 to 3 feet in diameter. Forest elder specimens living in optimal conditions can attain girths of 15 to 19 feet and heights over 130 feet.

Directions

Cold Mountain is an interior trail that has its southern end on the ALT and its northern end atop Cold Mountain.

The shortest route from a trailhead to the Cold Mountain–Art Loeb junction at Deep Gap is ALT-4. Starting at Camp Daniel Boone, follow the ALT uphill and to the northeast for 3.8 miles to Deep Gap. You can't miss Deep Gap; it is a well-worn loafing and camping spot on the main divide running north-south through the Shining Rock Wilderness. If you turn left at the gap and follow the rising ridgeline to the northeast, you will be walking Cold Mountain (entrance 30 degrees) toward its namesake peak. (See ALT-4, the preceding trail section, for further information.)

Notes

Part 2

Nonwilderness Pocket

East of FS 816
West of FS 816—and Nearby
Trails to the South

Roger Nielsen

The two Sams: double-humped Sam Knob on the right,
Little Sam Knob on the left

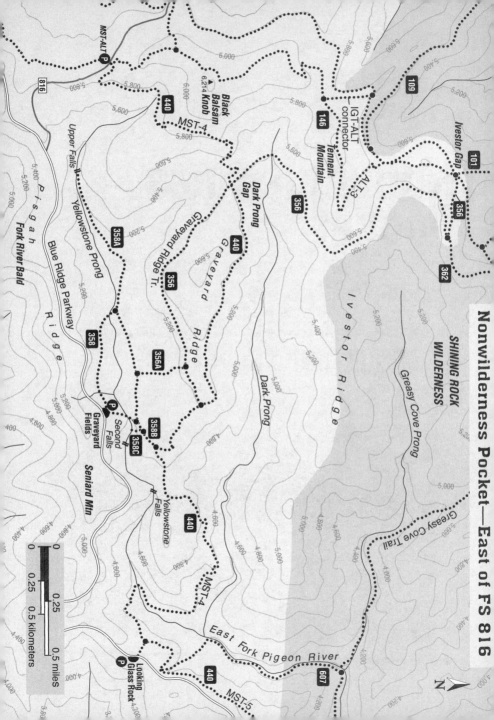

Nonwilderness Pocket—East of FS 816

Nonwilderness Pocket—
East of FS 816

Maggie Nettles

Painted trillium at Graveyard Fields

Trails

Mountains to Sea,
  Section 4

Graveyard Ridge

Graveyard Fields
  Trail System

Mountains to Sea Trail, Section 4

(FS 816 to junction with the access trail
leading from Looking Glass Rock Overlook)

Forest Service Trail 440 5.3 miles Mountains to Sea only, 5.4 miles including access trail

Dayhiking (low to high) Moderate to Strenuous
Dayhiking (high to low) Moderate
Backpacking (low to high) Strenuous
Backpacking (high to low) Moderate to Strenuous
Vehicular Access at or near Either End Western (higher elevation) terminus at the Mountains to Sea–Art Loeb Trailhead off FS 816, 5,900 feet; eastern (lower elevation) access at Looking Glass Rock Overlook, 4,495 feet
Trail Junctions MST-3, ALT-2, and ALT-3 at the MST–ALT Trailhead; Graveyard Ridge (two locations, see description); MST Access; access trail from Looking Glass Rock Overlook; MST-5
Topographic Quadrangles Sam Knob, Shining Rock
Blaze White circle
Usage Foot travel only
Features Waterfall; open views to Black Balsam's summit (see description); old-growth trees near the eastern end; wide variety of habitats

Section 4 is the most difficult, the longest, and the most botanically diverse of the five short MST sections detailed in this guide. Walked as described, the route winds west to east through upper-slope, ridgeline, lower-slope, and riverine habitats—from the cold-country conifers on Black Balsam Knob's high mountain-side all the way down to the rosebay rhododendron and doghobble beside Yellowstone Prong.

Most people do not hike this entire segment; the overwhelming majority start at its eastern end and walk the short downhill distance to the waterfall on Yellowstone Prong. That stretch is heavily tramped; the rest of the track is moderately used.

The left side of this section's first 1.6 miles, from FS 816 to its junction with the Graveyard Ridge Trail in Dark Prong Gap, is now the southeastern boundary of a roughly 600-acre controlled burn unit. If the series of burns take place as planned, the flames could scorch the young forest back to an earlier successional stage, restoring the views to Black Balsam Knob's summit.

MST-4's first 1.6 miles—descending, climbing, descending again—wind and switchback to the northeast, all of that distance traversing the southern-to-eastern mountainsides of 6,214-foot Black Balsam Knob. The footpath reaches its first junction less than 20 yards from the edge of section highpoint FS 816. Here, at the arrowed post, the two-trail treadway splits apart. The MST turns 90 degrees to the right and east; the ALT continues straight ahead toward Black Balsam Knob. After the route's blazed passage through a heavily shaded pocket of red spruce, it curls down the first of many switchbacks at 0.1 mile. Fifty yards further, you cross the first of more than a dozen boardwalks and railed bridges over seepage areas and rivulet runs. All these wooden walkways occur before the 0.6-mile mark, and all these seeps and spring-born rills are the high headwaters of Yellowstone Prong.

At 0.3 mile the course begins an easy and, if fire has restored the views to the left side of the trail, scenic downgrade on a former railroad bed. Two-tenths mile further, the trail crosses above the beginning gather of Yellowstone Prong, its waters usually either spilling or dribbling down a steep slant of moss-slick rock below the bridge.

The moderate, switchbacking climb begins at 0.6 mile (5,710 feet). After rising on boot-smoothed slabs of bedrock, the tread tops out at 5,890 feet and comes to a rock outcrop overlook open to the south at 0.8 mile.

The vegetation at or near this section's loftiest elevations—near the FS 816 trailhead and the upper portions of the ascent starting at 0.6 mile—has recently reached the sapling and young tree stage. Pin cherry, mountain ash, and serviceberry have led the charge to sunlight above the shrubs, closely followed by yellow birch, red spruce, Fraser fir, and two types of maple—red and mountain. The heath shrubs, deciduous blueberries and evergreen Catawba rhododendron, established the initial dominance of the woody plant tribe and remain plentiful in the understory of the young forest outside of the burn unit to the right of the trail.

The trek descends again at mile 0.9. Below the last in a series of switchbacks beginning at mile 1.1, the route ramps down more gradually to its well-signed four-way junction with the road-wide Graveyard Ridge Trail in Dark Prong Gap's open loafing area at mile 1.6 (5,400 feet).

The next 1.3 miles travel generally east along the north slope and crest of Graveyard Ridge, a Black Balsam Knob spur. The first 0.6 mile is Section 4's least demanding stretch; very short rises and dips interrupt the otherwise nearly effortless walking. Much of this rocky, slowly ascending segment tunnels through an evergreen tangle of Catawba rhododendron, mountain laurel, and fetterbush.

The sidehill tread crosses an intermittent spring run at mile 2.2, then gently undulates for the following 0.2 mile. Mountain winterberry is abundant along portions of this rolling path.

At mile 2.4 the MST begins its long downgrade to Yellowstone Prong with a zigzagging run of double switchbacks. Here the hiking descends a couple of times at an easy-to-moderate clip before easing up on the crest of Graveyard Ridge at mile 2.5. The route remains on or near the top of the fold as it makes an overall easy downhill run through recently reclaimed forest. A sidepath to the left at mile 2.7 leads to a bare-branch view of the upper pour of Dark Prong Falls. The rapidly returning forest will soon block most of the view.

At mile 2.9 the long brown tread arrives at its usually signed junction with the Graveyard Ridge Trail (5,200 feet), which heads to the right at 210 degrees. On its own again, Section 4 slowly loses elevation along the lower end of Graveyard Ridge. Here the forest, which frequently shades grass and fern, is composed of young, predominantly hardwood trees beneath the occasional much thicker northern red oak and red maple. At mile 3.3 the sidehill descent meets the usually well-signed junction (5,020 feet) with the Mountains to Sea Access Trail, a 0.2-mile connector that ties into the east side of the Graveyard Fields Trail. If you want to see nearby Lower Falls (0.3 mile one way), turn right (entrance 260 degrees) onto the access trail and follow this connector to its junction with the Lower Falls Trail before turning sharply left onto that route.

The line of march advances with an easygoing downgrade through an open grass-floored forest, often with only hardwoods that include silverbell and black cherry in sight above shrub level. At mile 3.5 the track rides the ridgeline for the last time, dipping to and rising from a saddle (4,940 feet, campsite, Yellowstone Falls entrenched nearby), before reaching the usually signed sidepath (mile 3.6) leading to the designated campsites well in the woods to the right.

Beyond the tent symbols, the long-trail tread descends in a lumpy, 1.4-mile half loop, bowed to the north, to its Yellowstone Prong crossing. Here, where the course bends to the north as it slants off the crest, the MST runs a gauntlet through thicket-growth rhododendron, mixing very short easy-to-moderate grades with much longer easy ones. At mile 3.8 you zigzag down a double switchback, the first pair of perhaps a dozen that put the brakes on the long descent.

The downhill hiking continues on predominantly easy grades interrupted with very short harder dips—often rock and waterbar step-downs. Where the mesh of evergreen heath thins out, you can see a diverse forest with hardwoods such as sweet birch, sugar and striped maple, Fraser magnolia, white ash, and white basswood.

The well-constructed trail continues to angle downslope, the route again lined with the dark glossy green of rosebay rhodo-dendron as it swings to the south to parallel Yellowstone Prong. Section 4 slants down to a wide grade and quickly passes a room-sized boulder at mile 4.8. The next 0.2 mile closely accom-panies the creek-sized prong's cascades upstream to the south-west.

The trail crosses the bridge (section low point at 4,360 feet) in front of a high cascade aptly known as Skinny Dip Falls at mile 5.0. Rock-bound Skinny Dip is a low angle falls consisting of three drops and two deep pools, perhaps 30 to 35 feet high altogether. Its popular, goose-pimple cold pools are unusually deep for a stream of Yellowstone Prong's size.

Wide and heavily trod, this section's remaining easy-to-moderate elevation gain is interrupted by a short, sharp dip to a runoff ravine. Here the downslope is still home for a number of old-growth trees; the two thickest are both yellow buckeyes. To locate the larger of the two, follow the notch of the intermittent rivulet (the one passing beneath the short boardwalk bridge about 60 yards beyond Skinny Dip's observation platform) downslope for approximately 30 yards. This impressive specimen, which recently measured 13 feet 6 inches in circumference, stands stout just to the left of the rivulet's notch. To find its slightly less bulky brother, whose girth measured 12 feet 10 inches, follow the faint path on the other side of the rill from the first buckeye a short distance toward a campsite, then turn diagonally to the right. It is about 25 yards from the far edge of the rivulet to the second big buckeye.

Section 4's eastern end is located at its usually well-signed junction with the blue-blazed access trail from the parkway. The long-march MST continues straight ahead; the access trail heads downhill and to the right to the Looking Glass Rock Overlook.

Nature Notes
Because of its shifting aspects, substantial change in elevation, and succession of environments ranging from ridgeline to riparian, MST-4 features the most diverse forest of the five MST sections detailed in this guide. Despite the overall diversity of its forest, Section 4 does not put on an especially good spring wildflower display. Wakerobin and painted trillium are common and particularly conspicuous when in fresh flower. The wakerobin's blossoms were shriveled and faded, and the painted's were faded and fallen by June 1 of a recent year. On that date bluebead lily, rose twisted-stalk, wood sorrel, and Appalachian twayblade—a small, inconspicuous orchid—were still in bloom.

On a recent June 23, only the tag ends of the Catawba rhododendron and mountain laurel blooms remained, a few flame azalea were still in flower, and the rosebay rhododendron was just beginning its show along Yellowstone Prong.

The last in a long series of glaciations, known as the Wisconsin Ice Age, began grinding southward some 75,000 years ago and continued, with occasional thaws, until roughly 15,000 years ago. During the peak of this onslaught, approximately 20,000 years ago, the glaciers entombed the northern half to two-thirds of North America. In the East these Pleistocene ice sheets, forming domes from 1 to 2 miles thick, flowed southward into present-day Pennsylvania, Ohio, and Indiana.

Even though the glaciers never scoured the South, the climate was still rock-cracking cold in the high Appalachians. Twenty thousand years ago, tundra-producing temperatures clenched the land here above 4,500 feet in permafrost. Downslope from the subalpine zone, Highland Dixie wore a skirt of boreal forest that flowed southward to middle Georgia.

Trees are not the sticks-in-the-mud that most people imagine. Many northern species were able to hobble ahead of the advancing glaciers in a slow-moving migration to the south. Then, as the wall of ice retreated and the land's prison melted to long flood, the conifers struck out from their base camps and reclaimed the highest peaks in the South. As the weather continued to warm, the evergreens followed their genetic imperatives further north and higher up the southern mountains. Today, the Southern Appalachian spruce-fir forest and its attendant community are marooned up high on islands of Canadian zone refugia.

The Fraser fir is confined to the most cramped living quarters of any eastern conifer. Its range is usually depicted as eight dots—disjunct sanctums, six smaller and two larger—from southwestern Virginia to the North Carolina–Tennessee border in the GSMNP. The pocket of Frasers in the Smokies remains this species' largest island in the sky.

Botanists believe the Fraser fir evolved quite recently, since the major climatic warming following the end of the ice age—a tenancy of only the last 5,000 to 8,000 years. The balsam fir, which still perfumes the land of moose and loons, seeded itself southward in front of the bulldozing ice. After the last glacial high tide, the warming earth sent the cold-adapted evergreens on the march again, eliminating the balsam from long stretches of low-elevation central Appalachia, forcing the southern race of balsams to climb higher or perish. As is often the case, genetic isolation led to speciation.

Until recently, high peaks like Black Balsam Knob made the rules, selecting and stratifying life in accordance to its genetically encoded ability to withstand heat or cold. Few hardwoods can climb to the top of the mountain, and the fir cannot descend deep into the nearby river valleys. Each species' highest roothold represents its elevational limit; above that limit its cells rupture and it freezes to death. Every tree has a specific freezing point. The Fraser can tolerate temperatures as low as minus 80 degrees.

Three short-needled conifers—Fraser fir *(Abies fraseri)*, red spruce, and eastern hemlock—find suitable habitat (for now) in the Shining Rock area. (See page 92 for a description of the eastern hemlock.) Only two short-needled evergreens, Fraser fir and red spruce, grow high on Black Balsam's southern slope at the upper-elevation end of this section. These two cold-adapted northerners can be readily differentiated by their cones and needles. (See the description of the red spruce, page 239, for botanical details.)

Fraser fir

While a few Frasers stray down below 4,500 feet in cool stream valleys, this tree does not occur in larger numbers until it climbs above the 5,400-foot contour line. From 5,400 to 6,000 feet it mixes with northern hardwoods and red spruce. Above

6,100 feet the fir increasingly mixes with only one large tree: the spruce. In the recent past the Fraser, its balsam scent a fragrant gift from the glaciers, was Southern Appalachia's signature tree above 6,300 feet. Above this elevation *A. fraseri* was dominant, occurring in dense, dark green stands that appeared black from a distance.

A small to medium-sized conifer, the sharp-pointed and conical-shaped Fraser is the only *Abies* species native to the southern mountains. Significantly taller and thicker specimens were frequently reported in the recent past. Today, most mature firs are less than 18 inches in diameter and under 50 feet tall. This

vital component of the spruce-fir forest has been decimated by acid deposition and an insect pest: the balsam woolly adelgid, the Southern Appalachians' first exotic and deadly adelgid. This tiny, aphidlike insect recently killed 95 percent of the mature firs in the GSMNP.

Mountain winterberry

Multiboled clumps of mountain winterberry (*Ilex montana*) are abundant along the 2-mile stretch of trail from mile 1.6 to mile 3.6. Also known

mountain winterberry

as mountain holly, this fairly common large shrub or small tree occasionally attains 25 feet in height. It is most frequently found on wide, moist hardwood ridges up to approximately 6,000 feet in the highlands of Southern Appalachia.

Throughout most of the year, this deciduous holly's drab foliage and tiny white flowers make it easy to overlook. But in late summer and autumn, *I. montana*'s shiny red fruits are bigger, brighter, and much more noticeable than its spring blossoms. As its common name suggests, the showy berries, often clustered two to four together, persist into winter.

The alternate leaves—finely saw-toothed, abruptly pointed at the tip, 2½ to 5 inches long—are usually bunched near the ends of short spur twigs. Summer's green fades to pale yellow in fall.

Clusters of the ¼-inch-wide flowers bloomed white at the ends of their twigs on a recent June 1, and the vibrant red berries called attention to the winterberry stands on a recent September 28 and October 24.

Directions

Section 4 has vehicular access at or near either end. Its western, MST–ALT Trailhead is located off FS 816 (Black Balsam Road), and its eastern access is located at the Looking Glass Rock Overlook at BRP milepost 417.

Western, MST–ALT Trailhead off FS 816

Approach from the south: From the BRP–access road from NC 215 junction, turn left onto the parkway and travel approximately 3.0 miles before turning left onto FS 816.

Approach from the north: From the BRP–access road from US 276 junction, turn left onto the parkway and travel approximately 8.3 miles before turning right onto FS 816.

The entrance to paved FS 816 is located between BRP mileposts 420 and 421. It is usually marked with some combination of signs large and small: Black Balsam Trailhead, Black Balsam Road, FS 816–Black Balsam Road. Travel FS 816 0.7 mile to the long strip of pull-off parking and MST post on the right side of the road. The MST–ALT Trailhead is the western end of Section 4 and the northeastern end of Section 3. The western end of

Section 4 is located at the MST post on the right (northeast) side of the road. The beginning two-trail treadway heads north; less than 20 yards in from the road, the trails split where the MST turns 90 degrees to the right and east.

Eastern access at the Looking Glass Rock Overlook

The short access trail leading to the eastern end of Section 4 begins across the BRP from the overlook. Turn left onto the MST and you will be walking Section 4 toward FS 816. Turn right and you will be following Section 5 toward the power tower where the MST crosses the parkway at Pigeon Gap. (See MST-5, page 52, for directions to its southwestern access at the overlook.)

Notes

Graveyard Ridge Trail

Forest Service Trail 356	3.4 miles

Dayhiking Easy in either direction

Backpacking Easy to Moderate in either direction

Interior Trail Southeastern (lower elevation) terminus at its junction with Mountains to Sea Trail, 5,200 feet; northwestern (higher elevation) terminus at its junction with Art Loeb and Ivestor Gap Trails at Ivestor Gap, 5,690 feet

Trail Junctions MST-4 (two locations, see description), Graveyard Ridge Connector, Greasy Cove, IGT, ALT-3

Topographic Quadrangle Shining Rock

Blaze Orange

Usage See description

Features Year-round views (see description); easy walking; late spring–early summer flowering shrub display

---

Graveyard Ridge, a moderately used interior trail, offers mild grades and frequent views of the nearby mountains. The easy walking will remain; most of the views to mile 1.3 will not. Though often rocky, this route gradually gains only 490 feet of elevation on former railroad bed and road. From mile 1.3 to its higher-elevation end at Ivestor Gap, the left side of the tread (hiked as described) is part of the boundary of a controlled burn unit. The success of a controlled burn is dependent upon numerous factors, so it is impossible to know what the forest to the left side of that segment will look like in the near future. One thing is certain: if the fires burn hot all the way to or from trail's edge, the flames will reopen some of the former views to the soaring, rim-rocked southern slope of Tennent Mountain.

Usage on Graveyard Ridge is situational: it depends upon the section of trail and the time of year. The treadway is foot travel only from its southeastern, lower-elevation junction with the MST to its junction with the MST in Dark Prong Gap (mile 1.3). From that gap to its northwestern end at Ivestor Gap, the trail is also open to horses and bikes year-round (never seen sign of a single horse, and only a couple of bikes). Additional usage swings with the gate at the beginning of the IGT. When the gate is open for the blueberry picking and hunting seasons, high-clearance vehicles can and do crunch this route's wide track. These vehicles usually remain on the uppermost 1.2 miles, from Ivestor Gap down to the saddle at mile 2.2.

Graveyard Ridge is described as it is most easily reached and most often intentionally hiked, from southeast to northwest, from either its lower-elevation junction with the MST or its nearby junction with the Graveyard Ridge Connector to its junctions with the ALT and IGT in Ivestor Gap.

This treadway's southeastern end is located near the lower, eastern crest of its namesake ridge, a Black Balsam Knob spur. Starting at its usually signed junction with Section 4 of the MST, this trek's first leg slowly rises east to west as it forms a flattened half loop that swings around the southern slope of the ridge. Much of the trailside forest along the first 0.6 mile is rapidly recovering from an unintentional 1999 fire.

The wide rail-line grade, especially along its lightly trod first 0.2 mile, is occasionally narrowed to single-file footpath by exuberant sun-gap vegetation. Here, early on and for now, the black cherry is the most common mature tree, and dense hedges of sapling beech flank portions of the tread. At 0.2 mile the Graveyard Ridge Connector ties in from downslope at its usually signed T-junction.

Maintaining course straight ahead, the sidehill hike traverses the south-facing slope above Graveyard Fields. Now the occasional larger trees are mostly northern red oak, and the abundant heath shrubs include mountain laurel and several highly sought after berry-bearing bushes. The downhill corridor is quickly filling in; red maple, pin cherry, and black locust are leading the charge toward sunlight.

At 0.6 mile you cross the fire boundary and enter a still-young forest of older trees including the first of the sharply spired red spruce. Catawba rhododendron is the dominant heath shrub in the now shady forest; red maple and yellow birch are the most numerous of the hardwoods seeking to establish a new canopy. The easygoing grade soon passes the first of the small Fraser firs, flat needled and balsam scented. At mile 1.3 the wide track crosses MST-4 at a usually well-signed four-way junction. This open, loafing-spot connection is located in Dark Prong Gap (5,400 feet) slightly less than half a mile from Black Balsam's grassy summit as the raven flies.

Beyond its second interior junction, the line of march makes a maneuver typical of mountain travel, be it rail or trail. Here the route makes a slow-curving half loop to the right around the hollow of a stream before making a similar curl to the left around a mountain and over a spur ridge. The idea is to cross the stream's steep-sided hollow high and cross the spur ridge low, thereby avoiding the strenuous elevation swings that would result from straight-line travel. In this case the old railway forms a backward-S configuration, bottom open to the east, top open to the west.

In the middle of the first curve, 30 yards past a designated campsite to the left, the course rock-steps Dark Prong at mile 1.6.

The branch-sized prong is Graveyard Ridge's only reliable year-round water source. The second half of the double curve sweeps around the sharp eastern slant of Tennent Mountain, a 6,070 footer. In the middle of this half loop, the gentle upgrade crosses over Ivestor Ridge, an eastward-running Tennent spur, at a shallow saddle (mile 2.2, 5,490 feet).

Starting at the gap, the right edge of the track doubles as the Shining Rock Wilderness boundary to the trail's higher-elevation end. From Ivestor Ridge, you finish the half loop to the north-west on Tennent's shoulder. Along the way, at mile 2.4 where the tread widens to the right, there is a partial winter view (for now) of the long sliding falls up high on Greasy Cove Prong. This small-volume waterfall needs recent rain to be noisy enough to catch your attention.

After coming parallel to the main divide, the sidehill hiking heads north just downslope from the ridge-running ALT. It then ranges across the upper-east flank of a small, unnamed knob before bending to the east (mile 2.9) and rising to its junction with the Greasy Cove Trail 0.2 mile further (5,650 feet; N 20 70, W 51 73). Graveyard Ridge switchbacks to the left and up at the junction. The entrance to Greasy Cove is located along the out-side curve of the switchback, to the right and east. The remain-der of Graveyard Ridge's single-track road leads west as it threads across the southern slope of Grassy Cove Top and affords open views of Tennent Mountain's northern rise to the south.

Graveyard Ridge ends where it connects with the IGT in Ivestor Gap: a take-a-break area, major trail junction, and heav-ily used portal into the Shining Rock Wilderness. The IGT and ALT pass through this impossible-to-miss gap. If you want to travel north on Section 3 of the ALT toward Shining Rock, turn right off the road at the usually signed, path-wide slot along the right edge of the road (entrance north) less than 50 yards from

Graveyard Ridge's IGT junction. From its first ALT junction, Graveyard Ridge and the Art Loeb share the road for the next 35 yards to the usually signed second ALT junction. If you want to hike the ALT to the south toward Black Balsam Knob, turn to the left off the road before passing through the vehicle-blocking, split-rail gate.

Graveyard Ridge ends at its junction with the IGT along the western edge of the gap. If you want to follow the IGT to the south-southwest toward its beginning at the Black Balsam Trailhead, turn left with the open road. The IGT makes a sudden transition from wide, single-track road to narrow path in Ivestor Gap. If you want to walk the IGT to the north toward Shining Rock, turn to the right onto the path that continues between the last two vehicle-blocking boulders along the right (northern) edge of the road. As you turn, you will be immediately to the right of the last boulder in the row and the wilderness sign behind it.

Nature Notes

Graveyard Ridge offers a fair spring wildflower display, and if the prescribed fires are successful, it may soon feature a good late-summer show of sun loving asters such as goldenrod. This route also affords a good heath shrub show that is often underway by June 5.

Round-leaved sundew

An exquisitely delicate killer, the round-leaved sundew (*Drosera rotundifolia*) offers its sweet, glistening bait to unsuspecting insects along short segments of this trail. To compensate for scant nourishment available in swampy and water-saturated habitats, sundews evolved the capability to attract and devour insects and pygmy arthropods. Small specialized leaves enable this predatory plant to capture its prey, usually bantam ants and other lilliputian insects. Each leaf is bristled with reddish tentacles, hairlike and glandular, that secrete a tiny droplet of sweet, sticky fluid—essentially a tasty, nondrying glue—to attract insects, which quickly become stuck in the longer outer tentacles. With an incredible burst of growth, these elfin tentacles pin the victim with their goo-tipped strands and push it into closer contact with the leaf, where shorter tentacles secrete digestive enzymes. The more the victim struggles, the quicker

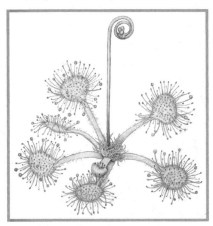

round-leaved sundew

the growth spurt. The enzymes reduce the bemired next meal to a nutrient-rich broth, a sundew smoothie, which is absorbed through the surface of the leaf.

The small round leaves of this plant of prey, no larger than ¾ of an inch across, are deployed in a rosette around the main flower stalk. Budding from a one-sided cluster along a 4- to 8-inch-long stem, the ¼-inch-wide, five-petaled flowers open white to pale pink and usually one at a time.

The round-leaved sundew, which has a huge range extending as far north as Alaska and Greenland, is considered rare in the mountains of North Carolina. In the Shining Rock area, linear colonies of this bug-eating herb are most often found where a mossy seep meets the high side of an old road grade, the wetter and sunnier the better. Look for small-plant red, then look closer. These unusual wildflowers are common along the upslope edge of the old road just beyond the Greasy Cove junction.

Thyme-leaved bluet

Extensive, low-lying beds of thyme-leaved bluets frequently edge the sunnier segments of this trail. Only 3 to 5 inches tall, these dainty and vibrantly hued perennials can be identified by their tiny rounded leaves and miniature four-petaled flowers. Bluets are collectively bountiful; dozens of the ⅓-inch-wide blooms show off their sky blue petals and yellow centers in a single square foot. This spring-blooming species flowered by the thousands on May 17 and June 8 of recent years.

Directions

Graveyard Ridge is an interior trail that has its southeastern end on MST-4 and its northwestern end at its junction with the ALT and IGT in Ivestor Gap.

thyme-leaved bluet

The shortest-distance route (0.9 mile) to Graveyard Ridge's south-eastern end begins at the Graveyard Fields Overlook. This route begins to the right of the Graveyard Fields sign and follows the loop for a short distance in a counterclockwise direction. From the usually well-signed MST Access Trail–MST junction, turn left and uphill onto the white-blazed MST, then hike a little less than 0.5 mile (rounding up and down makes this distance 0.4 mile in the MST-4 narrative) to the usually signed MST–Graveyard Ridge junction. Graveyard Ridge is to the left (entrance 210 degrees).

You can also gain the Graveyard Ridge Trail via the Grave-yard Ridge Connector from the Graveyard Fields Loop. Follow the 0.5-mile connector to its T-junction with the Graveyard Ridge Trail. This route is also 0.9 mile to its Graveyard Ridge junction. Graveyard Ridge's southeastern end, however, is to the right and an additional 0.2 mile away. (See Graveyard Fields, the following trail system, for further information.)

The shortest and easiest way to Graveyard Ridge's northwestern end is the IGT. Walk that trail for 2.2 miles to Ivestor Gap on the southern border of the Shining Rock Wilderness. At this obvious loafing spot—usually marked with a wilderness sign and vehicle-blocking boulders—the IGT leaves the road and continues nearly straight ahead on narrow treadway into the wilderness where the one and only road curves sharply to the right in the gap. Graveyard Ridge is the road continuing generally east from Ivestor Gap. (See IGT, page 69, for further information.)

Notes

Graveyard Fields Trail System

Forest Service Trails 358, 358C, 358B, 356A, 358A

Graveyard Fields Trail 358 (the loop) 1.1 miles
Lower Falls Trail 358C 0.1 mile
Mountains to Sea Access Trail 358B 0.2 mile
Graveyard Ridge Connector 356A 0.5 mile
Upper Falls Trail 358A 1.0 mile

Dayhiking Easy (loop only, see description for difficulty of the rest of the system)

Backpacking Easy to Moderate

Start The 1.1-mile loop starts and ends at the Graveyard Fields Overlook, 5,120 feet

Trail Junctions Within the Graveyard Fields Trail System: Lower Falls, Mountains to Sea Access, Graveyard Ridge Connector, Upper Falls
Graveyard Fields Trail System to other trails: MST-4, Graveyard Ridge

Topographic Quadrangle Shining Rock

Blaze Orange on a couple of carsonite signs for the loop (see description for the rest of the system)

Usage Foot travel only

Features (entire system) Yellowstone Prong; two waterfalls; year-round views until the forest recovers; access to Graveyard Ridge and Mountains to Sea Trails

As the plaque states, "A natural disaster occurred here 500 to 1000 years ago." A powerful wind, possibly a microburst, uprooted the primary growth spruce forest cloaking the southern slope of what is now called Graveyard Ridge. Over the years the dead-and-down conifers and their root wads rotted away, leaving only dirt mounds that resembled burial sites. Soon after settlers moved in nearby, the gently shelving flat north of Yellowstone Prong became known as Graveyard Fields. The scorched-earth wildfire of 1925 destroyed the recovered forest on the flat and even consumed the old mounds.

The Graveyard Fields system consists of five trails—one loop, two waterfall trails, and two connectors—totaling 2.9 one-way miles. Three official footpaths spoke away from the loop. The one at the eastern end forks into two trails: Lower Falls and Mountains to Sea Access.

In 1999 the most recent fire torched the trees over more than 80 acres of Graveyard Ridge's southern slope. Today, the ever-resilient forest is on the march again and, barring further disturbance, will steadily block most of the views that have been open for years.

With two waterfalls, easy blueberry picking, and other attractions so near the parkway, the Graveyard Fields area is popular beyond the point of overuse. The loop and the two waterfall trails are very heavily trod; the two connectors are lightly used in comparison. Graveyard Fields' function for hikers, especially those who have already walked to the waterfalls, is quick and easy access to the Graveyard Ridge and Mountains to Sea Trails.

Boardwalked in wet places, the Graveyard Fields loop is described as it is most often hiked, in a counterclockwise direction starting with the steps to the right side of the parking area. The wide, black-topped trail (paved to the first bridge at present) descends steadily through evergreen heath thickets, primarily Catawba and rosebay rhododendron, and scattered clumps of multiboled serviceberry. A wooden walkway with stairs completes the downhill run to the bridged crossing of Yellowstone Prong and its long slabs of water-worn bedrock. Across the bridge, the track turns right at the fork, then quickly arrives at its first usually signed junction at 0.2 mile. The MST Access and Lower Falls Trails share the treadway that quickly bends to the right.

The loop curls up and to the west onto a gentle slope still in the early stages of succession. Scattered young trees, mostly red maple and black cherry, are already over 30 feet tall. Blackberry canes, heath shrubs, and pin cherry saplings are rapidly crowding out the remaining herbaceous growth. Some of the open views will last for a few more years yet.

The main route reaches its second usually signed junction at mile 0.4. Here the Graveyard Ridge Connector heads to the right and nearly north where the loop continues its easy walking to the west.

The corridor becomes increasingly forested—primarily tall rosebay rhododendron and young hardwoods—along the 0.2-mile stretch to Graveyard Field's third and final usually signed junction at 0.6 mile. Here the loop turns left at the fork and quickly crosses the high, sturdy, hurricane-proof bridge over Yellowstone Prong. The Upper Falls Trail bears off to the right from the normally well-marked junction.

Across the bridge, the wide walkway's final half mile rises easily through small hardwoods—the multiboled mountain winterberry frequently the most abundant—mixed with the dense growth of rhododendron. The trail-ending climb up stair steps closes the loop back to the parking area.

The unblazed and moderately difficult Lower Falls Trail, which shares its first 60 yards with the MST Access Trail, ventures straight ahead at the usually signed fork. A long wooden stairway descends sharply to the observation deck in front of the small but fairly deep plunge pool. After heavy rain Lower Falls is a loud and powerful downrush of spindrift-throwing white froth. But at low-to-medium water levels, the 55- to 60-foot-high falls is a combination of slanting spills and arrowy slides between three short leaps as it rides gravity's will down the wide rockface.

The MST Access Trail, which shares its first 60 yards with the Lower Falls Trail, forks up and to the left at the usually signed junction (carsonite sign recently blazed yellow). This short, easily walked connector passes a large rock outcrop near its midpoint and ties into the MST near the middle of a bend usually marked with multiple signs. If you turn right and downhill onto the MST (Section 4), you will come to the access trail leading to the Looking Glass Rock Overlook after 2.0 miles. If you follow the MST to the left and uphill, you will reach FS 816 after 3.3 miles.

Recently blazed yellow on its lower-end carsonite sign, much of the easy-to-moderate Graveyard Ridge Connector slowly ascends through a formerly open area quickly recovering from the 1999 fire. Where the slope steepens, the tread gains elevation through a series of winding, half-loop switchbacks. The connector ties into the Graveyard Ridge Trail at an obvious and usually signed T-junction. To the right it is 0.2 mile to that route's lower, southeastern terminus on the MST. To the left it is 1.1 miles to the prominent four-way Graveyard Ridge–MST intersection at Dark Prong Gap and 3.2 miles to the Graveyard Ridge–Ivestor Gap junction in Ivestor Gap.

The unblazed Upper Falls Trail roughly parallels Yellowstone Prong upstream, approaching close enough for at least partial looks at the branch-sized brook several times in the first 0.1 mile. Most of the remaining views (soon to be blocked by the fast-growing forest) of the nearby peaks occur within the first 0.4 mile. The easy-to-moderate hike soon enters a solid young forest composed of rhododendron, northern hardwoods (the yellow birch is by far the most abundant broadleaf), and occasional red spruce. At the halfway point the footpath dips to and crosses a small feeder branch, often only a few inches deep. The final 0.3 mile rises slightly harder on a rocky track with numerous rock and waterbar step-ups. The trail forks near Upper Falls. The path to the right and up leads to a rock jumble in front of the waterfall. The path to the left and down takes you below a long slanted raceway further away from the falls.

This far west, Yellowstone Prong is a small-volume, branch-sized stream less than a mile from its source springs on Black Balsam Knob's upper-south slope. During hot and dry weather the 45- to 50-foot falls becomes a narrow ribbon of listless water that fans out slightly as it slides down the right side of the widening rockface. After dropping over the final ledge, the falls finishes with a narrow sliding run. After substantial rain during a wet spring, the surging water becomes white and airborne as it leaps free from the slanting ledges.

Note: A public-private partnership of the NPS, USFS, and BRP Foundation plans to fund the Graveyard Fields Enhancement Project: a cooperative effort to implement numerous changes and improvements in the Graveyard Fields area in the near future.

Nature Notes

The painted trillium is Graveyard Field's showiest and most widespread spring wildflower. Common and often growing in association with rhododendron, this member of the Lily family is easily identified by its bicolored bloom. Most of the painteds were in bloom or bud on May 14, and most were somewhat faded on May 26 of recent years. By August 25 the pollinated blossoms had produced surprisingly large, shiny red berries.

Catawba rhododendron, Graveyard Field's most striking spring-blooming shrub, is easily distinguished by its flamboyant flowers—large clusters of deep pink to rose-lavender blossoms. The Catawba, named after the First Nation tribe, was beginning to bloom on a recent May 26.

Serviceberry

Distributed throughout the Southern Appalachians, the serviceberry is common in the Shining Rock highcountry and par-

ticularly abundant in the Graveyard Fields area. Many springtime hikers are familiar with this tree's flowers; especially from a distance, serviceberry blossoms stand out against the wintry-looking hardwood slopes.

This member of the Rose family blooms earlier than any other white-flowering tree at similar elevations in the Southern Highlands. Over a recent five-year span, the frequently multiboled serviceberry reliably whitened the Graveyard Fields woods

serviceberry

from April 28 through May 15. The flowers appear on slender stalks in terminal clusters before the leaves break bud or just after the reddish leaves unfurl. Each starry blossom reveals five narrow, strap-shaped petals from ½ to 1 inch long.

The dark purplish red fruits, tiny applelike pomes from ¼ to nearly ½ inch in diameter, begin ripening in June when other soft mast is scarce. This tree's early ripening fruit accounts for one of its other names: Juneberry. Sweet and tasty, these juicy fruits attract a wide array of wildlife—fox, coyote, skunk, squirrel, deer, bear, and raccoon, as well as turkey, grouse, and smaller birds.

Ranging from the lowlands to approximately 6,100 feet in the southern mountains, this small hardwood usually attains a height of only 20 to 45 feet and a diameter of 10 to 16 inches. Especially on young boles, the serviceberry's smooth gray bark is distinctively patterned with dark vertical streaks gradually twisting around the trunk like rifling in a gun barrel. Its ovate, alternate leaves—pointed at the tip and finely saw-toothed on the margin—display a purplish red cast in the spring and again in the fall.

Old-time mountaineers knew this broadleaf as just plain "service" and pronounced the word as "sarvis." The common name originated during the days of circuit-riding preachers. Come the new year, traveling preachers made their first spiritual forays into the highcountry when these hardwoods flowered white along their paths.

Directions

The Graveyard Fields Trail system begins at the Graveyard Fields Overlook between BRP mileposts 418 and 419.

Approach from the south: From the BRP–access road from NC 215 junction, turn left onto the parkway and travel approximately 4.4 miles to the overlook on the left side of the road.

Approach from the north: From the BRP–access road from US 276 junction, turn left onto the parkway and travel approximately 6.9 miles to the overlook on the right side of the road.

Nonwilderness Pocket—West of FS 816

Nonwilderness Pocket— West of FS 816—and Nearby Trails to the South

Gary Crider

Misty camp along the MST

Trails

Art Loeb, Section 1

Art Loeb, Section 2

Mountains to Sea, Section 3

Devils Courthouse

Little Sam

Flat Laurel Creek

Sam Knob / Sam Knob Summit

Art Loeb Trail, Section 1

(Parkway to Pilot Mountain)

Forest Service Trail 146   **3.3 miles**

Dayhiking In Moderate
Dayhiking Out Moderate to Strenuous
Backpacking In Moderate to Strenuous
Backpacking Out Strenuous
Vehicular Access at or near Either End
  Northern (higher elevation) terminus off the
  parkway just south of Silvermine Bald, 5,515 feet;
  southern (lower elevation) terminus atop Pilot
  Mountain, 5,105 feet
Trail Junctions ALT-2, Farlow Gap (not included in this
  guide), access trail from the end of Forest Service
  229, ALT continuing to the east from Pilot Mountain
Topographic Quadrangles Sam Knob, Shining Rock
Blazes White rectangle
Usage Foot travel only
Features Year-round views from the top of Pilot
  Mountain; pinkshell azalea display; occasional
  old-growth oaks

This moderately used ridgetop and upper-slope segment of the
Art Loeb is known primarily for three features: its dense, spring-
blooming stand of pinkshell azalea on Pilot Mountain's north-
facing ridgeline, its views from Pilot's open highpoint, and its

cumulative difficulty for a relatively short stretch without any sustained steep grades. People walk all or part of this route to pay homage to the rare beauty of Pilot's pinkshells. Art Loeb's roller-coaster ride—down to gaps, up to peaks—gains and loses a surprising amount of elevation: over 4,600 feet in the 6.6 miles from parkway to Pilot and back again.

This segment of the ALT, which runs slightly aslant of north-south, is described as it is most often dayhiked, from the parkway or the access point near Deep Gap to the top of Pilot Mountain. Beginning at the parkway, the white-blazed footpath descends to the southeast atop Shuck Ridge, a Silvermine Bald spur. Here at the upper end of this section well above 5,000 feet, the forest is a mix of small-needled conifers and hardwoods capable of climbing into the mile-high cold. Red spruce and sapling Fraser fir mingle with black cherry, yellow birch, northern red oak, and three species of maple—striped, red, and sugar. Clumps of multiboled witch-hazel are especially common along this stretch of Shuck Ridge. Where broadleafs dominate the wide keel of the ridge, grasses, herbaceous wildflowers, and extensive colonies of hay-scented and New York ferns often blanket the forest floor.

After an overall easy-to-moderate downgrade, the boot-worn treadway seamlessly switches crests at 0.6 mile, forking away from Shuck Ridge and riding another crest—a spur off a spur— to the south. This narrow spine is much drier and supports a different forest than Shuck Ridge because it is south facing and because the sharpness of its rocky crest sheds rain much faster than a wide ridgetop. Now chestnut oak, American chestnut saplings, deciduous and evergreen heath shrubs, plus colonies of shiny green galax are common. The trek makes an overall moderate descent before reaching the flat of a shallow saddle (4,820 feet) at 1.0 mile.

The route tops a small, unnamed knuckle of a knob (4,860 feet) at mile 1.2, where the top of the fold forks again. Here the track loses elevation to the southeast again, on a predominantly hardwood ridge wider and moister than the one just before it. Following a downhill run to mile 1.3, the tread switchbacks sharply to the right off the crest where it drops steeply straight ahead. After regaining the ridgeline, the downgrade continues before easing to the three-way junction, quickly followed by a four-way junction in the flat of Farlow Gap at mile 1.5.

The gap's elevation, 4,555 feet, is just low enough to support a surprisingly diverse forest, a mix of northern and cove hardwoods that includes Fraser magnolia, yellow poplar, white ash, and silverbell (abundant and just past peak flowering on a recent May 10). The northern red oak is the thickest tree along this section and reaches its best growth in or near the deeper soils of the gaps.

Frequently used by mountain bikers, old FS 140A ties into the ALT from the right. The trail follows its roadbed for 40 feet to the four-way junction and loafing spot. The usually signed Farlow Gap Trail's western, upper-elevation end is to the left; the Art Loeb holds course straight ahead, just to the left of the prominent rock outcrop and the grassy campsite immediately beyond it.

After undulating through an open forest with numerous witch-hazel trees in the understory, the path begins the ascent to Sassafras Knob with an easy grade. An old-growth northern red oak, this one with a girth of 11 feet 1 inch, is rooted to the right just before the ALT briefly ties into 140A again at mile 1.7.

Section 1 continues the climb to the knob on a dry and narrow ridgeline dominated by oaks over evergreen heath. The track slowly turns to the south as it rises up Sassafras; three or four short stretches reach at least moderate difficulty before the trail eases up to the knob's highpoint (4,940 feet) at 2.2 miles.

Over Sassafras, the ridgetop route travels downward progressively harder to mile 2.3, where it switchbacks from one side of the fold to the other to smooth out the grade. After the last switchback swings over the spine, the line of march traverses the intervening slope before catching a ride atop the next ridge to the west. Sassafras and blackgum join the predominantly hardwood forest along the easy descent to the shelter at mile 2.5. Here you can find an intermittent spring—a headwater feeder of Laurel Fork—85 yards down the widest path from the front of the shelter.

The treadway curves close beside the shelter, then ramps down the ridge to the next saddle. On the way down, the trail passes an intermittent wet-weather spring—a high capillary of Bearpen Branch—just to the right of the route 40 feet before Section 1 angles to the right onto old FS 229. The course follows the easy walking of the former road's rocky bed to Deep Gap (4,580 feet) at 2.7 miles. A half dozen or more large northern red oaks stand in the gap. You will find the thickest one (11 feet 5 inches in circumference) about 7 long paces to the left of the track shortly before the prominent camp on the same side.

Old FS 229 ties into the trail from the left just beyond the same prominent camp in Deep Gap. Here the ALT forks to the right onto footpath (the access trail from old FS 229 ties in from the left 85 yards beyond the fork) and begins a progressively more difficult pull, the rating quickly ratcheting up from easy to strenuous. By early summer the moist, north-facing crest is covered with a lush growth of tall herbs and ferns, including the interrupted fern. Just when you think you're in for a straight-up-the-mountain grunt, the first of two dozen switchbacks starts zigzagging up the ridge below an all hardwood canopy at mile 2.8.

The next 0.4 mile switchbacks up Pilot Mountain. Here the fairly cold-tolerant sweet birch becomes less common as the especially cold-hardy yellow birch—a north-country species shoved deep down into Dixie by the Last Glacial Maximum— becomes more numerous with increased elevation.

Above the final switchback, a short straightaway leads to Pilot's rocky topknot, a former fire tower site now a look-off centered to the left and right, east and west. From the wide view to the left and east, you can easily identify the high conical peak and towered top of Mount Pisgah (12.2 miles, 5,721 feet) at around 36 degrees. To the right of Pisgah and much further away (48.6 miles), Mount Mitchell's summit (6,684 feet) and observation tower are often shrouded in clouds at around 52 degrees. Much closer and lower, Looking Glass Rock (4.7 miles) at around 70 degrees and Cedar Rock Mountain (3.9 miles) at around 111 degrees are readily recognized by their sharply sloping rockfaces. In short line of sight over Looking Glass Rock's left side, Black Mountain (8.6 miles) is the steep-sided peak on the second row of ridges past Looking Glass.

From the right and west side of Pilot, you can spot the usual high peaks along the parkway to the northwest, and row after row of ridges and ranges to the west and west-northwest as far as the air clarity will allow. Towered on the right side of its broad crown, Toxaway Mountain stands tall in its setting (11.8 miles, 4,777 feet) at around 217 degrees. The crest running to the right of Toxaway (west-northwest) is part of the long and winding Blue Ridge, which doubles as the Tennessee Valley Divide in this location.

To the right of Toxaway and beyond the Blue Ridge, three prominently pointed peaks look like a row of well-gapped sawteeth, each of the sharply sloped mountains the highest uplift in sight to its summit. First in line left to right, Terrapin Mountain (20.2 miles, 4,460 feet) is the shortest and dullest tooth at around 225 degrees. Closer and higher, Chimneytop Mountain (16.6 miles, 4,618 feet) rises to a crookedly conical apex at around 229 degrees. Whiteside Mountain (20.5 miles) thrusts its mostly bare-rock southeastern slope (not visible from Pilot) up to 4,910 feet at around 236 degrees.

When the air is clear look for Standing Indian (41.9 miles, 5,499 feet), its long, gently sloping ridgeline descending to the left (southeast) away from its summit at around 251 degrees.

The Art Loeb continues for approximately 14.7 miles to its lower-elevation, southeastern terminus.

Nature Notes

This short stretch of the ALT offers a good spring and late summer wildflower show. On a recent May 13 and 14 of different years, wood anemone, yellow mandarin, rose twisted-stalk, wakerobin and painted trilliums, lousewort, and bellwort were in fresh bloom. Bluebead lily, Canada mayflower, and Vasey's trillium were in bud, and the trout lily leaves were already yellowing at the extensive colony in Farlow Gap.

White snakeroot, pink turtlehead, white wood aster (abundant), angelica, goldenrod, false foxglove, several species of yellow asters, and southern harebell were in bloom or bud among others on August 7 and 20 of two recent years.

Witch-hazel

The witch-hazel (*Hamamelis virginiana*), a stooped understory tree usually 10 to 30 feet tall, is especially abundant along the middle four-tenths of this section's northernmost mile. Here

multiboled clumps of this species—its light colored bark often
blotched pale green with lichen—arch over the trail. This slightly
aromatic broadleaf is most common and noticeable on moist
hardwood slopes and along streambanks free from rhododendron.

Nearly everything about the witch-hazel is unique, unusual,
or distinctive. Its easily identified alternate leaves—3 to 5 inches
long, wavy edged, and widest beyond midpoint—have lopsided
bases and round-toothed margins. *H. virginiana* flowers later
than any other tree, shrub, or herb in the Southern Highlands.

It often begins blossoming during
the last half of October and,
depending upon elevation, may
continue blooming through
November into December. Each
small, bright yellow flower displays
four twisted, stringlike petals. Clustered blossoms resemble twisted
tufts of teased yellow hair.

Witch-hazel, once called win-
terbloom, has evolved an unusual
method of seed dispersal: it fires
them out over the forest floor.
About the same time the yellow
petals appear in the fall, the
rounded, woody seedpods that developed from the previous
year's blooms shoot their black, shiny seeds up to 30 feet from
the tree.

witch-hazel

Pinkshell azalea

People time their trips to Pilot Mountain to admire the
pastel-colored flowers of the pinkshell azalea (*Rhododendron
vaseyi*), a Southern Appalachian endemic native to perhaps only

half a dozen counties in North Carolina. Here, along this section of the Art Loeb, it blooms beside spruce just south of the parkway and amid hardwoods on the way up to Pilot Mountain. During a peak year these deciduous heath shrubs flower profusely, creating a wash of pink on the upper-north slope of Pilot Mountain, where they are much more abundant than along any other trail or trail section in this guide.

The pinkshell's blossoms, five to eight flowers per cluster, often break bud before the small elliptical leaves fully unfold. The five-petaled flowers, which have long upward curving stamens, range from white slightly tinged with pink to medium pastel pink. The two lower petals are splayed out and slightly larger than the others. Freckles ranging from reddish brown to yellowish green dot the bases of the top three petals. Usually 4 to 10 feet tall in the Shining Rock area, these showy shrubs were in peak bloom on May 11, 13, and 14 of three recent years. They were in bud and fresh bloom on May 1 during the unusually warm springs of 2011 and 2012.

pinkshell azalea

Starry campion

Clustered atop tall slender stems, the flowers of the starry campion are so deeply cleft that they appear to have numerous slender petals when, in fact, they have only five. The ¾-inch-wide blossoms form circles of fringed white spreading up and slightly out into star shapes. Most of this plant's upper leaves—

starry campion

2 to 4 inches long and lance shaped—occur in whorls of four along the stem.

Usually 14 to 28 inches tall, the starry campion is most common in rich, open woods. It is usually in bloom somewhere along this section of the ALT from August 1 to 20.

Directions

Section 1 has vehicular access at or near either end. Its northern trailhead is located off the parkway near Silvermine Bald between mileposts 421 and 422, and its southern access is located at the end of FS 229 (Pilot Mountain Road) near Deep Gap.

Northern trailhead off the BRP

Approach from the south: From the BRP–access road from NC 215 junction, turn left onto the parkway and travel approximately 2.0 miles to the trailpost and small pull-off parking area to the right of the road.

Approach from the north: From the BRP–access road from US 276 junction, turn left onto the parkway and travel approximately 9.3 miles to the trailpost and small pull-off parking area to the left of the road.

The ALT—marked by short trailposts on either side of the road—crosses the BRP here. The northern end of Section 1 is located at the small pull-off parking area on the south side of the parkway. The beginning of Section 1 rises gently for a few feet, then descends.

Southern access at the end of FS 229

Approach from the north: From the NC 215–access road from BRP junction, turn right onto NC 215 South toward Rosman and travel approximately 9.1 miles before turning left onto signed Clinic Road (SR 1328).

Approach from the south: From the three-way US 64–NC 215 intersection near Rosman, travel NC 215 North for approximately 7.7 miles before turning right onto signed Clinic Road (SR 1328).

From Clinic Road: Travel Clinic Road for slightly less than 0.2 mile, then turn left onto signed Shoal Creek Road (SR 1327). Follow Shoal Creek Road for approximately 2.2 miles to where it becomes dirt-gravel and continues straight ahead as FS 475 (N. Davidson River Rd.). Proceed 0.8 mile on FS 475 to a four-way intersection, then turn left and uphill onto FS 229 (Pilot Mountain Road, gated during winter weather and in spring before its track is cleared of tree debris). Travel this road for approximately 2.5 miles to its combination turnaround/parking area. Walk the continuing track 0.2 mile to where the upslope bank first dips below eye level, then take a bend-back turn to the left and up onto the path that ties into the Art Loeb after less than 50 feet. Following the ALT uphill and to the left leads you to the views atop Pilot Mountain after 0.6 mile.

Art Loeb Trail, Section 2

(Parkway to FS 816)

Forest Service Trail 146	1.5 miles

Dayhiking (low to high) Moderate
Dayhiking (high to low) Easy to Moderate
Backpacking (low to high) Moderate to Strenuous
Backpacking (high to low) Moderate
Vehicular Access at Either End Southern (lower elevation) terminus off the parkway south of Silvermine Bald, 5,520 feet; northern (higher elevation) terminus at the Mountains to Sea–Art Loeb Trailhead off FS 816, 5,900 feet
Trail Junctions ALT-1, MST-3 (see description), ALT-3 and MST-4 at the MST–ALT Trailhead
Topographic Quadrangle Sam Knob
Blazes White rectangle for ALT, white circle for MST
Usage Foot travel only
Features Rock outcrops; red spruce

This short section of the ALT is only 1.5 miles long and shares its northernmost 1.1 miles with the MST. The short, steep segment of ALT-2—the leftover, one-trail tread from the parkway to the crest of Silvermine Bald—is by far the least hiked link of the ALT in this guide. On many days, Art Loeb thru-hikers are the only ones to walk this 0.4-mile stretch. This section is described as the majority of thru-hikers trek it, from south to north—the climb first, then the mostly easy walking to FS 816.

Starting on the north side of the BRP, ALT-2 begins to switch-back right away as it heads northwest up the high southwest slope of Shuck Ridge, a Silvermine Bald lead. The forest on this rocky slope is a high-elevation mix of spruce-fir and hardwoods dominated by northern red oak and yellow birch. The red spruce is the tallest tree and increasingly controls the canopy as the route continues to climb. The understory is frequently thick with evergreen heath shrubs—fetterbush, mountain laurel, Catawba rhododendron. The round, shiny leaves of galax occasionally line the track.

The narrow path keeps right on slanting up Shuck as it winds through a series of switchbacks. The hiking is easy between switchbacks at first, but becomes steadily steeper and rockier as the trail gains 440 feet of elevation to the MST junction. On the way up, rock outcrops are seldom out of sight in the trail corridor. The grade is most often no harder than moderate between the numerous short sets of step-ups on rocks and erosion bars.

At 0.4 mile the ALT pops up to its prominent, usually well-signed T-junction with the MST (5,960 feet) on Silvermine Bald's crest. Here ALT-2 turns to the right (northeast) onto MST-3 and piggybacks on the treadway for 1.1 miles to FS 816. (See MST-3, the following trail section, for a description of this shared segment.)

Directions

Section 2 has either-end vehicular access. Its southern trailhead is located off the parkway between mileposts 421 and 422, and its northern, MST–ALT Trailhead is located off FS 816.

Southern trailhead off the BRP

The southern end of ALT-2 and the northern end of ALT-1 share the same small pull-off parking area on the south side of the parkway. Short trailposts mark the route to either side of the road. Section 2's southern end is located on the north, upslope side of the BRP across the road and nearly 50 yards from the pull-off parking area. (See ALT-1, the preceding trail section, for directions to its northern trailhead off the BRP.)

Northern, MST–ALT Trailhead off FS 816

The northern end of ALT-2, the southern end of ALT-3, the northeastern end of MST-3, and the western end of MST-4 all share the same trailhead off FS 816 (Black Balsam Road) north of the BRP. If you follow the level, white-blazed, two-trail tread-way (usually marked with a blazed post) into the dark spruce forest to the left (southwest) side of the road, you will be on the treadway shared by ALT-2 and MST-3 for 1.1 miles. (See MST-4, page 127, for directions to its western, MST–ALT Trailhead off FS 816.)

Mountains to Sea Trail, Section 3

(NC 215 to FS 816)

Forest Service Trail 440   **4.4 miles**

Dayhiking Easy to Moderate in either direction
Backpacking Moderate in either direction
Vehicular Access at Either End Southwestern (lower
 elevation) terminus off NC 215, 5,130 feet;
 northeastern (higher elevation) terminus at the
 Mountains to Sea–Art Loeb Trailhead off FS 816,
 5,900 feet
Trail Junctions MST-2, Devils Courthouse–MST
 connector, Little Sam, ALT-2 (see description), MST-4
 and ALT-3 at the MST–ALT Trailhead
Topographic Quadrangle Sam Knob
Blazes White circle for MST, white rectangle for ALT
Usage Foot travel only
Features Year-round views; two large rock outcrops;
 extensive fern colonies; Catawba rhododendron
 displays

MST-3 is the shortest (access trails added) and least difficult of the
five MST sections included in this guide; most of its sustained
grades are easy. Walked as described, this moderately used
upper-slope and ridgeline route winds southwest to northeast,
half-looping around the highpoint of Chestnut Bald before following the crest of Silvermine Bald.

Remaining above 5,000 feet for its entire length like Sections 1 and 2, this stretch rises to the highest elevation—approximately 5,985 feet on the crest of Silvermine Bald—along the 23-mile length of the five short MST sections included in this guide. This hike's best views, those with short sidepaths leading to rock outcrop overlooks, will remain in the future.

Starting on the east side of NC 215, MST-3 quickly enters a mix of highcountry conifers and cold-adapted hardwoods. Here the low canopy is largely composed of red maple, yellow birch, red spruce, and northern red oak. The subcanopy generally consists of mountain ash, pin cherry, mountain winterberry, serviceberry, mountain maple, and Fraser fir. Further down in the filtered light, the understory is ruled by two species of rhododendron—Catawba and rosebay.

The mild grade heads east-northeast on the slopes of Pisgah Ridge—a long, named string of knobs roughly paralleling the north side of the parkway—for its first half mile. The path is especially shaded and dark where red spruce grow in combination with the rhododendron. The course comes alongside the sliding waters of a small Bubbling Spring Branch tributary before making a bridged crossing over the stream at 0.5 mile.

Beyond the branch, the trek begins a two-thirds loop around the north side of an unnamed, 5,650-foot knob. At 0.8 mile the route skirts the base of a rock outcrop the size of a small apartment complex—impressively large even by local Shining Rock standards. After passing the bottom of the outcrop, the MST rises with the help of a pair of switchbacks. Just above the elbow of the second one, a short sidepath takes you to the top of the rock and its open views. (The narrow safe zone atop the outcrop is absolutely no place for run-ahead young children.)

The six nearest peaks—those you can identify in all weathers and pollution levels except cloud cover—include a courthouse, a bald, one named and two unnamed knobs, and a mount. Flat-topped and cliff-faced Devils Courthouse is to the far left edge of the view, if the trees still allow the look. The next two rounded crowns to the right of the courthouse are nameless knobs on Pisgah Ridge. (Further away, Toxaway Mountain's gently sloping and towered top is usually visible just off the second knob's left shoulder.) Next in line, Tanasee Bald stands in the crook of the BRP–NC 215 junction, south of the former and west of the latter. Herrin Knob's uplift is immediately south of the parkway, close to midway between Tanasee and Hardy and sharing the same ridgeline. Highest in near view at the far right edge of the prospect, Mount Hardy's broad summit with its distinctive Cyclops cliff face is just north of the parkway.

At mile 1.2 the treadway enters the most extensive fern colony along the trails included in this guide. Here finely wrought hay-scented ferns quilt both sides of the footpath, upslope and down, in varying widths and densities (briers are invading) for close to 0.2 mile. Beyond these light green fern fields, the easy hiking traverses a stretch of open young forest frequently underlain with much darker evergreen wood fern.

At mile 1.5, just beyond a very short dip on slab rock, a sidepath to the right will provide a view of nearby Devils Courthouse for a few more years yet. Starting at mile 1.6, Section 3 travels through a dark stand of planted red spruce before skirting the edge of the monocultural conifers for a longer distance. It then runs beside the spruce again, the track occasionally serving as a dividing line—spruce to the right, ferns to the left. The MST leaves the stand at mile 1.8 and continues its slow ascent on the western slopes of Chestnut Bald.

After crossing several boardwalks over seeps and spring runs (all intermittent during prolonged drought), you come to a posted T-junction just north of the BRP at mile 2.0 (5,660 feet).

Here the white-blazed MST turns sharply to the left, and the blue-blazed Devils Courthouse–MST connector to the right (entrance 160 degrees) leads 0.1 mile to the Devils Courthouse Trail on the other side of the BRP.

At mile 2.2 the route comes to a fork where the sidepath to the left leads to campsites before ending at the Little Sam Trail. A tenth-mile further, just beyond this section's second very large, view-providing outcrop, the tread arrives at its usually well-signed junction with the Little Sam Trail (5,740 feet), which strikes out to the left (entrance about due north) parallel to the length of the rock.

Advancing from the junction, the track half-loops around the high north slope of Chestnut Bald and gradually gains elevation along the way. The line of march quickly ranges through a recently open area still in early succession; mountain ash and pin cherry will remain abundant until the next wave overtops them. The trail enters NPS land at mile 2.9, gains the ridgeline, then immediately begins the moderate descent to the gap between the balds—Chestnut and Silvermine. At the very beginning of the downridge run, two short spurs to the right and less than 25 yards apart guide you to the same rock outcrop overlook, a wide wedge of a view open straight out to the southeast.

Cliffs rise from the parkway at the left edge of the view. Looking like the partial breach of a sperm whale stilled in stone, Looking Glass Rock is unmistakable at around 102 degrees. Low and nearby, Cedar Rock Mountain's two bands of gray cliff, one above the other, are also unmistakable at around 132 degrees. The close and distinctly conical mountain at around 162 degrees is Pilot, and Lake Toxaway reflects sunlight to either side of 192 degrees over 12.0 miles away. At the far right edge of the view, Toxaway Mountain stands flat topped and towered 13.3 miles away.

The route bottoms out in the gap's steadily shrinking grassy opening (mile 3.0, 5,825 feet). Here you can find an intermittent spring downhill to the left (north) side of the gap. Pushing onward to the sea, the trail slowly ascends the crest of Silvermine Bald, another of the named knobs along Pisgah Ridge. The steady upgrade is frequently lined by a dense hedge of heath shrubs, including the evergreen fetterbush.

At mile 3.3 the second sidepath to the right leads to another narrow view open to the south and Pilot Mountain, this one atop the high cliff that rises gray and craggy from the north side of the parkway between mileposts 421 and 422 (another potentially dangerous spot for run-ahead young children). Less than 15 yards beyond the clifftop, you arrive at the usually well-signed T-junction (5,960 feet) with ALT-2. The southbound Art Loeb, blazed with white rectangles, ventures downhill and to the right (140 degrees) toward its parkway crossing. Straight ahead, north-bound ALT-2 and the MST share the same treadway for the remainder of this section.

The next 0.7 mile rides Silvermine's high ridge (section highpoint at mile 3.5), gently rolling over two more small knuckles on the mountain's northeastern crest. Here the highcountry hiking passes through a forest where many of the mature red spruce have died in recent years. The mountain ash, abundant and beautiful in berry beginning in September, has quickly sprung up in the light gaps. Following the slight saddle at mile 3.6, the forest is frequently dominated by stands of planted red spruce for the next 0.4 mile. Hobblebush—a deciduous viburnum shrub with large, heart-shaped, opposite leaves—is common along parts of this same stretch.

At mile 4.0 the two-trail track bends to the north as it descends, leaving Pisgah Ridge and the parkway corridor as it forges ahead on the crest leading toward Black Balsam Knob.

A tenth-mile further, the MST enters a stretch of wide ridgeline with numerous low outcrops and a reviving forest that screens more of the remaining views every year. With 0.2 mile to go, the route dips to a red spruce flat and follows white blazes through the dark, needle-floored forest the rest of the way to FS 816.

Nature Notes

Section 3 has a fair spring wildflower show. Bluebead lily and painted trillium colonies are common. On a recent May 31, Canada mayflower and wood sorrel had just begun to bloom, wake-robins and painted trilliums were largely blown, and bluebead lilies were in perfect peak. The wake-robins were past peak and the painteds were only slightly past prime on a recent May 20 of a very sunny drought year. The late summer aster display was already a week past peak on a recent September 14.

The vivid, deep pink to rose-lavender blossoms of the abundant Catawba rhododendron had just begun to open at the section's western, lower-elevation end on that same May 31. The mountain laurels were in bud, and the few pinkshell azaleas were mostly past prime.

bluebead lily

Bluebead lily

Common along much of this section, the bluebead lily (*Clintonia borealis*) requires cool, moist, acidic soils usually above 5,000 feet in elevation. Its preferred habitat is the spruce-fir forest and the spruce-fir/northern hardwood mix. In bloom, this lily is one of the easiest of Southern Appalachian wildflowers to identify. The combination of habitat preference, leaf size and shape, and flower color make it unmistakable.

The leaves (two to five in number) and the berries of this native perennial are showier than the blossoms. The thick leaves, glossy and richly green, basal and broadly oval, are usually between 5 and 10 inches long. The slightly poisonous shiny blue berries are nearly ½ inch in diameter.

Four to eight pale yellow or greenish yellow flowers form loose, nodding umbels at the top of the slender stalks. Like most members of the Lily family, these ½- to 1-inch-long flowers feature three petals and three petal-like sepals.

Also known as Clinton's lily, these memorable herbs are likely to be blooming along Section 3 during late May and early June. Most of the colonies appeared to be at full flower over a recent Memorial Day weekend.

Painted trillium

Trilliums are unique among Southern Appalachian wildflowers, and the painted (*Trillium undulatum*) is unique among trilliums. In bloom, this native perennial cannot be mistaken for any other forb found in the Southern Highlands. Trilliums are distinctly three parted: they produce three leaves, flowers with three petals above three sepals, ovaries with three cells, and fruits with three ribs.

Most often standing between 4 and 12 inches tall, this species bears a single whorl of ovate leaves, usually 2 to 5 inches long. The lone flower's otherwise white petals are painted with a red or purplish red brush-stroke V on the inner base of each petal. These three inverted V's form a triangle of contrasting color, a bull's-eye guiding pollinators to the right place. The red

painted trillium

runs outward and darker in the veins, especially the midveins, emphasizing the three points of its botanical geometry. The blossoms are usually 1¼ to 2¼ inches wide, wavy margined, and slightly recurved.

Requiring cool forests and acidic soils, this member of the Lily family reaches the southernmost extent of its large range in the Southern Appalachians, where it is usually found beneath or near rhododendron or other heaths. Like the wood anemone, trilliums have evolved a method of seed dispersal known as ant farming.

Michaux's saxifrage

Michaux's saxifrage is occasional to common within its specialized niche: seeps below boulders, bluffs, and rock outcrops or the ledges, cracks, and crevices in the rocks themselves. This distinctive wildflower is usually 6 to 24 inches tall with a widely branching flower stalk. Its basal rosette of reddish green leaves—simple, 3 to 7 inches long, and prominently toothed—is diagnostic in combination with the right habitat. These basal leaves turn redder as the growing season progresses. Mature leaves are frequently tinged with red along their edges and veins, especially the midvein.

The flowers of this native perennial are tiny (¼ to ⅜ of an inch across), five petaled, star shaped, and bilaterally symmetrical: the narrow white petals are dissimilar but arranged so that they produce left and right mirror images. This Southern Appalachian endemic was blooming at the impressively large rock outcrop at mile 0.8 on a recent July 5.

The name saxifrage comes from Latin and the ancients' unsophisticated sense of cause and effect. The Latin word *saxum* (stone) was combined with *fragere* (to break). These early botanists called their saxifrage species "stonebreakers" because they believed these plants caused the cracks and fissures where they were rooted.

Directions

Section 3 has either-end vehicular access. Its southwestern trailhead is located off NC 215 just north of the BRP, and its northeastern, MST–ALT Trailhead is located off FS 816, also just north of the BRP.

Southwestern trailhead off NC 215

Approach from the south: From the NC 215–access road from BRP junction, turn left onto NC 215 North toward Canton and travel 0.4 mile to the large gravel parking area to the left of the road.

Approach from the north: From the four-way NC 215–NC 110–US 276 intersection, travel NC 215 South (also marked with a Love Joy Rd. street sign) approximately 17.3 miles to the large gravel parking area to the right of the road.

The southwestern end of Section 3, marked with a MST post, begins further downhill and across the highway from the parking area. The eastern end of Section 2 is located on the parking-area side of the highway.

Northeastern, MST–ALT Trailhead off FS 816

Section 3's MST–ALT Trailhead is located off FS 816 (Black Balsam Road) north of the BRP. This trailhead is the northeastern end of Section 3 and the western end of Section 4. If you follow the level, white-blazed, two-trail treadway (usually marked with a blazed post) into the dark spruce forest to the left (southwest) side of the road, you will be on Section 3 heading toward NC 215. (See MST-4, page 127, for directions to its western, MST–ALT Trailhead off FS 816.)

Notes

Devils Courthouse Trail

Park Service Trail	0.4 mile

Dayhiking Easy to Moderate
Backpacking Moderate (camping prohibited within the BRP corridor, which encompasses all of this trail and the top of the courthouse)
Start Devils Courthouse Overlook, 5,460 feet
End Lookout atop Devils Courthouse, 5,720 feet
Trail Junction Devils Courthouse–MST connector
Topographic Quadrangle Sam Knob
Blaze None
Usage Foot travel only
Features Craggy cliff face; year-round views from the walled lookout atop the summit; plaques sighted in to prominent peaks

The name Devils Courthouse came from a Cherokee tradition that was incorporated—perhaps with changes—into early settler folklore. According to the overlook plaque, "Within the mountain is a cave where, legend claims, the devil holds court. In Cherokee lore, this cave is the private dancing chamber and dwelling place of the slant-eyed giant, Judaculla."

Judaculla has long been associated with both Devils Courthouse and Tanasee Bald. In Mooney's *Myths of the Cherokee*, the slant-eyed giant, Tsul Kalu—anglicized to Jutaculla or Judaculla—was the great lord of the hunt, who resided in a dance hall in nearby Tanasee Bald.

Blacktopped for much of its length and busy, Devils Court-house is the second shortest trail in this guide (excluding the Graveyard Fields system) and the only one routed completely within the BRP corridor. This wide walkway heads from its view of the Devils Courthouse cliff face—its craggy profile unmistakable for miles around—to the walled lookout atop its summit. The courthouse cliff is composed of migmatitic mica gneiss and schist. (Migmatitic is the adjective form of migmatite: a metamorphic rock showing localized melting of light colored materials.)

After paralleling the parkway for 0.1 mile, the macadam tread curls to the right and enters the beleaguered spruce-fir forest on the courthouse's northwestern slope. Mountain ash, yellow birch, mountain maple, and Catawba rhododendron constitute much of the subcanopy and understory. (The Catawbas were showing off their corsage-sized flower clusters on June 4 and June 9 of recent years.) On the way up, the track rises moderately for 0.1 mile before easing to milder grades.

The route reaches its only junction at 0.3 mile, where the treadway turns sharply to the right. Here the blue-blazed Devils Courthouse–MST connector begins to the left opposite the trail's right turn. The nearly level 0.1-mile connector heads north across the parkway (over the tunnel) before tying into the MST.

The easy walking continues on rock-step stairs before leveling out on the courthouse's flat-topped summit. Three sighted-in tablets atop the stacked-rock walls line your eyes up with eleven prominent peaks ranging from nearby Tanasee Bald, Sam Knob, and Mount Hardy to out-of-state Rabun Bald (Georgia, 33.2 miles). The severe air pollution plaguing the Southern Appalachians often prevents even short range views from this popular lookout. Hot, still, high-pressure conditions three or more days after rain are particularly bad—for views and for your health. On a recent July 20 I could barely make out Toxaway Mountain, only 12.9 miles distant through the crud-choked sky.

If you want crisp, long-distance views, wait until the cooler weather that arrives immediately after a cold front with sky-scrubbing rain pushes through. Then you can really see into three other states—Georgia, South Carolina, Tennessee—and spot the observation tower atop Rabun Bald (with binoculars).

Nature Notes

The North Carolina Wildlife Commission has restored speed and ferocity to Shining Rock's skies. It accomplished this feat by bringing back the perfect aerodynamic form of the fastest being on earth: the peregrine falcon (*Falco peregrinus*). With a moderate measure of luck, you can now claim witness to the striking beauty of this bird on the wing, to the fluid grace of its fast arrowing flight. With even more luck and more time spent atop mountains open to the high blue, you might witness this raptor turn fighter plane if another large bird—raven or turkey vulture or red-tailed hawk—enters peregrine airspace while the proprietor is on patrol. Then the falcon tucks its dagger-tipped wings into one of the earth's most exquisite expressions of form and function as it drops from the sky toward the unsuspecting intruder. After scaring the wits and whitewash out of the interloper with a supersonic buzz, the feathered jet pulls out of its stoop and banks toward a close-quarter dogfight. Only no talons will turn to fist. After showing off big-stick speed, the intimidator talks softly as it escorts the eager-to-leave bogey out of its territory.

A medium- to large-sized falcon, this species measures 16 to 20 inches long and whips the air with wings spanning from 36 to 46 inches. The sexes are outwardly similar, but the female is 15 to 20 percent larger and 40 to 50 percent heavier than the male, which is known as a tiercel because it is roughly one-third smaller than the female.

The peregrine's long, wind-honed wings sweep backward beyond the elbows as they taper to points at their tips. The arc from one wingtip to the other, along the leading edge of the wing and across the bill, delineates the pronounced bend of a bow. Adults are colored dark bluish gray on their upper parts and mostly pale white with a variable amount of spotting and fine barring on their under parts. This bird of prey's hook-billed head is capped with black running from the base of its bill across the back of its head and below its eyes. This diagnostic field mark dips well below the eyes in the approximate shape of a cold-weather cap's earflaps. Immature birds are brown where the adults are blue-gray or black.

This bolt out of the blue is the fastest feathered arrow in evolution's quiver, a winged sky cheetah whose only traction is air. When this sleek and powerful raptor flies with a will in pursuit of fast prey, it regularly reaches speeds of 70 miles per hour as it closes in on its quarry. Seventy, however, is only a warm-up wind sprint compared to what *F. peregrinus* can do in a dive. When this falcon folds its wings and drops straight down, a stoop often plummeting thousands of feet in a few moments, gravity and natural selection join forces to test the tensile strength of feathers and air-filled bones as the bird accelerates beyond astounding into disbelief. Most top-end dive clockings range from 200 to 220 mph. Some are even higher.

In 1984 the North Carolina Wildlife Commission began a hacking program to reintroduce captive-raised peregrines back into the wild with the hope of re-establishing a breeding population in the state. This program continued until a total of ninety-two falcons (all of them hacked starting at three weeks old) had been released into the wild by 1997. In the Shining Rock region, biologists utilized a pair of craggy, 6,000-foot peaks, Sam Knob and Tennent Mountain, as hacking sites.

As you may already know, or guessed, the Devils Courthouse rockface is an aerie: a peregrine falcon nesting ledge. (Nearby Looking Glass Rock is also an aerie.) Peregrines nested on the courthouse's high cliff from 1999 through 2010. They did not set up housekeeping in 2011 or 2012.

Directions

Devils Courthouse begins at the Devils Courthouse Overlook located between BRP mileposts 422 and 423.

Approach from the south: From the BRP–access road from NC 215 junction, turn left onto the parkway and travel slightly less than 1.0 mile to the overlook on the right side of the road.

Approach from the north: From the BRP–access road from US 276 junction, turn left onto the parkway and travel approximately 10.5 miles (0.2 mile beyond the end of the Devils Courthouse Tunnel) to the overlook on the left side of the road.

Notes

Little Sam Trail

Forest Service Trail 347   **1.3 miles**

Dayhiking (low to high) Easy to Moderate
Dayhiking (high to low) Easy
Backpacking (low to high) Moderate
Backpacking (high to low) Easy to Moderate
Interior Trail Southern (higher elevation) terminus
    on Mountains to Sea Trail, 5,740 feet; northern
    (lower elevation) terminus on Flat Laurel Creek Trail,
    5,540 feet
Trail Junctions MST-3, Flat Laurel Creek
Topographic Quadrangle Sam Knob
Blaze Yellow
Usage Foot travel only
Features Succession forest; 360-degree view from the
    top of an impressive rock outcrop; occasional over-
    the-vegetation views until the forest recovers;
    Catawba rhododendron display

Short and easily walked, Little Sam is an upper-slope trail that
winds north-south, connecting MST-3 to Flat Laurel Creek.
From its upper-elevation end to its only stream crossing, the
route runs along the western and northern slopes of Chestnut
Bald. North of the branch, a headwater fork of Flat Laurel Creek,
the treadway switches to the northwestern slope of Silvermine
Bald. Most of Little Sam's grades are easy.

This interior trail is described from high to low, from south to north, from upper slope to Flat Laurel Creek. Beginning at its usually signed junction with the MST, Little Sam immediately parallels a long (close to 100 feet) gray whaleback rock outcrop to the left. A sidepath at the far end of the outcrop leads to the easy scramble up bare rock.

For now, the topknot spine of this impressive outcrop affords views of the worn and rounded rise of the local Appalachians, the land still wracked and wrenched from ancient orogeny, still a formidable geology rearing up to better than 6,000 feet. Prominent nearby peaks include the two scenic Sams (Sam Knob and Little Sam Knob), Devils Courthouse, Mount Hardy, Chestnut Bald, and Green Knob. Sam (6,060 feet) and Little Sam (5,862 feet at the benchmark and maned with red spruce) heave up ridged and rocky to the north. The craggy, cliff-face profile of nearby Devils Courthouse (5,720 feet) stands to the south-southwest, and 6,125-foot Mount Hardy—the highest reach of Fork Ridge— rears up almost due west. Less than a half mile to the east, conifer-clad Chestnut Bald lifts the land to just over 6,000 feet. Green Knob, a named peak on Fork Ridge in the Middle Prong Wilderness, rolls up to slightly over 5,900 feet to the northwest.

Beyond the lookout, the track makes a 60-yard, easy-to-moderate descent into recovered forest—primarily red spruce, mountain maple, Fraser fir, pin cherry, mountain ash, and yellow birch. At the end of this first downhill run, a brushy short-cut path back to the left (west) leads to campsites before connecting (after 0.1 mile) with the MST 0.1 mile before that trail's Little Sam junction (walking the MST to the northeast from its NC 215 Trailhead). After slightly less than 0.2 mile, the tread ties into a former railroad grade, easy walking enlivened with occasional dips to wet-weather runoff notches.

For now, until the forest grows up even more, the route still affords occasional between-branch and over-the-foliage views to the west and Mount Hardy. The gently descending rail-to-trail track is often a wide aisle through the flanking evergreen of Catawba rhododendron. At 0.9 mile the footpath veers sharply to the left and downhill at the usually signed fork (a campsite is straight ahead). Following a progressively steeper 70-yard descent, Little Sam crosses a branch-sized feeder—cold, clear, and usually rock-step shallow. The course quickly continues its mostly easy downgrade on a rocky rail line through a pleasing mix of conifers and highcountry hardwoods. Red spruce is by far the tallest evergreen, yellow birch the most common broadleaf.

A short dip leads to Little Sam's usually signed connection with the wide Flat Laurel Creek Trail. To the left it is 0.4 mile to Flat Laurel Creek's junction with the Sam Knob Trail and 2.6 miles to Flat Laurel Creek's southwestern trailhead off NC 215. To the right it is 1.1 miles to Flat Laurel Creek's northeastern, Black Balsam Trailhead at the paved end of FS 816.

Nature Notes

Frequently shaded by conifers and evergreen heath, Little Sam has a poor forest-floor wildflower display in spring. The shrub layer largely composed of Catawba rhododendron, however, provides the best and by far the most abundant source of spring color—showy deep pink to rose-lavender blossoms, big and beautiful as a corsage. Catawbas were just beginning to bloom in the sunny area on and around the rock outcrop on a recent June 2, and were in peak condition along the trail on a recent June 12.

Tall, eye catching, and distinctive, the pink turtlehead was conspicuous on a recent August 15.

Pin cherry

The pin cherry (*Prunus pensylvanica*) is an early succession species most often found in the northern hardwood forest and the northern hardwood/spruce-fir mix after a disturbance. Also known as fire cherry, this broadleaf is a roughrider; it charges up hills, taking and holding land until other longer-lived trees can invade. Functioning as a site-prep specialist, this pioneer provides cover, shade, and humus for the next stage of succession. The short-lived pin cherry typically attains heights of 25 to 50 feet before succumbing to an early death, which often occurs only twenty-five to thirty years after first colonizing a disturbed site.

pin cherry

This cherry's narrow, lance-shaped leaves are most often 2½ to 5 inches in length, long pointed, and finely serrated with reddish teeth. Both twigs and leaf stems are red to reddish brown. Especially on branches and young boles, pin cherry bark is smooth and distinctive, ranging from bronze to a satiny reddish brown. The numerous corky horizontal lines (lenticels) on the bark further differentiate this member of the Rose family.

Three to eleven blossoms typically occur on flat-topped or rounded clusters. The five-petaled corollas are ½ inch wide and creamy white. The pin cherries at Little Sam's upper-elevation end were almost finished blooming on a recent May 24, and were still flowering on May 31 during a recent exceptionally rainy spring. The resulting ¼-inch-thick fruits are bright red and sour tasting. Many birds and mammals, including ruffed grouse and black bear, feast on the soft mast.

Alternate-leaf dogwood

The alternate-leaf dogwood (*Cornus alternifolia*) is more common beside Little Sam than along any other similar-length segment of trail in this guide. This shrub- to small-tree-sized dogwood grows in fairly rich soils from the lowest Southern Appalachian slopes up to near the summits (up to approxi-

alternate-leaf dogwood

mately 6,500 feet) of the highest peaks. Few woody plants in the Southern Highlands exhibit such a wide elevational range.

Three facts help distinguish this species: its leaves resemble those of the flowering dogwood in size and venation (the veins follow the margin of the leaf); it is the only dogwood that does not have opposite leaves; and it is the only *Cornus* species along this trail and in the Shining Rock area highcountry above 5,000 feet.

Crowding near branch ends, the alternate, prominently veined leaves are usually 2½ to 4½ inches long and frequently appear to be opposite or whorled. The leaves are often not obviously alternate except on long twigs, and the alternate pattern is easier to recognize by looking at the branches.

Saplings are green boled and green twigged; mature specimens lose their youthful color. Just beginning to bloom on a recent June 12, the alternate-leaf lacks the large showy white bracts of the flowering dogwood. Instead, it produces flat-topped or rounded clusters of tiny white blossoms with four narrow petals and yellow stamens. The resulting fruits and their stems are more colorful than the flowers. Starting in the last half of August, this small hardwood presents clusters of blue-black berries atop bright red or orange-red stems.

Directions

Little Sam is an interior trail that has its northern end on Flat Laurel Creek Trail and its southern end on MST-3.

To reach Little Sam's northern end, walk 1.1 miles on Flat Laurel Creek Trail starting from its northeastern, Black Balsam Trailhead at the paved end of FS 816. Usually marked with a carsonite sign, Little Sam heads uphill to the left and nearly west away from Flat Laurel Creek. (See Flat Laurel Creek, the following trail, for more information.)

The shortest route to Little Sam's southern end requires hiking 0.7 mile on three different treadways. Walk the Devils Courthouse Trail for 0.3 mile. Up high, where the wide track curls to the right toward the overlook, turn left and follow the blue-blazed Devils Courthouse–MST connector for slightly over 0.1 mile to where it ties into the MST at a T-intersection.

At the three-way intersection, where the MST makes a 90-degree turn at its trailpost, continue straight ahead on the white-blazed trail. Follow the MST for a little less than 0.3 mile to the usually signed and always obvious Little Sam junction. The entrance is to the left and roughly north.

The blue-blazed connector crosses over the Devils Courthouse Tunnel; its junction with the MST is on the other side of the parkway from the Devils Courthouse Overlook. (See Devils Courthouse, the preceding trail, for directions to its overlook parking area.)

Flat Laurel Creek Trail

Forest Service Trail 346   3.7 miles

Dayhiking Easy in either direction
Backpacking (low to high) Easy to Moderate
Backpacking (high to low) Easy
Vehicular Access at Either End Northeastern (higher
  elevation) terminus at the Black Balsam Trailhead at
  the paved end of FS 816, 5,815 feet; southwestern
  (lower elevation) terminus at Flat Laurel Creek
  Trailhead off NC 215, 5,040 feet
Trail Junctions Art Loeb Spur and IGT at the Black
  Balsam Trailhead, Sam Knob (two locations,
  Black Balsam Trailhead and at the western end
  of Sam Knob), Little Sam
Topographic Quadrangle Sam Knob
Blaze Orange on carsonite signs, a few plastic blazes
Usage Hike, bike, and horse
Features Year-round, fire-managed views; Flat Laurel
  Creek; wet-weather waterfalls; flowering shrub
  display; late summer and early autumn aster display

Flat Laurel Creek offers effortless walking, open views of three
nearby knobs, an excellent spring and early summer flowering
shrub display, a surprisingly high waterfall, and the clear, quick-
spirited water of its namesake stream. Winding northeast-south-
west primarily along the lower slopes of three named peaks, this
trail follows the bed of a former road for its entire length. Hiked

as described, all of Flat Laurel Creek's sustained grades are easy and downhill.

The easternmost 1.5 miles of this route, from its Black Balsam Trailhead to its junction with Sam Knob Trail, is part of a heavily tromped loop most often hiked counterclockwise—Sam Knob first, then the return segment of Flat Laurel Creek. Compared to its portion of the loop, the rest of this trail is lightly traveled.

On late summer weekends during blueberry-picking season, the trailhead parking area is often overflowing with cars parked along the shoulder of FS 816. The trails, especially this one and Sam Knob, are not anywhere near as crowded as the mob scene at the parking area would suggest. Bike usage is occasional; horse usage is rare, almost nonexistent.

The Forest Service's current controlled burn regime will ensure the continuance of unobstructed views to the inside of the Flat Laurel Creek–Sam Knob loop most of the way to the Little Sam junction. After the track turns west, you can spot the rounded dome of 6,214-foot Black Balsam Knob to the northeast. Most of the looks from this stretch feature the two scenic Sams—Little Sam Knob (5,862 feet at the benchmark) and Sam Knob (6,060 feet). Little Sam, with a Mohawk of dark spruce arced across its crown and a high rockface centered just below its highpoint, is close by and a little south of west as the route starts out from its upper-elevation end. Early on, Sam rears high into the northwestern horizon. This impressively rugged peak, studded with cliff faces and rock outcrops, changes profile from different vantage points. Near the beginning of the hike, Sam presents the length of his summit, a slight sag between a pair of rounded knuckles. Further along, after the route turns west, he shows off his southern side—narrow, conical, and craggy.

This trail is described as it is most often begun, from high to low, from northeast to southwest, from FS 816 to NC 215.

Beginning on the western slope of Black Balsam Knob, the treadway of the former road (much of it was railroad bed first) gradually descends to the south along the perimeter of gently sloping land. Here the track is a firebreak dividing line. To the right, much of the land inside the Flat Laurel Creek–Sam Knob loop is actively managed with fire so that it will remain in the early succession stage of herbs, low shrubs, and young saplings. The upslope land to the left has fire-free rein to succeed as it will. Currently, the young forest is a mix of small-needled conifers—red spruce and Fraser fir—and hardwoods cold hardy enough to handle the high elevation: yellow birch, mountain ash, pin cherry, red maple, serviceberry, and the shrub-sized upland willow.

At 0.6 mile you rock-step across a small, clear-water branch—the upper flow of Flat Laurel Creek—before turning to the west onto Silvermine Bald's lower slope. The hike reaches its usually signed junction with Little Sam Trail, which heads uphill to the left and nearly west at mile 1.1. Now traveling northwest, the easygoing grade comes to and crosses a headwater fork of Flat Laurel Creek—clear, cold, and usually only rock-step deep—0.3 mile beyond the Little Sam junction. Once across, the route soon parallels the boulder-bedded rush of its namesake stream on the lower slopes of Little Sam Knob.

At mile 1.5 Sam Knob Trail ties into Flat Laurel Creek at the usually signed T-junction beside the stream. If you turn right and cross the creek on a slab of bedrock jutting out well past the stream's middle, you will be on Sam Knob heading back to the Black Balsam Trailhead.

Following the quickly falling creek straight ahead, the line of march passes between the peaks of the two Sams—Little Sam on the left, Sam on the right. At mile 1.8, where stacked rocks stabilize the tread's edge above a former landslide chute, the gap in the vegetation affords an unobstructed view, for now, of the rockfaces and protruding outcrops on Sam Knob's conical southern side. Here a careful descent provides a close-up view of a cascade-pool-cascade run upstream and an unusual view in the other direction. Looking downstream from the jumbo boulder, 25 feet long and boot shaped, the narrow notch rising from the streambed frames mountains in the distance—small upside-down Vs inside the larger right-side-up V.

Beyond this view, the course pulls away from the entrenched creek, which dives down the precipitous slope in a long white pour known as Flat Laurel Creek Falls, a drop hundreds of feet high.

The trailside forest becomes more diverse as the mild downgrade ranges to the south, then southwest. At mile 2.1 you come to an open loafing and lookout spot atop a rock outcrop, the last unobstructed view. Fork Ridge's nearby crest is straight out to the west. This long lead rolls downhill to the north from the noticeably high and conifer-capped summit of Mount Hardy all the way to the West Fork Pigeon River.

The route passes a wet-weather falls that spills down both sides of the tread at mile 2.4. During a recent rainy spring, this slide swelled to small-branch size following substantial overnight showers. After finishing its half loop around Little Sam Knob, the wide track winds to the southwest through an increasingly hardwood forest where yellow birch and red maple are the thickest trees in the still-maturing forest. At mile 3.0 you cross a concrete bridge beside a slanting, low-volume waterfall, sliding and spilling down its wide rockface for perhaps 65 vertical feet. The drop of this Bubbling Spring Branch tributary, a thin glide during drought, is at its foaming best right after significant rain.

The hike curls around the upper ends of several hardwood hollows; thickets of rosebay rhododendron still frequently hedge the upslope bank. Sweet birch becomes increasingly common as the trail loses elevation. At mile 3.6 Flat Laurel Creek leads past a double-sided wet-weather falls—a pair of flowing curtains spilling over a 10-foot-high ledge. A tenth-mile further you cross creek-sized Bubbling Spring Branch before curving up through an active car-camping site close to trail's end at NC 215.

Nature Notes

Flat Laurel Creek has a relatively poor display of spring wildflowers. Its spring and early summer flowering shrub show, however, is widespread, diverse, and colorful. Fetterbush, dwarf rhododendron (blooming on May 25 and May 17 of recent years), Catawba rhododendron, mountain laurel, flame azalea, rosebay rhododendron, and bush honeysuckle add their ornaments in sequence starting in late April (fetterbush). Catawba rhododendron was just beginning to bloom on May 31, and it was in peak beauty on a recent June 12 along the upper-elevation half of the trail, while neither mountain laurel nor flame azalea had broken bud yet.

Bluets lined the upper trail on a recent May 31. In July, look for the blooms of bush honeysuckle and rosebay rhododendron as well as flowers from a few herbs such as Michaux's saxifrage and St. John's-wort.

Flat Laurel Creek also features an excellent late summer wildflower show. During late August and much of September assorted asters plus two species of gentian brighten the trailside.

Longtime Flat Laurel Creek hikers remember the late summer wash of yellow, when goldenrod blanketed acres of the gently sloping land inside the loop formed by Flat Laurel Creek and Sam Knob Trails. Until November of 2008, when the Forest Service conducted a controlled burn inside the loop, succession had been steadily displacing the goldenrod. Now, however, the Forest Service plans to employ fire to return much of the 200 acres inside the loop (pockets of red spruce and rhododendron will be spared from the flames) to baldlike conditions. And now, once again, the prolific goldenrod will reliably yellow a portion of the open land inside the loop.

Yellow birch

Classified as a northern hardwood, the yellow birch (*Betula alleghaniensis*) is the most numerous of the larger but still-young trees along the Flat Laurel Creek corridor. Not only is this birch the most abundant tree beside this trail, but it is also the most common trailside tree—conifer or broadleaf—above 4,500 feet in the Shining Rock region. It is the dominant tree at the upper-elevation end of the northern hardwood forest in the southern mountains.

yellow birch

Here, less than 20 miles north of the South Carolina border, yellow birch is nearing the southern limit of its huge range, which stretches from southeastern Canada down to the northernmost mountains of Georgia. Like the many other trees that require cool and moist conditions, this species enters the hot South only within the narrow peninsula of the higher mountains.

This broadleaf's curling bark identifies it from sapling size to maturity. The satiny, yellowish silver to yellowish bronze bark peels into long, thin-layered, horizontal strips. No other hardwood in the Shining Rock area (nor any other Southern Blue Ridge tree found above 2,000 feet) can be mistaken for this species. Mature specimens, those over the century mark, lose their youthful curls except on young branches and exposed roots.

Paired at the end of short branchlets, the toothed leaves turn bright butter yellow in autumn. The aroma of wintergreen emanates from cracked twigs, though not as strong as the scent wafting from sweet birch (aka black birch).

Yellow birch seedlings often germinate on mossy logs. If the fallen log is moist enough, the seedling continues to grow, sending straddling roots downward around the log. Eventually, its "nurse log" decays, leaving the tree, like a rider without a horse, propped up on the bowlegged stilts of its own roots.

stiff gentian

Stiff gentian

Two gentians, stiff and bottle, bloom during late summer and early autumn along Flat Laurel's wet banks and seep margins, especially on the route's wetter, sunnier, higher-elevation half. Usually confined to the mountains in the South, the stiff gentian is readily distinguished from its relatives by its significantly smaller size (most often 6 to 16 inches tall) and by its much smaller and more numerous flowers. The narrow, upright corollas of this branching annual are generally ¾ to 1 inch long. Tight clusters of these slender blossoms, as many as fifty or more individual flowers per plant, characterize this erect and stiff-looking herb.

Five fused petals form the tubular flowers, which vary widely in color. The stiff gentians beside this trail's wide treadway feature flowers that range between lavender and purple.

Bottle gentian

Large for its genus, the bottle gentian usually stands from 1 to 2 feet tall. Its five-lobed blossoms, 1 to 1½ inches long, range from pale to dark blue to a rich and royal purple-blue. The color and tapered shape of the flowers remind many aging hikers of the old-fashioned lights they wound around the family Christmas tree during their youth. This native perennial is one of the "closed" gentians, which means its lobes are shut tight and bumblebees must bully their way inside the blossoms to complete their mission.

bottle gentian

Gentians are among the last of the non-aster herbaceous plants to remain in bloom during the increasingly colder nights of high-elevation October. Both species were in flower on various dates between September 3 and October 7 in recent years. On the latter date most of the bottle gentians were faded to light brown, while the stiff gentians were blooming more profusely than they were two weeks before and were still in perfect color.

Pioneers once added gentian to their gin and brandy. People still sip gentian-flavored drinks today. If you have ever drunk Moxie, a soft drink still produced in New England, you have experienced the unusual and highly distinctive flavor of gentian extract.

Directions

Flat Laurel Creek has either-end vehicular access. Flat Laurel Creek's northeastern, Black Balsam Trailhead is located at the paved end of FS 816, and its southwestern trailhead is located off NC 215 north of the parkway.

Northeastern, Black Balsam Trailhead at the paved end of FS 816

Flat Laurel Creek shares the trailhead with Sam Knob, Ivestor Gap, and Art Loeb Spur Trails. Usually signed and always well worn, Flat Laurel Creek is the former road that continues straight ahead from the far end of the paved parking area. (See IGT, page 74, for directions to the trailhead at the paved end of FS 816.)

Southwestern trailhead off NC 215

Approach from the south: From the NC 215–access road from BRP junction, turn left onto NC 215 North toward Canton and travel 0.7 mile before turning to the right and down onto a narrow dirt-gravel road.

Approach from the north: From the four-way NC 215–NC 110–US 276 intersection, travel NC 215 South (also marked with a Love Joy Rd. street sign) approximately 17.0 miles before turning to the left and down onto a narrow dirt gravel road. If you miss this turn, you will come to the large MST parking area to the right of the highway a little more than 0.3 mile beyond the turn.

The entrance to the dirt-gravel road is usually marked with a carsonite trail sign on one side of the road and a campsite sign (BR-1 and tent symbol) on the other. There is a small, pull-in parking area to the right a few yards down the dirt-gravel road. Flat Laurel Creek is the old road that continues through the car-camping sites beyond the parking area.

Notes

Sam Knob Trail
Sam Knob Summit Trail

Forest Service Trails 617 and 617A

Sam Knob 617	1.0 mile
Sam Knob Summit 617A	0.8 mile one way out
	to the end of both forks

Dayhiking In (617) Easy
Dayhiking Out Easy to Moderate
Backpacking In Easy to Moderate
Backpacking Out Moderate
Dayhiking (617A) Moderate
Backpacking Moderate to Strenuous
Start (617) The Black Balsam Trailhead at the paved
    end of FS 816, 5,815 feet
    (617A) Junction with Sam Knob Trail, 5,670 feet
End (617) Junction with Flat Laurel Creek Trail just
    across Flat Laurel Creek, 5,430 feet
    (617A) Dead-ends at both highpoints atop Sam
    Knob, 6,060 feet at the slightly higher northwestern
    hump
Trail Junctions (617) Art Loeb Spur and IGT at the
    Black Balsam Trailhead, Flat Laurel Creek (two
    junctions, at the Black Balsam Trailhead and at the
    end of Sam Knob)
    (617A) Sam Knob
Topographic Quadrangle Sam Knob
Blaze (617) Blue, (617A) no blazes

Usage (617 and 617A) Foot travel only

Features (617) Maintained meadow; spring and summer wildflower display; year-round views of Sam Knob and Little Sam Knob

(617A) Sam Knob and its numerous rock outcrops; year-round views from the upper slopes and summit of Sam Knob until the forest recovers; late spring–early summer flowering shrub display

---

Sam Knob and its spur, the Sam Knob Summit Trail, offer open views of and from Sam Knob—a distinctively shaped peak rugged with cliff faces and large rock outcrops. Short and easily walked, heavily traveled and highly scenic, Sam Knob forms a half loop bowed north from east to west, from its prominent trailhead to its Flat Laurel Creek junction.

This route is frequently hiked as the first leg of a counterclockwise two-trail loop, which includes a 1.5-mile segment of Flat Laurel Creek back to the trailhead. This loop lengthens to 4.1 miles if you take the side-trip spur to the top of Sam Knob and out to both highpoints.

Beginning on the woods road to the right of the stone outhouse, the well-worn treadway enters a quickly regenerating forest. Red and mountain maple, red spruce and Fraser fir, pin cherry, mountain ash, and yellow birch have blocked the views and made this stretch of the track more tunnel-like. The roadbed becomes gullied and rocky from straight-line erosion where it descends a little harder (this part of the trail may be rerouted in the future) before entering the wildlife opening at 0.4 mile.

Located in the gap between Sam Knob and a Black Balsam Knob spur, the mowed meadow provides sunny, open habitat for native and naturalized wildflowers plus unobstructed views of the high rolling and ridged horizon all around. Sam Knob, a shape-shifting mountain that offers a different profile from every cardinal point, looms nearly straight ahead.

The route reaches its usually signed junction with the Sam Knob Summit Trail on the western edge of the meadow at 0.6 mile. Here Sam Knob turns left, skirts the margin of the opening, then makes an overall easy-to-moderate downslope run slanted a little west of due south. The tread quickly becomes a firebreak between the controlled burn unit to the left and recently recovered forest to the right, where deciduous heath shrubs (blueberries) remain abundant at this stage of succession. (See Flat Laurel Creek, the preceding trail, for information concerning the controlled burns.) Rock steps and boardwalks—a job well done—prevent parts of this downhill stretch from becoming an eroded and bemired mess. Yellow birch and red maple are the thickest of the still-young trees.

With 0.1 mile remaining the footpath rock-steps a thin Flat Laurel Creek feeder. Across the branch, the open, fire-maintained grassy area to the left supplies close-up views of Sam's sweeping rise and rock outcrops to the north and Little Sam's rounded arc of red spruce to the southwest. The course dips to and crosses the cold and clear flow of Flat Laurel Creek at a stream-narrowing slab of bedrock, then ties into its usually signed T-junction with Flat Laurel Creek Trail. A left turn onto that track finishes the loop back to the Black Balsam Trailhead at the paved end of FS 816.

Sam Knob Summit is a short, dead-end spur that ascends to Sam's pair of gently rounded knuckles, the highpoints separated by the scallop of a shallow saddle. The roundtrip distance of the spur plus the forks to both humps is 1.6 miles. This trail is well routed and well constructed—with rocked-in switchbacks and rock steps—to reduce both erosion and difficulty. Most of the hiking is no more difficult than easy to moderate; almost all of the quick, step-up pitches are less than 10 yards in length. The resilient forest is rapidly recapturing Sam's upper slopes and summit, blocking both the formerly open views to nearby mountains and uphill views to Sam's rugged outcrops.

From the usually well-signed junction at the western end of the meadow, follow the arrowed sign for Sam Knob Summit to the right. After less than 50 yards, the path veers left, enters the young forest, then gains elevation easily on Sam's southeastern slope. For now, northern hardwoods control most of the canopy and subcanopy. Below the broadleafs, the shrub layer is composed of deciduous and evergreen heaths, primarily mountain laurel and Catawba rhododendron.

Switchbacking, rock-stepping, and steadily slanting uphill, this popular route swings around Sam's upper-south side, the slope studded with outcropped rock. At 0.5 mile a very short sidepath to the left dips to a rock outcrop overlook open to the south and Little Sam Knob.

A tenth-mile further you come to a fork where paths lead left and right up to their respective highpoints on Sam's crown. Pin cherry and mountain ash are the two most abundant trees atop Sam's summit at present. The easygoing left fork passes a low breach of quartz before ending at the northwestern highpoint, the taller of the two at 6,060 feet, after slightly less than 0.1 mile. This fork ends at a rock outcrop that will afford good views straight out until the trees grow higher. Saplings to the right will quickly screen open views of Cold Mountain, Shining Rock, and Grassy Cove Top. The large slab of rock a short distance to the left should offer wide-range views for a few decades to come.

Fork Mountain is the nearest uplifted fold to the right of the first overlook at 35 to 40 degrees. Four miles out at around 350 degrees, High Top is the pivot point and last peak you can see along the Fork Mountain crest as it descends to the north-west, then north. Lickstone Bald's well-defined highpoint (8.0 miles) is located on its namesake ridge at around 333 degrees.

The highest local peak (6.0 miles, 6,410 feet—122 feet higher than New England's loftiest summit, New Hampshire's Mount Washington), Richland Balsam's conifer-dark crown thrusts up just this side of the parkway at around 303 degrees. Lickstone Ridge rolls to the right and nearly north away from Richland Balsam. Piney Mountain's distinctive and unusually flat ridge-line lies to the left of Richland Balsam's shoulder (across the parkway). Piney's highest tectonic fold, slowly raising the land left to right, helps identify Richland Balsam from a wide range of angles and distances.

Nearby at around 283 degrees, Green Knob (1.5 miles) is the only named highpoint on Fork Ridge as it ascends to the south toward Mount Hardy. Rough Butt Bald's broad bulk (4.1 miles) is just across the parkway at around 265 degrees, and Mount Hardy's evergreen cap is just this side of the parkway at around 234 degrees.

The fork to the right, which ends after slightly less than 0.1 mile at a low huddle of view-providing outcrops (for now, saplings are already reclaiming the left side of the prospect), leads to the downhill edge of Sam's southeastern hump. Black Balsam Knob's gently sloping summit (1.1 miles, 6,214 feet) is impossible to miss at around 96 degrees. The craggy profile of Devils Courthouse (1.7 miles) is unmistakable at around 190 degrees, and Chestnut Bald, rounded and domed, mounts the sky just to the left of the courthouse (1.5 miles, barely over 6,000 feet). Across Flat Laurel Creek, Little Sam Knob's ridgetop Mohawk of spruce arcs over its high rockface only a half mile away at around 204 degrees.

Toxaway Mountain (14.5 miles), flat crowned and tipped with a tower, is easily recognized at around 208 degrees. Mount

Hardy rears up at around 234 degrees (2.6 miles, 6,125 feet), and Rough Butt Bald's silent reach is immediately across the parkway at around 264 degrees (4.1 miles).

Nature Notes

Sam Knob's two ends of recently regenerated forest are separated by a maintained meadow in the middle. (The east side of the lower-elevation end is now in a controlled burn unit.) This meadow supplies open habitat for numerous sun-loving wildflowers, a few of them, including fireweed, found rarely or

nowhere else along the trails in this guide. The meadow provides this treadway's best herbaceous wildflower show, starting in spring and lasting through the colorful aster display in late summer and early autumn. Now that a low-intensity fire regime has been instituted inside much of the loop formed by Sam Knob and Flat Laurel Creek Trails, goldenrod and other early-succession wildflowers should also be common along the eastern side of the lower stretch of this route.

fireweed

Fireweed

For now, the summer-blooming fireweed grows beside the Sam Knob Trail just before it enters the meadow, at the leading edge of succession from herbs to shrubs and saplings. In season, this tall perennial is easily identified by its clusters of pink to magenta blossoms above narrow lanceolate leaves. The four-petaled flowers, approximately an inch across, open starting from the bottom of the tall stem, a spikelike raceme. Much more common farther north and in the northern Rockies, this native herb is uncommon to rare throughout its range in the heavily forested Southern Appalachians. The fireweed reaches the southern limit (in the east) of its huge range in the high mountains of Tennessee and North Carolina. It was in flower on a recent July 2, 7, and 18.

Over the past decade, the leading edge of the returning forest has quickly surged to Sam Knob's crown. Flowering shrubs now provide the best and most abundant late spring and early summer beauty along the Sam Knob Summit Trail. Catawba rhododendron decorated Sam's high slopes on a recent June 12. On July 2 bush honeysuckle was in fresh bloom, mountain laurel and flame azalea were at their tag ends, and the Catawba rhododendron's flowers had already fallen.

Appalachian St. John's-wort

The Appalachian St. John's-wort (*Hypericum buckleyi*) is an unusual Southern Appalachian endemic inhabiting high-elevation balds, rock crevices, and rocky seepage slopes. This low woody shrub (usually less than 2½ feet high) often forms

Appalachian St. John's-wort

large mats on sunny, exposed sites. This plant's status as a Southern Appalachian endemic does not accurately convey the limits of its range. An older reference lists this species from only five counties, four in North Carolina and one in South Carolina. Haywood County, where

Sam Knob is located, and two of its bordering counties—Jackson and Transylvania—form the largest island of its discontinuous and miniscule range.

The Appalachian St. John's-wort is readily identified along this trail because it is the only low, rounded, dark green shrub growing out of the crevices in Sam Knob's rock outcrops and cliffs. The small paired leaves of this species are simple, opposite, entire (not toothed along the margins), and sessile (stemless) or nearly so. The bright lemon-yellow blossoms are five petaled and approximately ¾ of an inch wide. The distinctive flowers, crowned with a starburst of yellow stamens, were enlivening trailside rockfaces on July 5 and 11 of recent years.

Directions
Sam Knob, Ivestor Gap, Art Loeb Spur, and the northeastern end of Flat Laurel Creek all share the same major trailhead. Sam Knob's wide and often signed entrance is at the end of the vehicle-blocking boulders to the right of the stone outhouse. (See IGT, page 74, for directions to the Black Balsam Trailhead at the paved end of FS 816.)

Part 3

Middle Prong Wilderness

And Nearby Trails to the South

Josh Leventhal

View from meadow off
Green Mountain Trail

Middle Prong Wilderness

0   0.25   0.5 miles

0   0.25   0.5 kilometers

Middle Prong Wilderness and Nearby Trails to the South

Meadow rising from the edge of the MST

Trails

Bearpen Gap	Buckeye Gap
Mountains to Sea, Section 1	Mountains to Sea, Section 2
Haywood Gap	Green Mountain

Bearpen Gap Trail

Forest Service Trail 442	0.6 mile

Dayhiking Easy in either direction
Backpacking Easy in either direction
Start Bearpen Gap Parking Area, 5,560 feet
End Junction with Mountains to Sea Trail west of
    Rough Butt Bald, 5,380 feet
Trail Junction MST-1, MST continuing to the northwest
    to the GSMNP
Topographic Quadrangle Sam Knob
Blaze A few blue blazes
Usage Foot travel only
Features Easy walking away from the parkway;
    wildflower displays; MST access trail

Bearpen Gap is a short, botanically rich means to a very long
end: the Mountains to Sea Trail. This upper-slope route, the
third shortest trail described in this guide (excluding the Graveyard Fields system), offers easy, pleasant walking away from the
parkway. The road-to-trail treadway heads generally southwest
along the northwestern and western slopes of 5,925-foot Rough
Butt Bald.

If you haven't the time or inclination to hike all of MST-1 but
wish to walk beyond the end of Bearpen Gap, try combining this
trail with the 0.7-mile segment of the MST to Wet Camp Gap.
This will make an easy round trip of 2.6 miles, from the Bearpen
Gap Parking Area to the wildflowers and remaining views at the

maintained wildlife opening in Wet Camp Gap and back again. (See MST-1, the following trail section, for more information.)

Beginning behind its trailpost and vehicle-blocking rock jumble, Bearpen Gap quickly dips to the gradual downgrade of the old roadbed and enters the Nantahala National Forest. Here the trailside timber is a mix of highcountry conifers and cold-tolerant hardwoods: red spruce and sapling Fraser fir mingled with sugar maple, yellow buckeye, beech, black cherry, and yellow birch, the most common large broadleaf. (BBD has decimated Bearpen Gap's maturing beech; see front matter for details.) Mountain ash and two small maples, striped and mountain, catch what sun they can in the understory. At 0.4 mile the track crosses the first of two spring-run rivulets, high-elevation headwaters of Piney Mountain Creek to the west. Both rivulets provide habitat for a linear colony of umbrella-leaf.

Look for the Bearpen Gap–MST connection where another woods road rises from a bend-back angle on the right to join the Bearpen Gap treadway. If you continue straight ahead in the direction you were walking (245 degrees), you will be on the white-blazed MST (MST-1 in this guide) heading toward the sea. If you turn downhill and sharply to the right, you will be hiking toward the MST's western terminus atop Clingmans Dome in the GSMNP.

Nature Notes

Although it is only a short access trail, Bearpen Gap features an excellent spring wildflower display with a surprising diversity for its length.

Spring beauty is the earliest of the first wave of wildflowers. This native perennial was recently in bloom on April 19, while the super abundant trout lily had yet to break bud. The best time to catch the most species in bloom is between May 5 and

26. During those three weeks you can usually spot the blossoms of bluebead lily, sweet cicely, doll's eyes, yellow mandarin, Canada mayflower, wakerobin, foamflower, wood anemone, mayapple, and mountain meadow rue.

By summer the slope is lush with tall herbs—primarily asters, cohoshes, and parsnips—flanking the trail and covering up what remains of the vernal wildflowers. The square-stemmed crimson bee balm blossoms dark red beside the rivulets from mid-July through early September. The tall white wands of the black cohosh wave in the wind from late July through most of August. Late August to September 20 is the time for pale jewelweed, pink turtlehead (late August and early September), and assorted asters such as white snakeroot and goldenrod.

umbrella-leaf

Umbrella-leaf

The aptly named umbrella-leaf (*Diphylleia cymosa*) holds aloft the largest herbaceous plant leaf in the Southern Appalachians. Nonflowering stems support a single giant and jagged leaf 1 to 2 feet across. Flowering stems require two somewhat smaller leaves to provide enough solar-powered energy. All the platter-sized leaves are deeply cleft in the middle, and each half has five to seven toothed lobes. No other woodland wildflower in the southern mountains features leaves the size and shape of this species.

This 1½- to 4-foot-tall rhizomatous perennial devotes much more of its biomass to foliage than flower. A small cluster of white six-petaled blossoms—½- to ¾-inch wide with yellow-orange stamens—rises well above the two broad leaves. The berry and stem combination, dark blue berries atop long, bright red or orange-red stems, is more colorful than its small flowers. The umbrella-leaf colonies were in bloom and bud on May 23 and 25 of recent years, and they were all but finished blooming on a recent June 9. The berries and stems were conspicuous on September 5 and 14 of recent years.

This member of the Barberry family, which also includes the mayapple, is a Southern Appalachian endemic. Its genus is represented by only two species: this one and an almost identical plant in the mountains of Japan.

This large-leaved herb needs to keep its feet wet in cool, often shady mountain forests. While it sometimes grows beside small streams and in seeps, it is most numerous and conspicuous where large colonies stretch into lush, tropical-looking linear swaths down rocky seepage runs. Because of its stringent habitat requirements, this forb is uncommon to rare throughout much of its range. Here in these high moist forests, however, the umbrella-leaf is noticeably more common (occasional) than in the lower, warmer mountains further south.

Directions

Bearpen Gap begins at the Bearpen Gap Parking Area located between BRP mileposts 427 and 428. The route, marked with a short trailpost, begins at the far left corner of the parking area.

Approach from the south: From the BRP–access road from US 74 junction, turn left onto the parkway and travel approximately 15.7 miles to the parking area on the right side of the road.

Approach from the north: From the BRP–access road from NC 215 junction, turn right onto the parkway and travel approximately 4.2 miles to the parking area on the left side of the road.

Mountains to Sea Trail, Section 1

(Junction with Bearpen Gap Trail to junction with the access trail leading from Rough Butt Bald Overlook)

Forest Service Trail 440   4.0 miles Mountains to Sea only, 4.8 miles including both access trails

Dayhiking (low to high) Moderate
Dayhiking (high to low) Easy to Moderate
Backpacking (low to high) Moderate to Strenuous
Backpacking (high to low) Moderate
Vehicular Access near Either End Northwestern (higher elevation) access at Bearpen Gap Parking Area, 5,560 feet; southeastern (lower elevation) access at Rough Butt Bald Overlook at Buckeye Gap, 5,420 feet
Trail Junctions Bearpen Gap, MST continuing to the northwest to the GSMNP, Haywood Gap, access trail from Rough Butt Bald Overlook, MST-2
Topographic Quadrangle Sam Knob
Blaze White circle, no blazes within wilderness
Usage Foot travel only
Features Wilderness; late spring–early summer flowering shrub display; occasional old-growth trees; open meadow in Wet Camp Gap; diverse spring wildflower display

Primarily an upper-slope route, MST-1 is smack in the statistical middle of the five MST sections described in this guide. It ranks third in difficulty, and although it is the shortest of the five, its access mileage bumps it up to third in overall length for those who hike one short segment of the MST at a time. Section 1, which remains above 5,000 feet for its entire length, has no sustained grades more difficult than easy to moderate.

Walked as described, moderately used MST-1 half-loops to the south around 5,925-foot Rough Butt Bald before descending to Haywood Gap, then half-loops to the north around two more knobs before ending near Buckeye Gap. Dayhikers often walk this track only as far as the maintained meadow in Wet Camp Gap before turning back.

The northwestern end of this section follows the old road that continues straight ahead (245 degrees) from its occasionally signed Bearpen Gap junction. Walk the white-blazed MST for 0.1 mile to the metal posts of a former gate, then remain on the only route as it bends to the left and up onto a woods road. After an initial rise, the trail settles down to mild grades across Rough Butt Bald's southwestern slope. Here the forest is predominantly hardwood, including sapling American chestnut, with a small conifer component of red spruce and Fraser fir. At 0.4 mile you come to the first of the vehicle-blocking, piled-boulder barricades. A short distance farther, several steep-sided tank traps block the width of the road for the same reason.

At 0.7 mile the treadway enters a grassy wildlife opening, then quickly turns nearly 90 degrees to the left, crossing the narrow upper portion of the meadow before returning to blazed forest. Follow the road straight ahead and downhill if you want to see the rest of the wildlife opening and its remaining views. This mowed meadow lies in Wet Camp Gap, a saddle cradled in the ridgeline between Rough Butt Bald and Gage Bald straight ahead across the gap.

Now on single-file footpath, the trek continues along the southern and southeastern slopes of Rough Butt Bald. Here the MST threads through forest with a larger conifer component mixed in with the cold-adapted hardwoods, including mountain maple and the abundant northern red oak. After descending for most of 100 yards, the frequently undulating trail continues to gradually gain elevation. At 0.9 mile the sidehill track passes through a boulder field, much of the treadway rock now laid flat or in steps; a tenth-mile further it makes a double switchback before continuing the easy upgrade.

The course zigzags up through a closely set pair of double switchbacks before entering a pocket of red spruce, some of them thick and low branched. The character of both the trail and forest changes at mile 1.4. Now the often needle-cushioned tread is wider, level side to side, and much less rocky. The frequently open forest features a large conifer component mixed with northern hardwoods. In season, the forest floor is a scatter of grass, evergreen wood fern, and the long, linear leaves of fly poison surrounding the breach of low rock outcrops.

Less than 100 yards past the section highpoint (5,680 feet, mile 1.5), the path veers to the right onto the ridgeline leading east from Rough Butt Bald. Here you begin the 0.7-mile descent to Haywood Gap. This downhill run, a mix of easy and easy-to-moderate grades, quickly swings off the spine and begins a series of modified switchbacks—left, right, then back left again—as it works its way down the broad snout of the ridge.

The MST crosses the parkway at Haywood Gap (mile 2.2, 5,235 feet) and continues straight into the woods across the road. At mile 2.3, Section 1 reaches its usually signed junction with the Haywood Gap Trail (the left fork). Here the footpath turns to the right and nearly east onto moist north-facing slope.

All of the sustained grades along the frequently undulating final 1.7 miles are easy.

Across the parkway, the sidehill hiking closely follows the 5,200-foot contour as it half-loops to the north-northeast around 5,420-foot Parker Knob. It then gains elevation more steadily along its second end-run half loop, this one bowed to the north around 5,490-foot Burnt Birch Knob. Most of both half-loop humps travel through or along the boundary of the Middle Prong Wilderness, where the route is unblazed.

Because the elevation doesn't vary much, and because nearly all of the exposures fall within the relatively moist range—from northwest to east—the forest along the final 1.7-mile stretch remains much the same: an assemblage of cold-tolerant hard-woods mixed with the two small-needled conifers. Yellow birch is by far the most abundant broadleaf, and most of the thickest boles also belong to this northern hardwood. Yellow buckeye, sugar maple, red spruce, northern red oak, and black cherry also rise into the canopy overhead. Fraser fir, silverbell, and two more maples—mountain and striped—compete for sun in the dimmer light of the subcanopy and understory. Catawba rhododendron dominates the shrub layer, and the forest floor is frequently a dense weave of grass, ferns, and herbaceous wildflowers, especially verdant during rainy years.

After curving over Parker Knob's broad ridgeline and turning south at mile 2.6, the easygoing grade follows the sidehill along a gently shelving slope (mile 2.8) where most of the forest floor is covered with wind-combed grass by mid-May. At mile 3.2 the trail crosses the first of as many as half a dozen wet-weather rivulets as it rounds the seepage slope of a broad upper hollow. The MST turns northeast at the beginning of the second half loop (still mile 3.2), then crosses the most reliable (but still intermittent in drought) of the coldwater rills at mile 3.5 before entering an area where the hay-scented fern frequently patterns the forest floor in season.

The tread bends to the right over a spur at the northernmost point of the second half loop (mile 3.6) before heading mostly south on the home stretch. Sixty-five yards before the access trail, the track passes through an extensive and conspicuous colony of false hellebore (some already 18 inches high on a recent May 5). Section 1 ends at its usually signed T-junction with the access trail (to the right, entrance about 215 degrees) leading to the parkway's Rough Butt Bald Overlook.

Nature Notes

This MST section features a wide array of herbaceous spring wildflowers and a good late-spring flowering shrub show. The forest floor comes alive with first-wave wildflowers—early bloomers such as trout lily, spring beauty, wood anemone, wakerobin, and squirrel corn—from mid-April through May 5. On a recent April 18, spring beauty bloomed by the thousands all over the slopes just beyond the Haywood Gap Trail junction. On the next Saturday, April 25, the prolific trout lily and two species in the *Dicentra* genus—squirrel corn and Dutchman's-breeches—were blossoming along with the spring beauty.

Over thirty-five forbs were in bloom on May 24 of a recent year. A partial roster includes Vasey's and painted trilliums, speckled wood and bluebead lilies, umbrella-leaf, rose twisted-stalk, mountain meadow rue, and Canada mayflower.

On June 9, while Michaux's saxifrage, wood sorrel, tassel rue, and a few others bloomed beside the trail, the abundant and beautiful trio of flowering heath shrubs—flame azalea, mountain laurel, Catawba rhododendron—provided most of the vibrant hues, especially along the higher-elevation segment from Rough Butt Bald to Haywood Gap.

A second burst of wildflower color occurs during the last third of August and September. It is then that the large and attractive asters showcase their dominance in both the number of species and their sheer abundance. An extensive wild aster garden graced the meadow in Wet Camp Gap on a recent September 8.

Fly poison

Particularly common along short stretches of this MST section, fly poison is tall and eye catching when in bloom. This highcountry herb is readily identified by its dense cluster of small, creamy white blossoms and its long grasslike leaves. The ¼- to ½-inch-wide flowers wrap around the 2- to 4-inch-long cluster. This cluster (raceme is the botanical term) is borne atop a stem usually rising from 1 to 3½ feet high. The fly poison's petals do not fade and fall shortly after pollination; they persist on the raceme and slowly turn green or greenish purple as they age.

fly poison

The basal leaves, less than an inch wide and with unusual V-shaped ribs, grow up to 2 feet in length. But they don't stand that high; they droop under their own weight.

This species' numerous flowers open from the bottom up. On June 26 and 29 of recent years most of the fly poison along this section were blooming about halfway up their cylindrical racemes, so it is likely they ordinarily reach peak sometime during the first two weeks of July. This member of the Lily family is most common along the segment of trail from the meadow south of Rough Butt Bald to the parkway at Haywood Gap.

This native perennial is toxic, especially the underground bulb. The alkaloids present in all parts of the plant are deadly enough to kill wild boar or backpacker. As its name suggests, portions of the plant were once employed to poison flies.

white snakeroot

White snakeroot

White snakeroot (*Eupatorium rugosum*), which Native Americans once used to treat snakebite, is most common on rich, moist hardwood slopes up to approximately 6,000 feet in elevation. It is especially abundant on high, northwest- to northeast-facing slopes. This variable, rhizomatous perennial is usually 1½ to 4 feet tall and may have one or several stems. The paired opposite leaves are sharply toothed, ovately shaped, and most often 3 to 6 inches long.

This forb is a member of the Composite family, which means that it is an aster. Its tiny white flowers, tightly bunched and fuzzy, occur in rounded to flat-topped clusters. Large colonies of white snakeroot bloomed in profusion along this MST section on a recent September 8.

This plant is also poisonous, and milk from cows that have grazed it will cause milk sickness in humans, an especially serious disease for young children. During periods of the nineteenth century, milk sickness was the leading cause of death in the nation.

False hellebore

The false hellebore (*Veratrum viride*) is the first large-leaved herb to herald resurrection in the uplands of Southern Appalachia. During early spring, when the first wave of small wildflowers animate the forest floor, this member of the Lily family has often already thrust a foot or more of green above winter's brown thatch. Not only does the false hellebore grow fast and early, but its large leaves—dark green and pleated—also provide a welcome flourish of strikingly patterned foliage. This herb's alternate leaves, oval shaped and 6 to 12 inches long, curve up and outward from their stem-clasping bases.

false hellebore

Unlike most wildflowers, false hellebore is at its showy best well before it blooms. It also fades with summer's heat. This native perennial's leaves are already ripped and ragged by the time the small, star-shaped flowers, yellow-green and easily overlooked, appear in midsummer. After blooming, it turns brown and withers away. By late summer these 2- to 4-foot-tall plants have vanished, melted back to underground dormancy.

False hellebore is able to unfurl its conspicuously large and otherwise vulnerable leaves during early spring—when herbivores and some omnivores are ravenously searching the forest for fresh greens—because the entire plant is poisonous. Its leaves are laced with highly toxic alkaloids; its roots are even deadlier. The parallel-veined leaves are patterned with pleats for a purpose: the fancy foliage serves as a learning aide, a cue prompting lifelong memory after that first small bite.

Directions

Section 1 has vehicular access near either end. Its northwestern access is located at the Bearpen Gap Parking Area between BRP mileposts 427 and 428, and its southeastern access is located at the Rough Butt Bald Overlook at Buckeye Gap between BRP mileposts 425 and 426.

Northwestern access
at the Bearpen Gap Parking Area

The 0.6-mile Bearpen Gap Trail provides access to the northwestern end of Section 1. Bearpen Gap's old road ties seamlessly into Section 1's northwestern end. Continue straight ahead, west-southwest, from the Bearpen Gap–MST junction and you will be walking on the white-blazed MST toward its access trail to the Rough Butt Bald Overlook. (See Bearpen Gap, the preceding trail, for directions to its parking area.)

Southeastern access
at the Rough Butt Bald Overlook

The short access trail leading to the southeastern end of Section 1 begins across the BRP from the overlook. Turn left onto

the MST and you will be on Section 1 heading toward the
Bearpen Gap Trail. A right turn sets your feet on the western
end of Section 2 heading toward NC 215. (See MST-2, page 243,
for directions to its western access at the overlook.)

Notes

Haywood Gap Trail

Forest Service Trail 142   **4.0 miles**

Dayhiking In Moderate
Dayhiking Out Moderate to Strenuous
Backpacking In Moderate to Strenuous
Backpacking Out Strenuous
Start Junction with Mountains to Sea Trail at Haywood
   Gap off the parkway, 5,230 feet
End FS 97 (road gated except during hunting season),
   3,590 feet
Trail Junctions MST-1, Buckeye Gap
Topographic Quadrangle Sam Knob
Blaze None (primarily wilderness)
Usage Foot travel only
Features Wilderness; Haywood Gap Stream; Middle
   Prong; diverse forest; spring wildflower display

This lightly trod, mostly riverine route parallels and crosses Haywood Gap Stream and the Middle Prong as it loses elevation from south to north, from Haywood Gap off the BRP to FS 97 well above the water. For most of the way, the track remains within earshot or eyesight of the cold clear flow—on cloudless days a sun-dazzled and rock-split race of sluices and slides, of pours, pools, and cascades.

This trail becomes progressively flatter from south to north. The second half is comparatively mild; the northernmost mile is easy as a daydream. The southernmost 1.4-mile segment, however, is a Middle Prong special—a wilderness path, narrow and ungraded, occasionally rocky, fun for only the confident and reasonably firm of knee.

Haywood Gap's southernmost 2.3 miles are often hiked as the first or last leg of a three-trail loop. This loop is easier to follow counterclockwise, the MST and then all of Buckeye Gap first, because it is much easier to find the Buckeye Gap–Haywood Gap junction coming from this direction.

Beginning in the BRP corridor on the northeast edge of Haywood Gap, this route immediately drops into a high, north-facing hollow—cool, moist, and wildflower rich. Here in the open forest of the uppermost hollow, you pass beneath an over-story of yellow birch, sugar maple, and yellow buckeye. A few red spruce add the contrast of their dark conifer green to the palette. After an overall downgrade of at least moderate difficulty, the footpath enters the Middle Prong Wilderness, usually marked with a pair of signs.

The descent soon parallels the notched run from Sweetwater Spring. At 0.2 mile the track enters rosebay rhododendron, then doglegs down and to the left before crossing rivulet-sized Haywood Gap Stream. Now on the west side of the branch, the trail loses elevation, sometimes sharply, as it closely accompanies the quickly gathering waters of the stream. At mile 0.5 a gap in the rhododendron allows the first good look at the cascading brook. Following a 0.1-mile respite of easy downhill hiking, the tread-way leads across a short length (less than 40 yards) of once tightly parallel timbers, now slanting and slick, slowly rotting and sliding downslope.

At 0.7 mile the path dips to and crosses a small feeder draining Possum Hollow (below a high and narrow cascade—fast, white, and loud when the water is up), then quickly makes its first short dive to the now creek-sized stream. Here, close to the flow, the course offers good views of the boulder-bedded run. This unusual maneuver—abruptly dropping to near bank level (none of the pitches longer than 30 yards), then closely shadowing the current before rising above and further back from the fast-falling creek—becomes a pattern repeated three more times, the second and steepest at mile 0.8.

The trek begins a stretch of effortless sidehill walking at 0.9 mile, much of it on old railroad bed through a predominantly hardwood forest where black cherry is common. At mile 1.1, where the level grade continues straight ahead, the footpath angles down and to the right as it returns to the wilderness-clear water. It then closely escorts the brook on a former rail line shaded by sweet birch and narrowed by flanking doghobble. The route abandons the bed, then dips to ford (rock-step crossing when shallow, feet-wet ford when higher) the suddenly larger stream at mile 1.4 (4,310 feet). This ford is a short distance below where Buckeye Creek and Haywood Gap Stream combine waters and lose their names to the Middle Prong.

Once across, you enter rhododendron and pick up the gradual grade of the rail line again. The prominent sidepath up and to the right at mile 1.5 leads to a campsite. Ninety yards further, where there is a gap in the trail along the outside edge of a bend in the Middle Prong, you must do whatever you think is best— go low or stay high—to negotiate the bottom of the small bluff.

The rest of Haywood Gap, with a few short exceptions, follows the old aisles of railroad and road, most of the grades mild as milk. At first, the riverine forest is often numerically dominated by the birches, yellow and sweet, which share the canopy with white ash, white basswood, and northern red oak. Red maple replaces sugar maple as the course continues to lose elevation. The wide track parallels the fast-falling Middle Prong as it slowly rises higher above and further away from the white-water cascades. The route begins to swing away from the Middle Prong at mile 2.0 in order to cross a sidestream where its banks present no problems. Two-tenths mile further, you rock-step across Grassy Ridge Branch and continue straight ahead up the low bank.

The line of march arrives at the roughly right-angle four-way intersection that marks its junction with the Buckeye Gap Trail at mile 2.3 (4,010 feet; N 20 22, W 56 57). Haywood Gap continues on its wide promenade straight ahead; the path to the left leads to a campsite, and the narrow tread running to the right and up (entrance 125 degrees) is Buckeye Gap.

The sidehill grade returns to its view-providing position above the prong at mile 2.4. Here your feet feel the occasional corduroy rows of old railroad ties, reminders that most of this cove was clear-cut to the quick, leaving no merchantable boles standing. The track crosses the very small volume Camp Two Branch, its name another reminder of the logging era, at mile 2.5. Haywood Gap continues above the creek-sized stream, affording frequent looks at the foaming cascades and short pools between drops. At mile 2.9 the trail begins an easy-to-moderate downgrade. After swerving to the left, the route makes one last steep drop to the fast-flowing water, where it fords the Middle Prong just downstream from a 10-foot-high cascade and plunge pool at mile 3.0 (3,750 feet).

According to the Forest Service map, Haywood Gap leaves the wilderness immediately after the ford. Now on the west side of the stream and traversing the lower slopes of Little Beartrail Ridge, the hike no longer closely follows the prong, which quickly slips away and becomes deeply entrenched well below and out of sight from the treadway. A tall, straight, second-growth hardwood forest, including mature silverbell, grips the steep downslope to the right of the woods road. The yellow poplar is the tallest, thickest, straightest, and most numerous tree in the resurgent forest. Here the downhill sweep of a yellow poplar stand adds the ancient grace of its vertical symmetry.

After rising back up to the 3,800-foot contour, much of the final mile gradually loses a little more than 200 feet of elevation. With 0.1 mile remaining the route crosses rock-step-shallow Little Beartrap Branch, cascading above and below tread at full flow. Haywood Gap's northern, lower-elevation end ties into FS 97 at the outside middle of a sharp curve.

Nature Notes

On a recent April 18 Haywood Gap's uppermost hollow—high, lush, largely hardwood—was densely stippled with thousands of spring beauty, the first and only widespread wildflower color of spring. A week later trout lily and Dutchman's-breeches bloomed by the hundreds while wakerobin and wood anemone (abundant and blooming on a recent May 9) were just starting to open. A huge colony of waxy-leaved mayapples promised more flowers for their appointed month, and the tall, fancy-leaved species of false hellebore was already several feet high.

The remainder of the route, which quickly descends into the riparian zone of rhododendron and doghobble, has a good spring wildflower display, including most of the common moist-site species plus larkspur and rose twisted-stalk. April 25 to May 10 is the best time to see the highest number of blooming forbs.

The herb layer in this high hollow is 2½ to 3½ feet tall by mid-June. On a recent August 31 and September 11 the area was full of flowering white snakeroot, brightening the woods in the uppermost hollow.

On a recent August 10 and 25, one of the upper-elevation seeps had turned into a pocket of vibrant color with the red of crimson bee balm, the orange of spotted jewelweed, the pink of pink turtlehead, the yellow of a large aster, and the orange-red stems and blue-black berries of umbrella-leaf.

Yellow buckeye

Identifying the yellow buckeye (*Aesculus octandra*) is a cinch in the Southern Appalachian highcountry for two simple reasons. Buckeyes are the only trees in the eastern forest with opposite leaves and five palmately compound leaflets (leaflets from a single center splayed out like spokes on a wheel). No

other buckeye climbs into the cold of the higher elevations in the southern mountains, and no other buckeye occurs beside the trails in this guide. The five saw-toothed leaflets are usually 4 to 7 inches long on mature trees and often even larger on saplings.

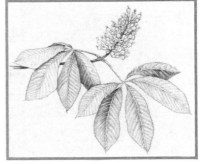

yellow buckeye

Yellow buckeye is the first broadleaf to break bud in the spring; on a recent April 25, it was the only hardwood already leafed out in Haywood Gap's highest hollow. This tree's elevation range spans from the river bottoms to approximately 6,200 feet in the Southern Appalachians. It is most common and grows best in the deep rich soils at middle and upper elevations. The yellow buckeye is a major component of the cove and northern hardwood forests, and occasionally mingles with red spruce and Fraser fir.

A medium to large-dimensioned tree, *A. octandra* is by far the largest of the buckeyes. It reaches its most impressive size in the mountains of Tennessee and North Carolina. Specimens from 13 to 15 feet in circumference and 110 to 130 feet tall were common in the most fertile coves before industrial logging. The national record yellow buckeye—136 feet tall and 19 feet 1 inch around—adds grandeur and wonder to the nearby GSMNP.

Early settlers likened the shiny, dark brown nut (poisonous) with its large pale scar to the eye of a deer.

Trout lily

The trout lily belongs to the first wave of spring wildflowers, the relatively small ones that push their way through the warm-

trout lily

ing soil so that they can leaf and flower before trees and the taller second wave of forbs steal their sun. Like the mayapple and umbrella-leaf, this herb requires energy from two leaves to bear a blossom. The trout lily's paired basal leaves, shiny and often prominently mottled with purple-brown, are usually 3 to 7 inches long when the plant blooms. The single leaves of nonflowering lilies are smaller, less colorful, and much less conspicuous across a colony.

The solitary yellow flowers nod from 3- to 8-inch stems. The 1- to 1½-inch-wide corollas consist of three petals and three sepals that arch gracefully backward toward each other until their tips often almost touch. Short rust-colored washes or speckled streaks frequently flare up from the center onto the lowermost third of the similarly colored sepals and petals. The blooms close back up at night and during cold cloudy days.

Locally abundant in rich, moist, predominantly deciduous woods, this diminutive member of the Lily family often occurs in dense colonies covering large patches of the forest floor. Like many other spring ephemerals, whose above-ground season between too cold and too shady is short, the trout lily grows and reproduces slowly. Because it takes individual plants seven or more years to produce their first blooms, flowering specimens are often somewhat scarce across a colony.

This herb's most widely accepted common name arose from the fancied resemblance of its mottled leaves to the speckled sides of Southern Appalachia's only native trout (actually a char), the now beleaguered brook trout.

Squirrel corn and Dutchman's-breeches

Two of the most unusual wild-flowers in the southern mountains— squirrel corn and Dutchman's-breeches—join the first color bearers of spring on Haywood Gap's highest hardwood slope. These low, native perennials are closely related; they share the same genus: *Dicentra*. Both have finely divided, deeply cut leaves, and both bear small creamy white flowers (approximately ¾ inch in height) that resemble manmade

squirrel corn

forms. Dutchman's-breeches display two inflated spurs that form the V-shaped legs of tiny pantaloons, cuffs up, waist down. The squirrel corn's shape is the Valentine's Day heart. It is so named because squirrels are fond of its yellow, kernel-like tubers. The flowers and foliage of these spring ephemerals quickly fade away after their short time in the sun.

Dutchman's-breeches

Directions

Haywood Gap's southern trailhead is located off the parkway at Haywood Gap between BRP mileposts 426 and 427, and its northern trailhead is located off FS 97. Haywood Gap has either-end vehicular access, however, only when FS 97 (Lickstone Road) is open. Except during hunting season, FS 97 is gated 0.3 mile in from its entrance off NC 215. (Contact the Forest Service for opening and closing dates.)

Southern trailhead at Haywood Gap

Approach from the south: From the BRP–access road from US 74 junction, turn left onto the parkway and travel approximately 16.7 miles to Haywood Gap. Look for the usually signed gap 1.0 mile beyond the Bearpen Gap Parking Area.

Approach from the north: From the BRP–access road from NC 215 junction, turn right onto the parkway and travel approximately 3.2 miles to usually signed Haywood Gap.

A sturdy wooden guardrail lines the south side of the BRP in Haywood Gap. The white-dot blazed MST (Section 1) crosses the parkway at the higher end of the guardrail opposite the on-grass parking area. Enter the woods on the parking-area side of the road and walk 55 yards to the MST sign, which marks the MST–Haywood Gap junction. Here where the MST turns to the right and nearly east, Haywood Gap Trail bears left, then curls down and to the right, quickly descending into the head of a hollow.

Northern trailhead off FS 97

Approach from either north or south: The directions to the entrance of FS 97 are essentially the same as those for Fork Mountain Trail. (See Fork Mountain Trail, page 65, for directions to its trailhead beside the West Fork Pigeon River.) If you are traveling from the south on NC 215 North, cross the NC 215 bridge over the Middle Prong, then immediately turn left onto dirt-gravel FS 97 just before Sunburst Campground. If you are traveling from the north on NC 215 South, turn right onto FS 97 immediately after Sunburst Campground and immediately before the bridge over the Middle Prong.

From FS 97: FS 97 makes three looping switchbacks in succession. The first switchback (mile 1.3) is to the right, the second to the left, and the third back to the right again. Recently marked with a 97H sign, Haywood Gap's northern trailhead is located to the outside of the third switchback's curve. An opening to the left funnels trail users toward the path on Haywood Gap's old roadbed.

If the gate is open, travel FS 97 a little less than 1.9 miles to the middle of the third switchback and park there. If the gate is closed, park there (the Forest Service requests that you do not block access through the gate) and walk the easy uphill grades of the road for a little less than 1.6 miles to the middle of the third switchback.

Buckeye Gap Trail

Forest Service Trail 126   **3.0 miles**

Dayhiking (low to high) Moderate
Dayhiking (high to low) Easy to Moderate
Backpacking (low to high) Moderate to Strenuous
Backpacking (high to low) Moderate
Interior Trail Southern (higher elevation) terminus
   on Mountains to Sea Trail, 5,540 feet; northern
   (lower elevation) terminus on Haywood Gap Trail,
   4,010 feet
Trail Junctions MST-2, Haywood Gap
Topographic Quadrangle Sam Knob
Blaze None (wilderness)
Usage Foot travel only
Features Wilderness; spring wildflower display;
   occasional old-growth trees; Grassy Ridge Branch

Buckeye Gap's dissimilar halves make it a Dr. Jekyll and Mr. Hyde
type of trail. The higher half follows a rail-to-trail treadway as it
gradually loses elevation on the upper-west slope of Fork Ridge,
a major lead rising southward to Mount Hardy. Here, above a
mile high, much of the young forest has recently regenerated
from formerly open land. Beyond where the course turns down
and to the west off the railroad bed onto ridgetop, the lower
half drops 1,280 feet in 1.4 miles, occasionally sharply and
often on narrow path. This stretch descends into a recovered
forest of taller and older trees.

This lightly used interior route is often trekked as the eastern leg of a three-trail loop—MST (parts of Sections 1 and 2), Buckeye Gap, and Haywood Gap, beginning and ending at the parkway from either Haywood Gap or the Rough Butt Bald Overlook. Buckeye Gap is described starting from its most easily reached and located end, from high to low, from south to north, from its MST-2 junction north-northwest of Mount Hardy down to its Haywood Gap Trail junction near the Middle Prong.

Beginning near the highest headwaters of Buckeye Creek, the track follows the easy, slightly descending grades of the former railway to the north. The washboard ripples of the vegetation-covered ties are still plainly visible in places. The forest often alternates between open hardwoods (yellow birch the most numerous as usual at this elevation) and evergreen pockets of rhododendron, red spruce, and Fraser fir. Below the hardwoods, the light-gap growth often pinches the tread to narrow footpath by early summer, while the conifers and heath shrubs generally maintain and frame a wide and shady aisle. Colonies of evergreen wood fern frequently add their finely cut symmetry to the upslope edge of the route.

The sidehill hiking repeatedly dips to slender threads of spring water, all of the rivulets running westward to nourish Buckeye Creek. At mile 1.1 the line of march crosses the downflow most likely to withstand prolonged drought. Early succession species such as pin cherry and mountain ash continue to screen the last of the open views.

At mile 1.6 (5,290 feet) the trail swerves down and to the left off the wide track onto ridgeline, a Fork Ridge spur ramping down to the northwest (west while the path remains on its crest). Now the Mr. Hyde half of the route rides the top of the fold downhill, losing nearly 300 feet in 0.3 mile as the hardwoods become more dominant with the loss of elevation. Most of the sustained grades are easy to moderate or moderate; the steeper pitches are much shorter. At mile 1.9 you begin a span of effortless walking along a wide ridgetop flat, a rich wildflower garden in spring and late summer. Striped maple and yellow buckeye are unusually abundant along this nearly level stretch.

At mile 2.1, just before the footpath heads downridge more sharply, Buckeye Gap's thickest trailside tree—an old-growth sugar maple 11 feet 2 inches in circumference—stands 14 paces to the right (N 19 71, W 56 21 at the treadway directly opposite the tree). This maple's shaggy, light gray bark is blackened by fungus low on its trunk, a common occurrence that helps identify old-timer sugar maples.

Still descending at a quick clip, the track bends to the right and down, doglegging off the keel onto a rich, north-facing slope at mile 2.2. Less than 20 yards after leaving the crest, the trail passes another old-growth sugar maple (this one with a girth of 10 feet 3 inches) 4 paces to the right of the route. During the bare-branch season, you can spot a larger sugar maple (circumference 11 feet 5 inches) approximately 35 yards to the left of the trail and opposite the maple just mentioned. Eighty yards further down the steeply dropping path, look for the flaky, reddish brown bark of another old-growth tree: a lunker silverbell with a circumference of 10 feet 5 inches is located 15 long paces to the right of the treadway (N 19 80, W 56 26 at the tree). Hollowed out and topped out, this giant of its species had seen much better centuries before the one-two punch of Hurricanes Frances and Ivan stripped off most of its remaining larger limbs in 2004. By 2012, this hardy old silverbell had not only lived into a new decade but had also generated a vigorous growth of new branches.

The downhill hiking continues on grades ranging from easy to moderate through a tall, second-growth hardwood forest with a dense ground cover of ferns and herbaceous wildflowers. The course rock-steps Grassy Ridge Branch between cascades at mile 2.5.

Across the sidestream, the trail angles downslope on an ungraded wilderness track, losing a little over 500 feet of elevation to the northwest in its final 0.5 mile. Despite its nearly 20 percent overall gradient, the descent works its way down— passing an occasional rock outcrop or large boulder on the downslope edge—with only a few short surges steeper than moderate. The upper end of the downgrade provides glimpses of the brook's quick white cascades. Further down, the slope falls away through an open forest of white ash, black cherry, white basswood, and sweet and yellow birch shading a luxurious herb layer—an aster garden in late summer.

Buckeye Gap ties into Haywood Gap Trail at a roughly right-angle four-way intersection. Haywood Gap passes through the junction to the left and right; left heads upstream toward the parkway at Haywood Gap. The fourth tread, the sidepath continuing straight ahead before bending to the right, leads to a campsite above the Middle Prong.

Nature Notes

Buckeye Gap's lower-elevation half, the stretch beyond where the treadway swerves down and to the west off the old railroad grade, features an excellent spring and fall wildflower display. On a recent April 25, much of the slope to the left just above the flat at mile 1.9 was slick with acres of densely packed trout lily, their yellow blossoms bright in the sun. On that same day spring beauty flowered in white drifts, squirrel corn and Dutchman's-breeches were abundant and blooming, and yellow mandarin and blue cohosh were in early flower.

On a recent May 8 yellow mandarin, foamflower, sweet

cicely, rose twisted-stalk, and wakerobin provided a second wave of color on the lush hardwood slopes, and many more were in bud or leaf.

On one sunny October 9, the moist slopes near the lower-elevation end of the route hosted aster gardens that included white snakeroot, goldenrod, whorled wood aster (white blooms), white wood aster, and heart-leaved aster (lavender blossoms). On that same date blue cohosh and doll's eyes were easily identified by their colorful and conspicuous berries. The cohosh held aloft bright, blueberry-hued berries. The doll's eye's bright red stems and shiny white berries with black dots make it unmistakable.

Carolina silverbell

Carolina silverbell

Commonly known as pea-wood in the old days, the Carolina silverbell (*Halesia tetraptera*) is also occasionally called snowdrop tree or mountain silverbell today. Throughout most of its range, which is confined to the South, this broadleaf is a shrub or small tree. But in these fertile, well-watered mountains, it regularly grows to heights of 65 to 80 feet and girths from 6 to 8 feet. The largest specimens rise to over 100 feet and measure from 10 to over 12 feet around. It is hard to believe that the tall, straight silverbell in the Southern Blue Ridge is the same species as the stooped understory tree in the upper Piedmont foothills of Georgia and South Carolina.

This hardwood's alternate leaves—usually 3 to 6 inches long, finely saw-toothed, and long pointed at the tip—are not particularly distinctive. The appearance of its bark, fruit, and flower, however, is unique in the Shining Rock region. The bark on seedlings and saplings is longitudinally lined with light yellow-gray streaks. Body armor on mature trees is typically dark reddish brown or blackish brown and divided into small, flaky squares.

Dangling in clusters beneath the branches, the countless bell-shaped blossoms wave back and forth in the spring winds. The flowers are white, four-lobed, and ½ to 1 inch long. The resulting chestnut-colored fruits have four broad, symmetrical wings running the length of the seedpod. The Buckeye Gap silverbells were in full bloom on a recent May 2 of a rainy and cool spring, and a few flowers were still swinging in the wind on May 8 of another year.

H. tetraptera most often remains an understory tree, but it frequently gains and holds the canopy where it makes its best growth. At mile 2.2, as the treadway descends toward Grassy Ridge Branch, the trail passes through a small stand of mature silverbells. This stand was much more noticeable and impressive before Hurricanes Frances and Ivan slashed through the forest.

Wood anemone
Primarily a northern species—another glacial gift to the South—the wood anemone (*Anemone quinquefolia*) is most common in the cool, moist northern hardwood forest and in the mix of northern hardwoods and spruce-fir in the Shining Rock area. On a recent May 8, the wood anemone was abundant and blooming on the wide spur-top flat at mile 1.9. This delicate native perennial, usually only 4 to 8 inches tall, exhibits a solitary, 1-inch-wide white flower with four to nine petal-like sepals and numerous pale yellow stamens and pistils.

Also known as windflower, this forb generates two sets of leaves, one upper and the other basal. The whorl of upper leaves

is usually three in number, and each of those leaves is usually divided into three sharply lobed leaflets. The specific name *quinquefolia* refers to the basal leaves, which tend to be five segmented.

The wood anemone is a true spring ephemeral. Once pollination occurs, the sepals fall off and the fruit quickly develops. Soon afterward, the leaves die back and all the above-ground green vanishes, leaving nothing but the memory of them until the following spring.

wood anemone

This wildflower's seeds often disappear from sight too. Ants not only help disperse anemone seeds, they also plant them in their well-aerated tunnels. Like trilliums, the wood anemone has evolved tender, fleshy extensions on the sides of their seeds that offer ants a nutritious food reward for their effort, a process known as ant farming. Not only does each seed come ready made with a built-in food bribe (called an elaiosome), but that fleshy food is also shaped to serve as a handle, allowing the workaholic insects to quickly march to underground safety with the otherwise slippery seeds. After consuming the edible handle—obtaining more energy to haul in more anemone seeds—the ants ditch the impenetrable seed casings in their fertile compost pile. There the seeds germinate and sprout, making more anemones and more ant food, a beneficial symbiosis for both. Looking through evolution's ever-adaptive eye, the result is the same as if the seeds had sprouted six legs, walked away from the competition of their rooted progenitors, then buried themselves in a fertile underground spot away from seed predators. Even with a liberal allowance of time, that is still not a bad trick for the brainless.

Directions

Buckeye Gap is an interior trail that has its southern end on the MST and its northern end on Haywood Gap Trail.

The shortest distance to Buckeye Gap's southern end is on MST-2 starting from its western access point at the Rough Butt Bald Overlook. Following an old railroad bed, Section 2 crosses branch-sized Buckeye Creek at mile 1.0. One-tenth mile further, the MST curls up and to the right where the former railroad bed continues straight ahead. The level grade of the old railway (entrance 30 degrees; N 18 63, W 55 91) is Buckeye Gap. (See MST-2, the following trail section, for further information.)

The Buckeye Gap–Haywood Gap junction can be difficult to locate while walking Haywood Gap Trail in the early spring before Buckeye Gap's entrance becomes defined with use. Hiking Haywood Gap Trail from high to low, from south to north, you will cross Grassy Ridge Branch at mile 2.2. Less than 0.1 mile beyond that crossing, you will come to what looks like a four-way junction after recent use. The path to the left leads to a campsite; Haywood Gap continues straight ahead. The narrow, sometimes faint path to the right and up (entrance 125 degrees) is Buckeye Gap. The junction (N 20 22, W 56 57) is located in a small area of recently recovered forest. (See Haywood Gap, the preceding trail, for further information.)

Mountains to Sea Trail, Section 2

(Junction with the access trail leading from Rough Butt Bald Overlook to NC 215)

Forest Service Trail 440   4.6 miles Mountains to Sea only, 4.7 miles including access trail

Dayhiking Easy to Moderate in either direction

Backpacking Moderate in either direction

Vehicular Access at or near Either End
Western (higher elevation) access at Rough Butt Bald Overlook in Buckeye Gap, 5,420 feet; eastern (lower elevation) terminus off NC 215, 5,130 feet

Trail Junctions Access trail from Rough Butt Bald Overlook, MST-1, Buckeye Gap, Green Mountain, MST-3

Topographic Quadrangle Sam Knob

Blaze White circle, no blazes within the wilderness

Usage Foot travel only

Features Wilderness; extensive fern colonies; views from open areas until forest recovers; Catawba rhododendron display; sidepath to Mount Hardy.

Often following old railroad beds, MST-2 ranks fourth in both difficulty and length (access trails included) of the five MST sections described in this guide. Most of the hiking is easy; there are no sustained grades of even moderate difficulty. The MST-2 treadway remains within the Middle Prong Wilderness for all but a few-tenths mile of its length.

Trekked from mountains to sea as described, this moderately used, predominantly upper-slope hike half-loops to the north around Mount Hardy. Like Sections 1 and 3, MST-2 remains above 5,000 feet, and nearly all of it ranges between the 5,200-foot and 5,800-foot contours. Most of the exposures span from northwest to northeast. The flora found on these cool and moist slopes is much the same throughout this section—a pleasing mix of cold-hardy broadleafs and conifers in the canopy; the glossy evergreen of rhododendron in the understory; and the intermingled patterns and textures of grass and fern on the forest floor.

The yellow birch is by far the most numerous tree species along this section. Red and sugar maple, yellow buckeye, and northern red oak share the canopy with the omnipresent birch. Mountain ash, serviceberry, and mountain maple are common in the subcanopy and understory.

Fraser fir and red spruce comprise the conifer component. Although they are abundant within small pockets throughout, these two short-needled evergreens are most common along this section's highest elevations, where the trail rises to and descends from its Fork Ridge crossing.

The trailside understory is frequently controlled by Catawba and rosebay rhododendron. These evergreen heath shrubs heighten the sense of straight, aislelike travel where they line a railroad grade. The evergreen wood fern often grows beneath the shade of the conifers and Catawba rhododendron. Pale green and delicate as a lace doily, the prolific hay-scented fern forms almost pure monocultural colonies in the sunnier areas.

The railway walking quickly enters the Middle Prong Wilderness. Here, on this first stretch, the trail contours to the northeast on the flank of Wolf Bald, a named knob on Hardy's western shoulder. The track crosses the first of many intermittent rivulets at 0.3 mile. All of the headwaters south of the route's first ridge contribute to Haywood Gap Stream, the western fork of the Middle Prong. At 0.7 mile the long-trail treadway turns to the right up to and over the crest of a Mount Hardy spur, then continues to the east, gradually gaining elevation on wide grade again.

At mile 1.0 you cross the drought-proof upper run of Buckeye Creek, the eastern headwater fork of the Middle Prong. The sidehill route arrives at its Buckeye Gap Trail junction (5,540 feet; N 18 63, W 55 91) a tenth-mile beyond the stream. Where Section 2 veers sharply to the right and up, the logging grade continuing nearly straight ahead (entrance 30 degrees) is the Buckeye Gap Trail.

Now heading east along Mount Hardy's northern slopes, the wilderness path rises through recently regenerated forest before skirting the downhill edge of an opening, which extends up to the nearby ridgeline and eastward almost to the Green Mountain Trail. (A backpacker-caused fire burned most of the opening in February of 2011.) Back in young woods, the narrow tread winds and undulates upward on a seepage slope of wet-weather spring runs, dipping to their notches and then ascending easy and easy-to-moderate grades toward the gap.

At mile 1.6 a spur to the right and up (entrance 140 degrees; N 18 53, W 55 55) leads to the top of Mount Hardy. Look for this sidepath immediately before the usually signed MST bends to the left and crosses a small boggy spot. At mile 1.7, Section 2 arrives at its T-intersection with the Green Mountain Trail at the small, pack-drop opening in Fork Ridge's southernmost saddle (section highpoint at 5,805 feet; N 18 58, W 55 51). The entrance to Green Mountain is to the left and nearly north.

Over the gap, the course continues its winding half loop around Hardy, losing elevation on mostly easy or easy-to-moderate grades frequently shaded by rhododendron and conifer. At mile 2.1 the track begins a stretch of nearly effortless walking atop a wide spur ridge that lasts 0.3 mile before it angles off the crest. Following a pair of modified switchbacks, the footpath descends to and crosses a pair of rivulets, the first at mile 2.5. A tenth-mile further the trail ties into the straight run of another logging grade.

Section 2's southernmost segment ranges outside of the wilderness from approximately mile 2.8 to mile 3.0. After returning to the wilderness and entering older woods, the route switches from railroad bed to sidehill path at mile 3.1. The MST dips down and sharply to the right onto a wide aisle at mile 3.3. Forty-five yards beyond this turn (N 18 16, W 55 02), you can spot a wet-weather waterfall in the distance to the left (306 degrees) under certain conditions: there must still be a gap in the trees, and there must have been substantial recent rainfall, the more the better. If both of these conditions are met, you will see a high, narrow ribbon of foaming white bisecting its gray, water-worn rockface.

The line of march soon makes a horseshoe-bend switchback down onto another logging grade heading in nearly the opposite direction. Here the hike approaches and parallels the west fork of Bubbling Spring Branch before skirting its streambed rocks and crossing an intermittent rivulet on the right side of the larger watercourse at mile 3.6. The brook quickly slants down and away from the trail, which continues its mild grades to the northeast.

The track enters a steadily shrinking meadow in a shallow saddle at mile 4.1. As part of the biological wilderness, this former wildlife opening's few acres will rapidly regenerate to young forest. At last tromp through, the meadow was already a jailbreak of briers, saplings, and shrubs. The top crag of Devils

Courthouse is nearby and will remain visible from the upper end of the opening for a few more years yet.

At mile 4.4 the trail reaches a usually signed fork; the MST follows the prominent path leading uphill and to the right, where the former access road to the opening continues straight ahead. The route parallels NC 215 to the south before dipping to and rock-stepping across Bubbling Spring Branch at mile 4.6. The short remainder rises to the Middle Prong Wilderness sign and section end at the MST post beside NC 215.

The sidepath to the top of Mount Hardy—sporadically brushed out, unblazed, and usually unmapped—is 0.6 mile long and gains approximately 370 feet of elevation. Hardy's benchmark is set in a knot of low rock immediately to the right of the path (N 18 26, W 55 63; 6,110 feet) at slightly less than 0.5 mile. Beyond the benchmark, the most prominent path skirts the left (east) side of the summit before heading downhill toward the BRP.

Nearly 0.1 mile beyond the benchmark, where the path is still on the left side of the crest, there is a low huddle of stand-up rock to the right of the track, nearby but unseen from the tread. Flagging frequently marks the entrance toward the rock. Hardy's crown has three of these small knots of stand-up rock. GPS readings and the slight downhill slant to the other two convinced me that this clump (N 18 20, W 55 63), which has initials carved on a rockface and is occasionally flagged, is Hardy's highpoint: best rounded-off estimation—6,125 feet.

Nature Notes
The dense and extensive shade from rhododendron thwarts a good wildflower display along much of this MST section. The

abundant and richly hued blossoms of the Catawba rhododendron more than atone for the paucity of forest-floor flowers. The pageant usually peaks during the first two weeks of June. The stream-flanking rosebay, the Catawba's larger and later-blooming cousin, usually opens its white to pale-pink flowers by July 4.

On a recent April 26, spring beauty and trout lily were common and blossoming along the first few tenths of a mile starting from this section's Rough Butt Bald Overlook access point. Wood sorrel, easily identified by its circle of three valentine-heart leaflets and its small white blooms etched with pink lines, was in color on a recent June 20. Pink turtlehead, spotted jewelweed (orange blossoms), black cohosh (tall white wands), plus asters such as white snakeroot and goldenrod enlivened late summer hikes on a recent August 24 and September 4. Goldenrod (still blooming on a recent September 27) is especially prolific in the upslope opening before the Green Mountain Trail junction.

Red spruce

Section 2 frequently winds through pockets of spruce-fir forest mixed with northern hardwoods. The only native spruce found in the Southern Appalachians, the red spruce (*Picea rubens*) is by far the tallest conifer at these elevations, generally between 5,200 and 5,800 feet. Although it is found sporadically in northern-exposure coves below 4,200 feet, this cold-adapted evergreen is most common between 5,000 and 6,100 feet in the Shining Rock area.

Three short-needled conifers—red spruce, Fraser fir, and eastern hemlock—find suitable habitat (for now) in the Shining Rock region. These three trees can be quickly differentiated by their needles and cones. Spruce needles, closely set and spirally arranged, bristle around their twigs in all directions. Usually longer than the hemlock's needles (⅓ to ⅔ inch long) and shorter than the fir's fragrant needles (½ to 1¼ inches long), the ½- to ¾-inch-long needles of the spruce are four sided, sharp pointed, and entirely green. In contrast, hemlock and fir needles are flat, soft pointed, and streaked with two white stripes on their undersides.

If you want to further verify your visual identification, place a needle between your forefinger and thumb and try to roll it back and forth. The keeled spruce needle will readily roll, the flat fir needle will not. Another tactile test to determine a spruce is to tap the palm of your hand against the tips of the needles; if you feel a sting from the sharp points, it is a spruce.

The pale reddish brown cones of red spruce are 1¼ to 2 inches long and hang downward from the branches. The tiny cones of the hemlock, which is increasingly scarce above 5,200 feet (and increasingly wiped out by the hemlock woolly adelgid), average only ¾ inch long, and the 1½- to 2½-inch-long cones of the Fraser stand upright on the branch.

Evolved to shed northern snow, the graceful lower limbs of *P. rubens* sweep away in shallow concave arcs, canting upward at their needled outer ends like turkey vulture wings. A medium to large tree, this species is intermediate in size between the much smaller Fraser fir and the larger eastern hemlock. The dimensions given in most guidebooks—50 to 80 feet in height and 1 to 2 feet in diameter—are northern dimensions. Down here in the moist, deep-soiled, and relatively warm Southern Highlands, these steeple-topped evergreens grow to impressive proportions. Primary growth spruce in nearby GSMNP—unswervingly straight, crowns conical, 90 to 120 feet tall—rise pagodalike above all other trees at higher elevations. Both national co-champion red spruce are rooted in the park. The slightly larger of the two is 123 feet tall and 14 feet 1 inch in circumference. The largest of its kind ever recorded, a Southern Appalachian giant, was 162 feet tall and 14 feet 11 inches in circumference.

Hay-scented fern

Only two ferns, the hay-scented and the New York, establish extensive, nearly monocultural colonies of thousands and thousands of ground-carpeting vascular plants in the southern mountains. Like the New York, the hay-scented emerges from the duff at regular intervals, creating a uniform symmetry similar to an agricultural crop. Two factors account for this fern's patterned appearance and abundance. Its underground rhizomes produce evenly spaced, cloned colonies. And, like the New York, this pteridophyte promotes its dominion by poisoning many other competitors, an evolutionary advantage that allows it to spread across acres of the forest floor.

hay-scented fern

The hay-scented's alternate pinnae—thin textured, yellow-green, and delicate—produce the light sweet scent of newly mown hay, especially during and right after rain. You can sniff the same scent by rubbing your fingers on their foliage. Its arching, finely cut, deciduous fronds are most often 12 to 30 inches high. Because their beds are often intermingled, it would appear that the two species have developed at least a detente level of immunity to the other's poison. While the hay-scented is the most plentiful fern along this section of the MST, it falls to second place (New York is first) in the Shining Rock–Middle Prong area as well as the entire Southern Appalachian region.

Evergreen wood fern

Gracing cool, moist slopes, the evergreen wood fern is mountain bound at the southern end of its extensive range. Here, in the Shining Rock region, this species is predictably abundant in the high mix of the spruce-fir and northern hardwood forests.

evergreen wood fern

Large, dark green, and glossy, the evergreen wood can be identified with minimal familiarity with botanical nomenclature. Its clustered, arching fronds (the visible parts of the plants) are usually 16 to 30 inches long, and its foliage is finely wrought and lacy. The oval or narrowly triangular blade (the leafy part of the plant) tapers gradually to a pointed tip. The rachis (the main stem above where the foliage begins) is prominently grooved.

When most other ferns have been frostbitten to brown crumples in the fall, this fern, true to its name, remains green. Over the winter, the fronds slowly turn yellow-green and ragged as they bend to the ground. The old fronds are still there and recognizable when the new crosiers break ground in the spring.

Directions

Section 2 has vehicular access at or near either end. Its western access is located at the Rough Butt Bald Overlook at Buckeye Gap between BRP mileposts 425 and 426, and its eastern trailhead is located off NC 215.

Western access at the Rough Butt Bald Overlook

Approach from the south: From the BRP–access road from US 74 junction, turn left onto the parkway and travel approximately 18.0 miles to the overlook on the right side of the road.

Approach from the north: From the BRP–access road from NC 215 junction, turn right onto the parkway and travel approximately 2.0 miles to the overlook on the left side of the road.

The short access trail leading to the western end of Section 2 begins across the BRP from the overlook. Turn right onto the MST and you will be on Section 2 heading toward NC 215. Turn left and you will be walking Section 1 toward its Bearpen Gap Parking Area access point.

Eastern trailhead off NC 215

Section 2's eastern trailhead is located off NC 215 just north of the BRP. This trailhead is the eastern end of Section 2 and the southwestern end of Section 3. (See MST-3, page 167, for directions to its southwestern trailhead off NC 215.)

Green Mountain Trail

Forest Service Trail 113   **5.6 miles**

Dayhiking In Strenuous to Rugged
Dayhiking Out Moderate to Strenuous
Backpacking In Rugged
Backpacking Out Strenuous
Start West Fork Pigeon River Trailhead, 3,115 feet
End Junction with Mountains to Sea Trail north
   of Mount Hardy, 5,805 feet
Trail Junctions Fork Mountain (at trailhead), MST-2
Topographic Quadrangle Sam Knob
Blaze None (primarily wilderness)
Usage Foot travel only
Features Wilderness; rhododendron tunnels; Fork
   Ridge; rock outcrops; year-round views; steepest
   sustained grades in the combined wildernesses

Rugged, chock full of character, and infrequently trekked end to
end, Green Mountain is the most difficult trail detailed in this
guide. The first mile of this scenic footpath features frequent
calf-busting, heart-hammering, straight-up-the-ridge grunts—
the full treatment. Green Mountain's total elevation change—
predominantly up, some down, not counting the many dips
around ridgeline rock—is over 3,700 feet. This memorable route
is rated PG: you need to be in pretty good shape to enjoy it, its
steep grades sometimes provoke involuntary cursing from those
who are carrying excess weight on their bellies or their backs,

and parents should not allow their young children to attempt it. But if you're fit and firm of knee and searching for a challenge along with highcountry beauty, try Green Mountain from bottom to top and back down again.

The longest of the four trails or trail sections mostly within the Middle Prong Wilderness, Green Mountain closely follows the crest of Fork Ridge from north to south, from its trailhead beside the Middle Prong to its upper-elevation junction with MST-2 just below Mount Hardy. Most hikers who set sole on this treadway walk it northward from its high-elevation end for various distances, usually no further than Green Knob, before turning back. The steep portion of the track, from the river to Green Knob, is lightly traveled. The top of Fork Ridge is the wilderness boundary for the trail's first 1.9 miles; the forest falling away to the east is within the wilderness.

After a warm-up of 30 yards, the route heads straight up the abrupt rise of the ridge—no switchbacks, no wiggling side to side—just straight up through the sharply slanting aisle of heath shrubs. This rigorous first pull kicks off with a fast-climbing ascent rated rugged, then eases up for a few feet at 0.1 mile before the tilt of the land steepens again. After the demanding first 0.2 mile, which really gets on the elevator and easily earns a strenuous-to-rugged rating for dayhikers, the trail slabs to the right of the crest and bypasses a rock outcrop on easy grades. Riding the narrow ridgetop again, the route is shaded by a forest of hardwoods above evergreen heath. The oaks, especially the chestnut oak, control the canopy over the next layer down, the subcanopy broadleafs— Fraser magnolia, sourwood, sassafras, striped and red maples, among others. The evergreen heaths, two species of rhododendron and mountain laurel, often form archways and tunnels.

Most of the two-tenths mile, ridgeline run to the top of a narrow-crested knob at 0.6 mile (4,010 feet) is strenuous.

Following the quick descent to the first gap (3,900 feet) at 0.7 mile, the uphill hiking continues on the long lead of Fork Ridge. After a respite of gentle grades, the climb becomes progressively more difficult to a whaleback slab of outcrop open straight out to the east-southeast at mile 1.1.

This overlook offers a good but short view of a high horizon of tall peaks. Nearby Fork Mountain is the first ridgeline across the deeply entrenched drainage of the West Fork Pigeon River. Less than 2.0 miles away, Birdstand Mountain is the prominent and named knob on Fork Mountain at nearly east. Part of Grassy Cove Top's rounded dome is visible over Fork Mountain and to the right of Birdstand at around 103 degrees. Sam Knob heaves the land up to 6,060 feet in the upper basin of the West Fork at around 145 degrees. The broad and gently sloping crown of Black Balsam Knob, the highest summit in sight at 6,214 feet, is easily recognized just to the left of and slightly over a mile further away than Sam.

The elevation gain continues on narrow crest often studded with rock outcrops. Where the ridge rises more sharply into rock, or it roaches to a point—all rock and rhododendron—the tread slips off the top of the fold and skirts below the obstacle before working its way back to the keel again. This bypass maneuver becomes an oft-repeated pattern. After nearly 0.4 mile of mostly easy walking, Green Mountain ascends past the first huddle of red spruce at mile 1.5.

For the next half mile, from 1.5 to 2.0, the trail's southward lift is much less challenging than along the first mile. At mile 1.6 the course picks its way uphill just to the left of a thin line of rock. Here the ridgeline's highest taper resembles a row of large fins. A mild upgrade enters the wilderness (5,070 feet) at mile 1.9. The remainder of the southbound route is surrounded by the Middle Prong Wilderness.

The trail ascends through elevation zones where black cherry and striped maple become noticeably more common. At mile 2.0 you trek past the first pocket of mature spruce. The predominantly hardwood forest changes significantly as Green Mountain climbs into colder weather. Yellow birch supplants sweet birch; northern red oak replaces chestnut oak. Sassafras, cucumbertree, and other less cold-hardy species are left behind and below in the warmer zone, unable to take root higher than their genetic imperatives will allow. As the footpath advances up the ridge, red spruce and Fraser fir become much more numerous as the trailside forest becomes increasingly less diverse.

Now high and designated wild, the route rolls up Fork Ridge, rising on mostly easy grades to small knobs (only two moderate runs to mile 2.6) before dipping to shallow saddles. For much of the distance from mile 2.2 to 2.5, the treadway tunnels through dense thickets of evergreen heath roofed with Catawba rhododendron. Beyond the shallow saddle at mile 2.6, the track ranges through dark green spruce mixed with hardwoods such as yellow buckeye, yellow birch, and serviceberry. Many of the rounded outcrops are furred with rockcap ferns.

From the top of a more prominent knob (5,780 feet) at mile 3.0, the remainder of the hike rides the high ridge, porpoising up and over each knuckle before finishing the arc downhill to the next gap or shallow saddle. Here the trail descends for 0.1 mile, then rises and dips again before heading up on mostly easy or easy-to-moderate grades to mile 3.3, where a sidepath to the left leads to a rock outcrop look-off open (for now) to the northeast.

The trail gains the flat atop Green Knob (5,905 feet, the only named highpoint on Fork Ridge along the way to Hardy) at mile 3.7. The line of march splits atop the peak; the left-hand sidepath quickly leads to a recently open but now bare-branch view to the east. In season, this view features Flat Laurel Creek Falls (aka Double Sam Falls) approximately a mile and a quarter away. Flat Laurel Creek flies into foam where it leaps off the high, gently sloping basin of its upper watershed, cascading as much as 350 to 400 feet toward its meeting with the West Fork Pigeon River far below. This falls is closely flanked and framed by the two scenic Sams—Little Sam Knob on the right, Sam Knob to the left. Black Balsam Knob rears up right behind the Sams.

The next mile undulates like a sine wave. Following the wide ridgecrest to the south, the highcountry hiking holds its course downhill to a gap (5,740 feet) at mile 3.9. It then makes an easy-to-moderate ascent to the next knob (5,890 feet) at mile 4.3 before losing elevation to the next gap at mile 4.5. The route makes another upridge run to the first bump on the last prominent knob at mile 4.7. This long knob's three highest knuckles become larger and slightly higher to the south.

The high-elevation stretch of Fork Ridge, from Green Knob to trail's end, provides habitat for a cold-weather flora. Much of the area has either recently recovered to forest or is in full-throttle succession to that end. Red spruce and yellow birch dominate the canopy. Below those two, mountain and red maple, mountain ash, serviceberry, and Fraser fir catch the filtered light. The shrub layer is primarily composed of evergreen and deciduous heaths—Catawba rhododendron and those highly sought after deciduous berry bushes. Evergreen wood fern is often found in the shade of the maturing spruce. Occasional bed-sized moss cushions, plush and soft, tempt you to touch.

At mile 4.8 a prominent sidepath to the left leads to a rock outcrop overlook open to the southeast. Perched on the upper-western rim of the West Fork's watershed, this prospect will provide open views of the nearby mountains for a few more years yet. Double-humped Sam Knob stands at around

75 degrees, conifer-pated Little Sam Knob at about east, the high and wide crown of Black Balsam Knob a little further away between the two Sams, the rounded summit of Chestnut Bald at around 124 degrees, and craggy Devils Courthouse at around 135 degrees.

At mile 5.2, near the crown of the last knob's largest and last knuckle (5,915 feet, trail highpoint), there is a camp to the right of the tread. After steady descent the track comes to a T-junction at mile 5.4. Here where the trail turns left and south, the sidepath to the right crosses a small, intermittent seepage flow after 55 yards before heading uphill.

Sixty yards beyond the fork, the route reaches the first of two sidepaths to the right. Both of them head to the same place: an area of environmentally correct campsites (proper distance from both trail and water) tucked in the conifers or out in the large opening. Still grassy from a recent fire, parts of the ridgecrest will afford views for some years yet. Following a short but sharp downgrade, the remainder of the trail gently undulates to its ending T-junction with the MST in the first gap north of Mount Hardy.

Excluding the Middle Prong beside its lower-elevation end, Green Mountain's only near trailside water is the intermittent seep to the right at mile 5.4.

Nature Notes

Green Mountain, which follows a high ridgeline frequently shaded by either rhododendron or conifer, does not provide a good spring herbaceous wildflower display. As usual, however, the next layer up—the heath shrubs—more than compensates for the lack of a forest-floor show. On a recent June 6, painted trillium were largely spent while wood sorrel and bluebead lily were still in bloom. On that same date mountain laurel was slightly past prime at the lower elevations and Catawba rhododendron was in full glory at the highest elevations. On September 7, assorted asters animated many of the remaining early succession areas, and by October 21 the wildflower flourish was over, but the fall color was spectacular.

Black cherry

From mile 1.6 to mile 2.7, black cherry (*Prunus serotina*) is often common beside this route where the ridgecrest is wider and deeper soiled. The dark scaly bark of this cherry sticks out in a mixed stand. Broken into small platy scales with upturned edges, the bark is dark brownish gray to nearly black. The centers of the scales often appear slick and shiny.

black cherry

Black cherry is one of the earliest hardwoods to leaf out in the southern mountains; only the yellow buckeye breaks bud substantially earlier at similar elevations. The foliage, twigs, and bark of this cherry emit the distinctive aroma of bitter almond or hydrocyanic acid. The finely saw-toothed alternate leaves are usually 2½ to 5½ inches long and sharp pointed at the tip. When eaten fresh and raw, the leaves release prussic acid, a poison.

Unfolding from the ends of the outermost branches when the leaves are not yet fully grown, numerous small white flowers with orange stamens cluster tightly on racemes 4 to 6 inches long. Birds and other wildlife, including bears, eat the resulting fruits when they ripen in late summer.

The black is the largest native cherry in North America. This member of the Rose family reaches its largest dimensions in the deep, rich, well-watered soils of the Southern Highlands. People accustomed to the small, scraggly specimens (easily identified by their heavy infestations of tent caterpillars) along the roadsides of Piedmont Georgia and the Carolinas can scarcely believe the height and straight-boled beauty of mountain-grown cherries. Achieving its best growth in coves and on north-facing slopes, *P. serotina* often reaches 75 to 100 feet in height and 7 to 10 feet in circumference. Primary growth trees in never-cut forests often become much larger. In the nearby GSMNP, an impressve cherry along Ramsay Cascades Trail measured 124 feet in height and slightly over 13 feet in girth.

mountain maple

Mountain maple

Multiboled clumps of mountain maple (*Acer spicatum*) are often common along the segment of highcountry treadway beyond mile 2.5. This shrub- to small-tree-sized maple prefers cool forests, especially in rocky soils below larger broadleafs. Primarily a northern species, mountain maple climbs nearly to the summits of Southern Appalachia's highest peaks and rarely descends below 3,000 feet.

This short-trunked hardwood is usually considered a shrub over most of its extensive range (north-south from Hudson Bay to northernmost Georgia). But in the Southern Blue Ridge,

A. spicatum occasionally becomes a small tree 20 to 30 feet in height.

This maple can be identified by its bark—light brown and somewhat shaggy—its distinctive leaves, and its upright flower clusters. Its leaves are usually 3 to 5 inches long and wide with either three or five short lobes. When there are five lobes, the two lowermost ones are smaller than the top three. Somewhat wrinkled in appearance, the leaves also have heart-shaped bases and margins coarsely serrated with single teeth.

Canada mayflower

The ¼-inch-wide greenish yellow flowers occur on erect, candlelike clusters up to 5 inches long. Some of the mountain maples were in bloom on a recent June 6.

Canada mayflower

The Canada mayflower—a small, spring-blooming herb usually only 2 to 6 inches in height—often forms large, densely packed colonies that carpet the forest floor. Also known as wild or false lily-of-the-valley, this rhizomatous perennial is more widely distributed to the north. Here in the Shining Rock area, this forb is fairly common in moist cool woods up to approximately 6,000 feet. It is most abundant where the spruce-fir forest mixes with northern hardwoods.

The Canada mayflower's colonial growth habit, small size, and distinctive clasping leaves make it easy to identify even when not in flower. The one to three (usually two) glossy, deep green leaves are ovately shaped and most often 1½ to 3 inches long.

Small, dense clusters of diminutive, star-shaped flowers are borne atop the short, often slightly zigzag stems. Two petals and two petal-like sepals, white and strongly fragrant, give the individual flowers (3/16 of an inch long) a four-cornered appearance.

Directions

Green Mountain and Fork Mountain share the same trailhead parking area between the West Fork Pigeon River and NC 215. (See Fork Mountain Trail, page 65, for directions to this trailhead.)

The Green Mountain Trail begins on the other side of the highway from the long pull-off parking area beside the West Fork Pigeon River. Look for the sometimes faint treadway approximately 35 feet from the south side (south is the parking area side) of the bridge over the Middle Prong. You should see a slight gap in the woods just before the road bank rises higher. Don't follow the path along the Middle Prong; follow the trail that climbs sharply straight up the ridgecrest.

Notes

The Wilderness Act

The Wilderness Act of September 3, 1964, established the National Wilderness Preservation System, the first of its kind in the world. The idea of wilderness means different things to different people. Some describe any patch of woods bigger than their backyard as wilderness. Others won't call an area true wilderness unless it meets rare conditions: that it takes at least a week to walk across, that there is no sign of human habitation even from the vistas, and that all of the original predators are still on patrol. Knowing that the term is nebulous, as much spiritual as physical, the framers of the law attempted to define the qualities and purposes of wilderness. The following are salient ideas from the act.

A wilderness

- is an area of undeveloped federal land retaining its primeval character and influence, without permanent improvements or human habitation;
- has at least 5,000 acres of land or is of sufficient size to make practicable its preservation and use in an unimpaired condition;
- generally appears to have been affected primarily by forces of nature, with the imprint of man's work substantially unnoticeable;
- is hereby recognized as an area where the earth and its community of life are untrammeled by man, where man himself is a visitor who does not remain, and which has outstanding opportunities for solitude or a primitive and unconfined type of recreation;

- is devoted to the public purposes of recreational, scenic, scientific, educational, conservation, and historical use;
- is preservation that will secure for the American people of present and future generations the benefits of an enduring resource of wilderness— unimpaired for future use and enjoyment.

What is permitted in wilderness?

- Primitive recreation such as dayhiking, backpacking, and camping
- Hunting and fishing in accordance with state and federal laws
- Collecting berries, nuts, and cones for personal use
- Scientific research compatible with wilderness values
- Primitive facilities, if critical to the protection of the land
- Nonmotorized wheelchairs

What is prohibited in wilderness?

- New road construction
- Timber harvesting
- Structures of any kind, except those primitive facilities deemed necessary to protect the land
- Mechanical transport (bicycles, wagons, carts)
- Public use of any motorized vehicles or equipment
- Removal of plants, stone, or moss for personal or commercial use
- Removal of historical or archeological artifacts by the public

Environmental and Courtesy Guidelines

The Forest Service has implemented two environmental rules for the Shining Rock and Middle Prong Wildernesses: no fires and no more than ten people per group. These rules have the force of law; violators are subject to a fine. The Forest Service also strongly suggests that you camp at least 100 feet away from any water source.

Before the Hike

- As the Forest Service rule clearly states, limit group size to no more than ten for backpacking or dayhiking in the wilderness.
- Plan ahead—remember that large, easily accessed streams with swimming holes and open areas with views will be heavily used during warm-weather holidays and weekends. Also remember that the Graveyard Fields area and the trailheads along FS 816 will be very heavily used during blueberry picking season.
- Take a backpacking stove so you won't have to build a fire for cooking.
- Repackage food supplies in sealable bags or plastic bottles so there will be fewer boxes and tinfoil pouches to burn or carry out.

On the Trail

■ Don't litter—not even the smallest candy wrappers or cigarette butts. If you pack it in, pack it out—all of it. This includes all kleenex and toilet paper that you don't bury.

■ Take the dump du jour at least 100 feet from the trail and at least 150 feet from a campsite or water source. Dig a cat hole with boot heel or plastic trowel, then cover everything up well.

■ Do not cut across switchbacks. Cutting across switchbacks tramples vegetation, starts erosion, and encourages more shortcut taking.

■ Step to the high side so you don't cave in the low side of the trail when moving aside to let other hikers pass.

■ Don't pick, pluck, dig up, or cut up any flowers, plants, or trees—not even the tiny ones you think no one will miss.

No-Trace Camping

■ Try to camp at least 100 feet away from both water and trail.

■ Don't use worn out, naked-ground campsites. Let them heal. Use lightly worn existing campsites or, better yet, move well away from trail and stream, then make a no-trace camp that will rarely, if ever, be used again. Be creative. If your route rises to a wide ridge and then turns to follow that ridge, try looking for a flat spot well away from the tread on the crest opposite the trail. If your route runs through a gap with a gentle slope to one side, walk down that side and find a flat spot. If your trail sidehills around the nearby highpoint of a knob, walk up to the top of the knob and camp there. If your trail closely parallels a stream, cross the stream and make a no-trace camp on that side. Create your own peace and quiet, your own solitude.

◼ Don't cut standing trees or pull up vegetation to make room for your tent or tents. Be gentle; think of yourself as a guest. Fit in, tuck in—don't hack in.

◼ Don't enlarge an existing campsite. There is no need for large groups to circle the wagons against the night. Fit in and tuck in.

◼ Absolutely no campsite construction—leave the blueprints and hard hats at home: no boot bulldozing, trenching, or building log furniture or shelves; no hammering nails in trees, digging latrines, etc.

◼ Remember that organic scraps are definitely litter. No one wants to see your campsite compost pile crowned with eggshells and spaghetti noodles. And no one wants a skunk or raccoon to raid his or her camp because the previous tenants were sloppy campers. Once again, pack it out.

◼ Use biodegradable soap and dispose of waste water at least 150 feet from campsite or water source.

◼ Don't wash dirty dishes directly in a spring or stream. Don't use soap on yourself or your clothes directly in a spring or stream.

◼ Limit length of stay to one or two nights per campsite.

◼ Avoid building campfires. Carry a portable camp stove for cooking. If you do start a fire at a non-wilderness camp, keep it small and use only dead and down wood.

■ Don't build fire rings—tear them down.
■ Erase all evidence of a campfire built with no fire ring. Scatter the ashes, replace the duff, and camouflage the burned area.

Backcountry Courtesy

■ Don't take a dog hiking with you unless it is well trained. Leave behind dogs that may growl or bark at other hikers.
■ Be considerate—do nothing that will interfere with someone else's enjoyment.
■ Try to keep your voice volume at normal speaking levels. No one wants to drive for hours and backpack for miles only to be kept awake by drunken whoops and loud music.
■ Remember that backcountry campsites are first come, first served. Don't whine, argue, or try to crowd in if someone already has the camp you really wanted. Move on down the trail.
■ Help preserve the illusion of solitude, for yourself and for others. Make yourself unobtrusive, as invisible as possible. Use earth-tone tents and tarps and, if possible, camp far enough off the trail so that other hikers can't see you and vice versa.

Addresses and Map Sources

Both wildernesses as well as the FS land south of the Shining Rock Wilderness and east of NC 215 to either side of the parkway are located within the Pisgah Ranger District of the Pisgah National Forest. The FS land immediately south of the parkway and west of NC 215 belongs to the Nantahala Ranger District of the Nantahala National Forest. The BRP corridor is also federally owned, but it is administered and managed by the NPS. For more information call, write, or check the website.

Pisgah National Forest
Pisgah Ranger Station
1600 Pisgah Highway
Pisgah Forest, NC 28768
(828) 877-3265

USDA Forest Service
Supervisor's Office
160 Zillicoa Street
Suite A
Asheville, NC 28801
(828) 257-4200
www.fs.usda.gov/nfsnc
(good for all NC national
forests)

Nantahala National Forest
Nantahala Ranger District
90 Sloan Road
Franklin, NC 28734
(828) 524-6441

Supervisor's Office (address
and phone # same as for
Pisgah National Forest)

**Blue Ridge Parkway
(headquarters)**
Blue Ridge Parkway
199 Hemphill Knob Road
Asheville, NC 28803
(828) 271-4779
www.nps.gov/blri

Maps of the Pisgah National Forest, the Nantahala National Forest, and the combined wildernesses are available from the

FS offices for a small fee. The title of the map of the two wilder-nesses is "Shining Rock and Middle Prong Wildernesses."

Maps of the BRP are currently available at visitor centers, campgrounds, and by mail.

Topographic Quadrangles (1:24,000) are available from the United States Geological Survey. To order maps from the federal government, call (303) 202-4700 or go to the website at http://store.usgs.gov. You can also download and print free copies of sections of USGS topo maps from the same website.

Mileage Finder

Trail	Page	Total Miles	Trail Segment	Miles
Old Butt Knob	4	4.0	No interior junction.	4.0
Shining Creek	15	4.2	Big East Fork Trailhead to Old Butt Knob Trail	0.8
			Old Butt Knob to ALT-3 near Shining Rock Gap	3.4
Big East Fork	23	3.6	No interior junction.	3.6
Greasy Cove	29	3.3	Bridges Camp Gap and Big East Fork Trails to ALT– Greasy Cove connector	2.9
			ALT–Greasy Cove connector to Graveyard Ridge Trail	0.4
Bridges Camp Gap	*38*	1.3	Trailhead to first MST-5 junction . . .	0.04
			Shares treadway with MST-5 to second MST junction	0.06
			Second MST-5 junction to Big East Fork and Greasy Cove Trails.	1.2
MST-5	44	4.8	Access trail from Looking Glass Rock Overlook to first Bridges Camp Gap junction.	0.3
			Shares treadway with Bridges Camp Gap to second Bridges Camp Gap junction.	0.06
			Second Bridges Camp Gap junction to end of section	4.4
Fork Mountain	56	7.2	No interior junction.	7.2
Ivestor Gap	66	4.3	Black Balsam Trailhead to IGT–ALT connector	1.0
			IGT–ALT connector to Fork Mountain Trail.	0.7
			Fork Mountain to first ALT-3 junction	0.08

Trail	Page	Total Miles	Trail Segment	Miles
Ivestor Gap	66		Shares treadway with ALT-3 to second ALT-3 junction.	0.03
			Second ALT-3 junction to junction with Graveyard Ridge and ALT-3 in Ivestor Gap	0.4
			Ivestor Gap to Little East Fork Trail. . .	1.7
			Little East Fork to Old Butt Knob and ALT-3 in Shining Rock Gap	0.4
Art Loeb Spur	75	0.4	No interior junction.	0.4
ALT-3	77	7.9	MST–ALT Trailhead to Art Loeb Spur	0.5
			Art Loeb Spur to IGT–ALT connector	1.1
			IGT–ALT connector to first junction with IGT	1.0
			Shares treadway with IGT to second IGT junction	0.03
			Second IGT junction to junction with Graveyard Ridge and IGT in Ivestor Gap	0.4
			Ivestor Gap to ALT–Greasy Cove connector	0.4
			ALT–Greasy Cove connector to Shining Creek Trail	1.4
			Shining Creek to Old Butt Knob and IGT in Shining Rock Gap (90 yards from Shining Creek to opening in gap)	0.05
			Shining Rock Gap to Deep Gap and Cold Mountain junction	3.0
Little East Fork	88	5.0	No interior junction.	5.0
ALT-4	98	3.8	No interior junction.	3.8
Cold Mountain	107	1.5	No interior junction.	1.5

Trail	Page	Total Miles	Trail Segment	Miles
MST-4	118	5.3	MST–ALT Trailhead to Graveyard Ridge Trail at Dark Prong Gap 1.6	
			Graveyard Ridge at Dark Prong Gap to lower-elevation end of Graveyard Ridge Trail. 1.3	
			Graveyard Ridge to MST Access 0.4	
			MST Access to access trail from Looking Glass Rock Overlook. 2.0	
Graveyard Ridge	129	3.4	Lower-elevation end at MST-4 to Graveyard Ridge Connector 0.2	
			Graveyard Ridge Connector to MST-4 at Dark Prong Gap. 1.1	
			MST-4 at Dark Prong Gap to Greasy Cove Trail . . . . . . , ... 1.8	
			Greasy Cove to junctions with ALT-3 (two junctions less than 35 yards apart) and IGT in Ivestor Gap 0.3	
Graveyard Fields Trail System	137			
Graveyard Fields (the loop)		1.1	Trailhead to Lower Falls and Mountains to Sea Access (counterclockwise on loop) 0.2	
			Lower Falls and Mountains to Sea Access to Graveyard Ridge Connector. 0.2	
			Graveyard Ridge Connector to Upper Falls 0.2	
			Upper Falls back to trailhead 0.5	
Lower Falls		0.1	Junction with Mountains to Sea Access along the way 0.1	
Mountains to Sea Access		0.2	Junction with Lower Falls along the way. 0.2	
Graveyard Ridge Connector		0.5	No interior junction. 0.5	
Upper Falls		1.0	No interior junction. 1.0	

Trail	Page	Total Miles	Trail Segment	Miles
ALT-1	146	3.3	BRP to Farlow Gap Trail (trail not in this guide)	1.5
			Farlow Gap to access trail near Deep Gap	1.2
			Access trail near Deep Gap to the top of Pilot Mountain	0.6
ALT-2	156	1.5	BRP to MST-3	0.4
			Shares treadway with MST-3 from mile 0.4 to end of section at the MST–ALT Trailhead	1.1
MST-3	159	4.4	NC 215 to Devils Courthouse– MST connector	2.0
			Devils Courthouse–MST connector to Little Sam Trail	0.3
			Little Sam to ALT-2	1.0
			Shares treadway with ALT-2 from mile 3.3 to section end at the MST–ALT Trailhead	1.1
Devils Courthouse	169	0.4	Trailhead to Devils Courthouse– MST connector	0.3
			Devils Courthouse–MST connector to top of Devils Courthouse.	0.1
Little Sam	174	1.3	No interior junction.	1.3
Flat Laurel Creek	180	3.7	Black Balsam Trailhead to Little Sam Trail	1.1
			Little Sam to Sam Knob Trail	0.4
			Sam Knob to NC 215	2.2
Sam Knob	190	1.0	Black Balsam Trailhead to junction with Sam Knob Summit Trail	0.6
			Sam Knob Summit to Flat Laurel Creek Trail	0.4

Trail	Page	Total Miles	Trail Segment	Miles
Sam Knob Summit	192	0.8 out to both forks	Sam Knob Summit to fork 0.64	
			Left fork 0.09	
			Right fork 0.09	
Bearpen Gap	202	0.6	No interior junction 0.6	
MST-1	206	4.0	Bearpen Gap Trail to Haywood Gap Trail 2.3	
			Haywood Gap to access trail from Rough Butt Bald Overlook 1.7	
Haywood Gap	216	4.0	MST-1 to Buckeye Gap Trail 2.3	
			Buckeye Gap to FS 97 . . . . 1.7	
Buckeye Gap	226	3.0	No interior junction . . , ... 3.0	
MST-2	234	4.6	Access trail from Rough Butt Bald Overlook to Buckeye Gap Trail 1.1	
			Buckeye Gap to Green Mountain Trail 0.6	
			Green Mountain to NC 215 . . . . 2.9	
Sidepath from MST-2 to the top of Mount Hardy	238	0.6	No interior junction 0.6	
Green Mountain	244	5.6	No interior junction 5.6	

Connectors and Access Trails **Miles**

Devils Courthouse–MST connector 0.1

IGT–ALT connector 0.2

ALT–Greasy Cove connector. 0.2

Access trail from Rough Butt Bald Overlook to the southeastern end
of MST-1 and the western end of MST-2 . . . . 0.14

Access trail from Looking Glass Rock Overlook to the eastern end
of MST-4 and the southwestern end of MST-5 . . . . 0.09

Access trail from Wagon Road Gap Parking Area to the
northeastern end of MST-5 . . . . 0.4

Access trail from the end of FS 229 to ALT-1 near Deep Gap 0.2

Road Walks

FS 816: MST–ALT Trailhead to the IGT gate
at the Black Balsam Trailhead. 0.56

US 276: Vehicle-blocking boulders at the entrance
of Big East Fork Trail to the vehicle-blocking boulders
at the entrance of Shining Creek Trail. 0.13

Camp Daniel Boone: ALT-4 Trailhead kiosk to the lower-elevation end
of Little East Fork Trail 0.34

NC 215: NC 215 end of Flat Laurel Creek Trail to where the MST
crosses NC 215 . . . . 0.32

FS 97 (Lickstone Rd) and NC 215: Northern end
of Haywood Gap Trail on FS 97 to the gate on FS 97 . . . . 1.56

Northern end of Haywood Gap Trail on FS 97
to the entrance of Green Mountain Trail off NC 215 . . . . 1.90

Northern end of Haywood Gap Trail on FS 97
to the entrance of Fork Mountain Trail off NC 215. . . . . 1.96

List of Species Profiles

Trees and Shrubs

Wildflowers and Ferns

Other Wildlife

* Asterisk indicates illustration.

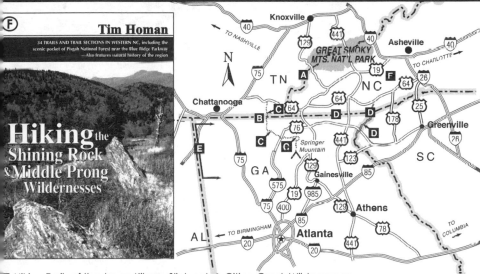